KU-527-566

C152024533

THE USBORNE
INTERNET-LINKED
CHILDREN'S
WORLD
ATLAS

Stephanie Turnbull and Emma Helbrough
Designers: Stephen Moncrieff and Andrea Slane
Consultant cartographic editor: Craig Asquith

Cartography by European Map Graphics Ltd
Map design by Laura Fearn and Keith Newell
Consultant: Dr. Roger Trend, Senior Lecturer in Earth Science
and Geography Education, University of Exeter

KENT
ARTS & LIBRARIES
C152024533

CONTENTS

Here you can see dramatic cloud formations at sunset over a desert in California, U.S.A. Below is a large sandstone arch, shaped by the weather over many years.

INTERNET LINKS

This book contains descriptions of many interesting Web sites where you can find out more about maps and places around the world. For links to these sites, go to the Usborne Quicklinks Web site at **www.usborne-quicklinks.com** and enter the keyword "atlas". There you will find links to take you to all the Web sites.

Site availability

The links on the Usborne Quicklinks Web site will be reviewed and updated regularly. If any sites become unavailable, we will, if possible, replace them with suitable alternatives.

Occasionally, you may get a message saying that a Web site is unavailable. This may be temporary, so try again a few hours later, or even the next day.

Internet links

For links to all the Web sites described in this book, go to **www.usborne-quicklinks.com** and enter the keyword "atlas".

Help

For general help and advice on using the Internet, go to the Usborne Quicklinks Web site and click on "Net Help".

To find out more about using your Web browser, click on your browser's Help menu and choose "Contents and Index". You'll find a searchable dictionary containing tips on how to find your way around the Internet easily.

What you need

The Web sites described in this book can be accessed using a standard home computer and a Web browser (the software that enables you to display information from the Internet). Here's a list of the basic requirements:

- A PC with Microsoft® Windows® 98 or a later version, or a Macintosh computer with System 9.0 or later

- 64Mb RAM

- A Web browser such as Microsoft® Internet Explorer 5, or Netscape® Navigator 4.7, or later versions

- Connection to the Internet via a modem (preferably 56kbps) or a faster digital or cable line

- An account with an Internet Service Provider (ISP)

- A sound card to hear sound files

Computer not essential

If you don't have use of the Internet, don't worry. This atlas is a complete, self-contained reference book on its own.

Extras

Some Web sites need additional programs, called plug-ins, to play sounds, or to show videos, animations or 3-D images. If you go to a site and you do not have the necessary plug-in, a message should come up on the screen.

There is usually a button on the site that you can click on to download the plug-in. Alternatively, go to Usborne Quicklinks and click on "Net Help". There you can find links to download plug-ins. Here is a list of plug-ins that you might need:

- **QuickTime** – lets you play video clips.

- **RealPlayer**® – lets you play video clips and sound files.

- **Flash**™ – lets you play animations.

- **Shockwave**® – lets you play animations and enjoy interactive sites.

Computer viruses

A computer virus is a program that can damage your computer. A virus can get into your computer when you download programs from the Internet, or in an attachment (an extra file) that arrives with an e-mail. We strongly recommend that you buy anti-virus software to protect your computer and that you update the software regularly. You can buy anti-virus software at computer stores or download it from the Internet. To find out more about viruses, go to Usborne Quicklinks and click on "Net Help".

Macintosh and QuickTime are trademarks of Apple computer, Inc., registered in the U.S.A. and other countries.

RealPlayer is a trademark of RealNetworks, Inc., registered in the U.S.A. and other countries.

Flash and Shockwave are trademarks of Macromedia, Inc., registered in the U.S.A. and other countries.

Note for parents

The Web sites described in this book are regularly checked and reviewed by Usborne editors and the links in Usborne Quicklinks are updated. However, the content of a Web site may change at any time and Usborne Publishing is not responsible for the content of any Web site other than its own.

We recommend that children are supervised while on the Internet, that they do not use Internet Chat Rooms, and that you use Internet filtering software to block unsuitable material.

Please ensure that your children read and follow the safety guidelines below. For more information, go to the Net Help area on the Usborne Quicklinks Web site at **www.usborne-quicklinks.com**

Internet safety

- Ask your parent's or guardian's permission before you connect to the Internet. They can then stay nearby if they think they should do so.

- If you write a message in a Web site guest book or on a Web site message board, do not include your e-mail address, real name, address or telephone number.

- If a Web site asks you to log in or register by typing your name or e-mail address, ask the permission of an adult first.

- If you receive e-mail from someone you don't know, tell an adult and do not reply to the e-mail.

- Never arrange to meet anyone you have talked to on the Internet.

WHAT IS AN ATLAS?

An atlas is a collection of maps. This atlas helps you explore our world and find out more about its varied landscapes, famous cities and amazing sights.

What maps show

A map is an image that represents an area of the Earth's surface, usually from above. Unlike a photograph, which shows exactly what an area looks like, a map can show features of the area in a clear, simplified way. It can also give different information, such as place names. Symbols are often used to mark features such as volcanoes and waterfalls.

Which way is up?

Although the Earth doesn't have a top and a bottom, north is usually at the top of maps. But it is sometimes more convenient to reposition a map, so north might not necessarily be at the top. Some maps have a compass symbol that indicates where north lies.

Wolf volcano

Darwin volcano

San Salvador

Fernandina

Alcedo volcano

La Cumbre volcano

Santa Cruz

Isabela

Sierra Negra volcano

Cerro Azul volcano

This simple map of the central Galapagos Islands names the main islands and their volcanoes.

Floreana

This is a satellite image of part of the Galapagos Islands. Using the map on this page, can you identify the islands shown in the photograph?

Physical and political

Physical maps indicate natural features such as mountains, deserts, rivers and lakes. Political maps focus on the division of the Earth's surface into different countries. Look on pages 18–19 for a political map of the world, and on pages 20–21 for a physical map. Most of the maps in this atlas show physical features as well as country borders, cities and towns.

Map scales

The size of a map in relation to the area it shows is called its scale. Some maps have a scale bar, which is a rule with measurements. It tells you how many miles or km are represented by a certain distance on the map. Other maps show these relative distances just as numbers. For example, the figure 1:100 means that 1cm on the map represents 100cm on the Earth's surface.

The scale of a map depends on its purpose. A map showing the whole world is on a very small scale, but a town plan is on a much larger scale so that features such as roads can be shown clearly.

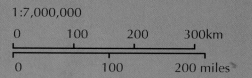

This map of Europe is on a small scale so that it all fits onto one small map.

This map of Denmark is on a larger scale to show more detail.

Internet links

For links to the following Web sites, go to **www.usborne-quicklinks.com**

Web site 1 Look at physical and political maps of different countries.

Web site 2 Find street maps of any town or city in the world.

Using this atlas

The maps in this atlas are grouped by continent. There are seven continents, which are (from largest to smallest): Asia, Africa, North America, South America, Antarctica, Europe and Australasia and Oceania. Each map section is accompanied by photographs and satellite images showing some of the continent's most impressive sights. You can look up many of these places on the maps.

This is Mount Rushmore, a huge sculpture of four U.S. presidents, which is one of the most famous sights in the U.S.A. Throughout this atlas you will see pictures of many more well known landmarks from around the world.

THE EARTH FROM SPACE

Modern technology has enabled scientists to make more accurate maps of the world than ever before. Even remote places, such as deserts, ocean floors and mountain ranges, have been mapped in detail, using information from satellites that observe the Earth from space.

What is a satellite?

Artificial satellites are machines that orbit, or travel around, the Earth. They observe the Earth using a technique called remote sensing. Instruments on the satellite monitor the Earth from a distance, and send back pictures of its surface. Satellites also monitor moons and other planets.

This satellite monitors the Earth 24 hours a day. It uses powerful radar that pierces through clouds. This means that the satellite can provide images of the Earth in all weather conditions.

Satellite movement

Some satellites orbit the Earth at a height of between 5km (3 miles) and 1,500km (930 miles), providing views of different parts of the planet. Others stay above the same place all the time, moving at the same speed as the Earth rotates to give a constant view of a particular area. These are called geostationary satellites. They travel at a height of around 36,000km (22,370 miles).

Internet links

For links to the following Web sites, go to **www.usborne-quicklinks.com**

Web site 1 Look at detailed satellite pictures of any part of the world.

Web site 2 See satellite images that show which parts of the Earth are in daylight or darkness at this very moment, plus up-to-date weather conditions across the globe.

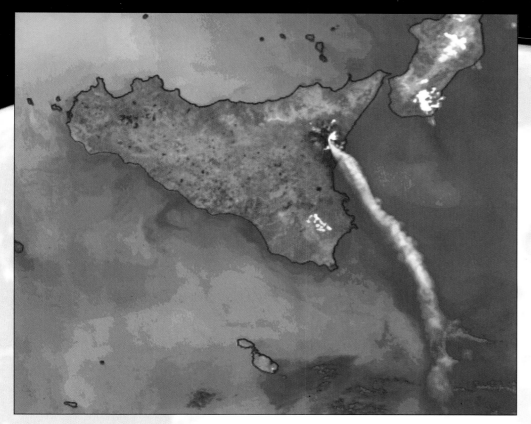

This satellite image of Sicily was taken in July 2001. It shows the volcano Mount Etna erupting. You can see smoke from the volcano on the right of the picture.

Satellite uses

Satellite pictures can be used to help predict and monitor natural hazards such as volcanic eruptions. They can also help scientists to observe the effects people have on the environment, for example the destruction of rainforests in South America. Satellite images are often artificially shaded to highlight relevant features, for example forests, so that they are easier to see.

Remote sensing

Satellites use a range of remote sensing techniques. One type is radar, which can provide images of the Earth even when it is dark or cloudy. Radar works by reflecting radio waves off a target object. The time it takes for a wave to bounce back indicates how far away the object is.

Powerful cameras provide pictures of the Earth's surface. Often, infrared cameras are used. Different surfaces reflect infrared rays differently, so infrared images of the Earth are able to show its various types of land surfaces, such as deserts, grasslands and forests.

This satellite image of the Earth is shaded to show different types of land. Deserts and other dry regions are red, and areas with lots of vegetation are orange.

DIVIDING LINES

The Earth is divided up with imaginary lines that help us measure distances and find where places are. There are two sets of lines, called latitude and longitude.

This arctic fox lives in northern Canada, very near the Arctic Circle line of latitude.

Latitude lines

Lines of latitude run around the globe. They are parallel to each other and get shorter the closer they are to the two poles. The latitude line that runs around the middle of the Earth is called the Equator. It is the most important line of latitude as all other lines are measured north or south of it.

Longitude lines

Lines of longitude run from the North Pole to the South Pole. All the lines are the same length, and they all meet at the North and South Poles.

The most important line of longitude is the Prime Meridian Line, which runs through Greenwich, in England. All other lines of longitude are measured east or west of this line.

Other lines

The Equator is not the only named line of latitude. The Tropic of Cancer is a line north of the Equator. The Tropic of Capricorn is at the same distance south of the Equator. Between these lines are the hottest, wettest parts of the world. This region is called the tropics.

The Arctic Circle is a latitude line far north of the Equator. The area north of this includes the North Pole and is called the Arctic. On the other side of the globe is the Antarctic Circle. The area south of this includes the South Pole and is known as the Antarctic.

Latitude lines   *Longitude lines*

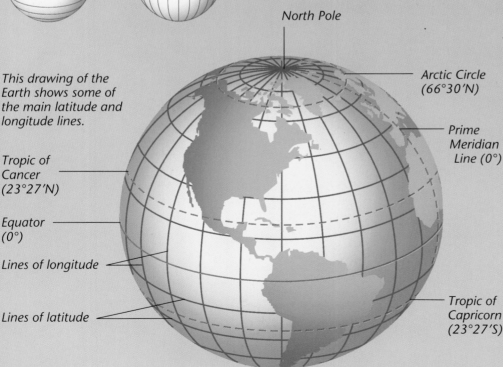

This drawing of the Earth shows some of the main latitude and longitude lines.

North Pole

Arctic Circle (66°30'N)

Prime Meridian Line (0°)

Tropic of Cancer (23°27'N)

Equator (0°)

Lines of longitude

Lines of latitude

Tropic of Capricorn (23°27'S)

Internet links

For a link to a Web site where you can find out more about the Earth's lines of latitude and longitude, and test your knowledge with a great latitude and longitude quiz, go to **www.usborne-quicklinks.com**

Using the lines

Lines of latitude and longitude are measured in degrees (°). The positions of places are described according to which lines of latitude and longitude are nearest to them. For example, a place with a location of 50°S and 100°E has a latitude 50 degrees south of the Equator, and a longitude 100 degrees east of the Prime Meridian Line.

Exact locations

The distance between degrees is divided up to give even more precise measurements. Each degree is divided into 60 minutes ('), and each minute is divided into 60 seconds ("). The subdivisions allow us to locate any place on Earth. For example, the city of New York, U.S.A., is at 40°42'51"N and 74°00'23"W.

The steamy rainforests of Malaysia lie near the Equator. Many apes, like the one shown here, live in these rainforests.

This is a map of New Zealand, with a grid formed by lines of latitude and longitude.

Using a grid

Lines of latitude and longitude form grids on maps. The maps in this book look similar to the one on the left. The columns that run from top to bottom are formed by lines of longitude and marked with letters. The rows running across the page are formed by lines of latitude and are numbered.

All the places listed in the map index on page 130 have a letter and a number reference that tell you where to find them on a particular page. For example, on the map on the left, the city of Christchurch would have a grid reference of C3.

HOW MAPS ARE MADE

The process of making maps is called cartography. Map-makers, or cartographers, compile each map by gathering information about the area and representing it as an image as accurately as possible.

Internet links

For a link to a Web site where you can click on examples of all kinds of map projections, including cylindrical, conical and azimuthal projections, go to **www.usborne-quicklinks.com**

Creating maps

Many sources are used to create maps. These include satellite images and aerial photographs. Cartographers often visit the area to be mapped, where they take many extra measurements.

In addition, cartographers use statistics, such as population figures, from censuses and other documents. As the maps are being made, many people check them to make sure they are accurate and up-to-date.

Map projections

Cartographers can't draw maps that show the world exactly as it is, because it is impossible to show a curved surface on a flat map without distorting (stretching or squashing) some areas. A representation of the Earth on a map is called a projection. Projections are worked out using complex mathematics.

There are three basic types of projections – cylindrical, conical and azimuthal, but there are also variations on these. They all distort the Earth's surface in some way, either by altering the shapes or sizes of areas of land or the distance between places.

A cartographer uses an electronic distance measurer to check the measurements of an area of land.

Cylindrical projections

A cylindrical projection is similar to the image created by wrapping a piece of paper around a globe to form a cylinder and then shining a light inside the globe. The shapes of countries would be projected onto the paper. Near the middle they would be accurate, but farther away they would be distorted.

Cartographers often alter the basic cylindrical projection to make the distortion less obvious in certain areas, but they can never make a map that is completely accurate.

This picture of a piece of paper wrapped around a globe illustrates how a cylindrical projection is made.

Below is a type of cylindrical projection called the Mercator projection, which was invented in 1596 by a cartographer named Gerardus Mercator. It makes countries the right shape, but makes those near the poles too big.

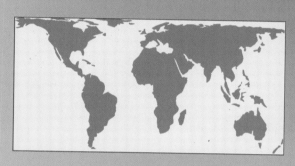

This cylindrical projection makes countries the right size in relation to each other, but some parts are too long. The projection was created in 1973 by Arno Peters. It is called the Peters Projection.

Conical projections

A conical projection is similar to the image you would get if you wrapped a cone of paper around part of a globe, then shone a light inside the globe. Where the cone touches the globe, the projection will be most accurate.

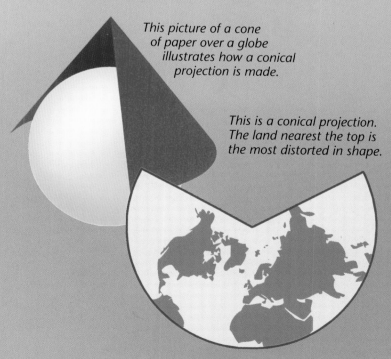

This picture of a cone of paper over a globe illustrates how a conical projection is made.

This is a conical projection. The land nearest the top is the most distorted in shape.

Azimuthal projections

An azimuthal projection is like an image made by holding paper in front of a globe, and shining a light through it. Land projected onto the middle of the paper would be accurate, but areas farther away would be distorted.

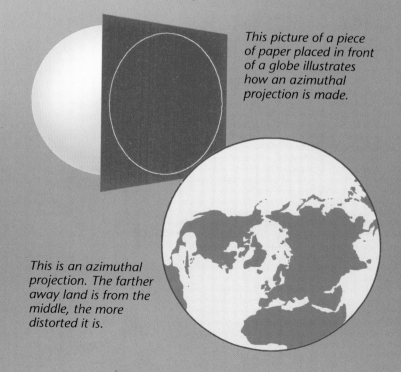

This picture of a piece of paper placed in front of a globe illustrates how an azimuthal projection is made.

This is an azimuthal projection. The farther away land is from the middle, the more distorted it is.

THEMATIC MAPS

Maps that represent information on particular themes, like the ones on these pages, are known as thematic maps. They help you to identify patterns and make comparisons between the features of different areas.

Earth's resources

The Earth contains all kinds of useful resources. Rocks and minerals can be used as building materials, and fuels such as coal, oil and gas contain energy that can be turned into heat and electricity.

Countries with large amounts of natural resources can become very rich. For example, Saudi Arabia, in western Asia, has large oil and gas reserves, which it exports all over the world.

This is an oil field, where oil is extracted from the ground using pumps. It is then piped to refineries and turned into products such as motor fuel.

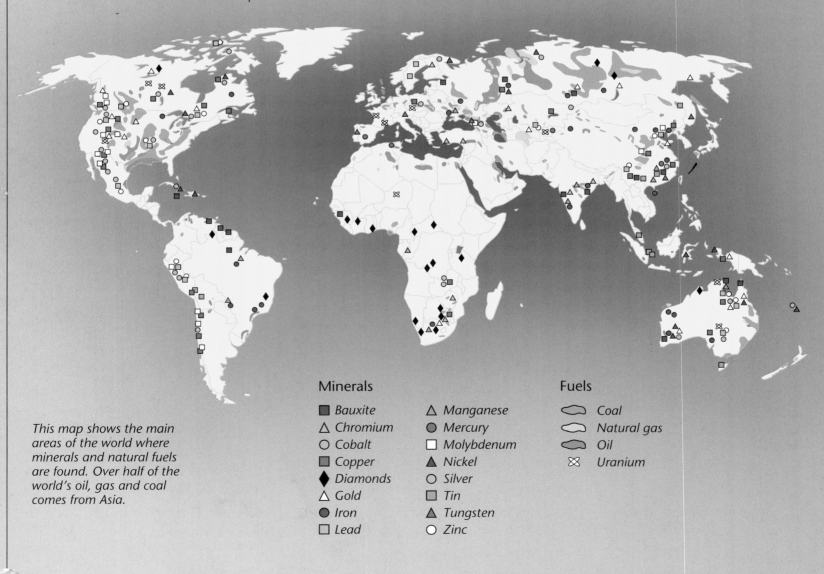

This map shows the main areas of the world where minerals and natural fuels are found. Over half of the world's oil, gas and coal comes from Asia.

Minerals

- ■ Bauxite
- △ Chromium
- ○ Cobalt
- ▢ Copper
- ◆ Diamonds
- △ Gold
- ● Iron
- ▢ Lead
- △ Manganese
- ● Mercury
- ☐ Molybdenum
- ▲ Nickel
- ○ Silver
- ☐ Tin
- ▲ Tungsten
- ○ Zinc

Fuels

- ⬭ Coal
- ⬭ Natural gas
- ⬭ Oil
- ⊠ Uranium

Different climates

The long-term or typical pattern of weather in a particular area is known as its climate. Climates vary across the world and depend largely on each area's latitude. The hottest parts of the world are those closest to the Equator.

Climate is also affected by other factors, such as wind and the height of the land. Oceans influence climate too – places near the sea normally have a milder, wetter climate than areas farther inland.

In this map, land is divided into five climate types. Dry areas are generally hot, but temperatures there can fall very low too. Some dry places, such as the Gobi Desert in eastern Asia, are extremely cold in winter.

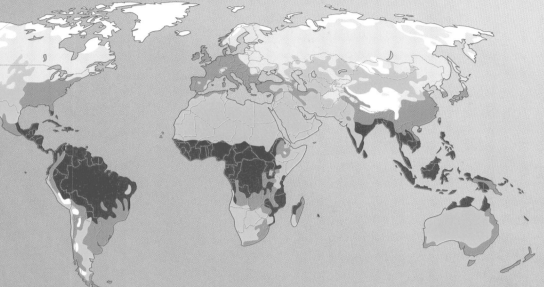

- Polar
- Cold
- Temperate
- Dry
- Tropical

World population

There are more than six billion people in the world, and the population is still growing. Experts think it may reach more than nine billion by 2050. The number of people living in a given area is known as its population density. Europe and Asia are the most densely populated continents in the world. About a third of the world's population lives in China and India alone.

This map shows the average population density by country. The shading indicates the number of people per sq km (0.386 sq miles).

Internet links

For a link to a Web site where you can discover how many people there were on Earth when you were born, and find out about the effects of population growth, go to **www.usborne-quicklinks.com**

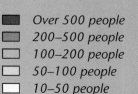

- Over 500 people
- 200–500 people
- 100–200 people
- 50–100 people
- 10–50 people
- Fewer than 10 people

HOW TO USE THE MAPS

E ach continent section in this atlas begins
with a political map showing the whole
continent. The rest of the maps are larger
scale maps showing the various parts of the
continent in more detail.

Political maps

The shading on the political
maps in this atlas is there to
help you see clearly the
different countries that make
up each continent. The main
purpose of these maps is to
show country borders and
capital cities. Alongside
them there are facts and
figures about the continents
and their features.

*This is a section of the political map of
South America. You can see the whole
map on pages 36–37.*

Environmental maps

The majority of the maps in
this atlas are environmental
maps, like the one on the right.
The shading on these maps
shows different types of land,
or environments, such as
desert, mountain or wetland.

The main key on the opposite
page shows what the different
shading means. It also shows
the symbols used to represent
towns, cities and other
features. There is a smaller key
on each environmental map
repeating the most important
information from this key.

Finding places

To find a particular place or
feature on the environmental
maps, look up its name in
the index on pages 130–143.
Its page number and grid
reference is given next to the
name. You can find out how
to use the grid on page 11.

*The map on the right is part of the
environmental map of the U.S.A. The
numbered labels at the top explain some
important features of these maps.*

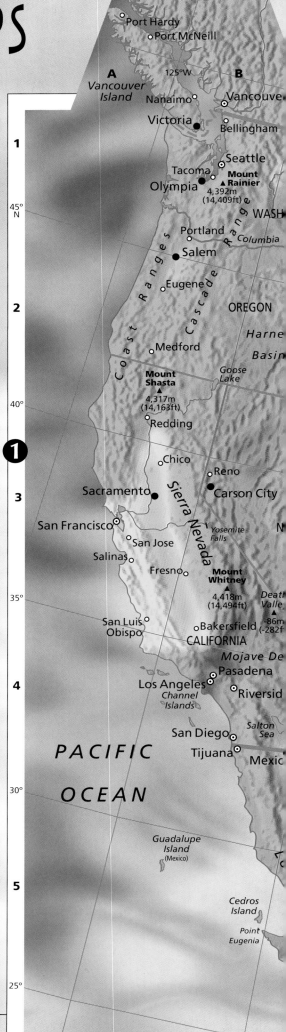

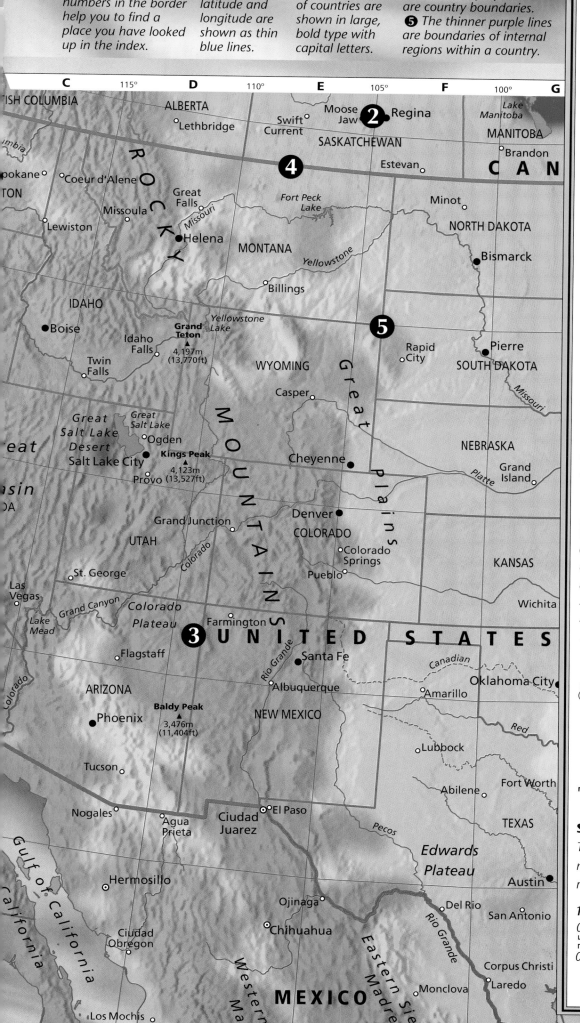

❶ *The letters and numbers in the border help you to find a place you have looked up in the index.*

❷ *Lines of latitude and longitude are shown as thin blue lines.*

❸ *The names of countries are shown in large, bold type with capital letters.*

❹ *The thick purple lines are country boundaries.*

❺ *The thinner purple lines are boundaries of internal regions within a country.*

| C | 115° | D | 110° | E | 105° | F | 100° | G | 85° |

BRITISH COLUMBIA
ALBERTA
Lethbridge
Swift Current
Moose Jaw ❷ Regina
Lake Manitoba
MANITOBA
SASKATCHEWAN
C A N
Spokane
Coeur d'Alene
❹
Estevan
Brandon
ONT
Mara
Great Falls
Fort Peck Lake
Minot
Missoula
Missouri
NORTH DAKOTA
Lewiston
Helena
MONTANA
Yellowstone
Bismarck
rior
IDAHO
Billings
Yellowstone Lake
❺
Boise
Grand Teton 4,197m (13,770ft)
WYOMING
Rapid City
Pierre
SOUTH DAKOTA
aukee
Lake Michigan
Idaho Falls
Twin Falls
Casper
Missouri
Great Salt Lake Desert
Great Salt Lake
Ogden
Kings Peak 4,123m (13,527ft)
Cheyenne
NEBRASKA
IND
Ind
eat
asin
DA
Salt Lake City
Provo
M
O
U
N
T
A
I
N
S
Denver
COLORADO
Grand Island
Platte
South Bend
Grand Junction
Colorado
Colorado Springs
Pueblo
Great Plains
KANSAS
Evan
St. George
Las Vegas
Lake Mead
Grand Canyon
Colorado Plateau
Farmington
❸ U N I T E D   S T A T E S
Wichita
deau
Kentucky Lake
Colorado
Flagstaff
Rio Grande
Santa Fe
Albuquerque
Canadian
Oklahoma City
Amarillo
TENN
Jackson
his
Ch
Hunt
ARIZONA
Baldy Peak 3,476m (11,404ft)
NEW MEXICO
Red
PI
an
A
M
Phoenix
Tucson
Lubbock
on
Fort Worth
Nogales
Agua Prieta
Ciudad Juarez
El Paso
Pecos
Abilene
TEXAS
Mobile
Hermosillo
Ojinaga
Del Rio
San Antonio
Edwards Plateau
Austin
Orleans
Gulf of California
Ciudad Obregon
Chihuahua
Rio Grande
Corpus Christi
Mississ Delta
M E X I C O
Monclova
Laredo
f Me
Los Mochis
Western Sierra Madre
Eastern Sierra Madre

Main key

Land cover:

Boreal forest
Temperate forest
Tropical forest
Temperate grassland
Savanna
Semi-desert and scrub
Hot desert
Wetland
Mountain (Only high mountains are marked.)
Tundra
Ice
Cultivation
Urban

Cities and towns:

■ National capital
● Internal capital
⊙ Major city or town
○ Other town

Boundaries:

―― International boundary
- - - International boundary through water
―― Internal boundary
- - - Internal boundary through water

Water features:

Sea
Lake or reservoir
Seasonal lake
Dry lake/salt pan
River
Seasonal river
Waterfall/dam

Other features:

▲ 2,490m (7,988ft) Height above or below sea level (Only a selection of elevation points are given. Places below sea level have a minus sign in front of the height.)

∴ Ruin or other place of interest

⊓⊔⊓⊔ Ancient wall

Scale:

This tells you the size of the map in relation to the area it represents. For example:

1:10,900,000

| 0 | 200 | 400km |

| 0 | 100 | 200 | 300 miles |

GREENLAND
(Denmark)

ICELAND

NORW

Arctic Circle

ALASKA
(U.S.A.)

C A N A D A

UNITED
KINGDOM

DENMA

NETH.

IRELAND

BELG.

LUX.

SWI

FRANCE

UNITED STATES
OF AMERICA

SPAIN

Azores
(Portugal)

PORTUGAL

TUNIS

Tropic of Cancer

MOROCCO

Canary Islands
(Spain)

Hawaiian
Islands
(U.S.A.)

WESTERN SAHARA
(Morocco)

ALGERIA

THE BAHAMAS

MEXICO

CUBA

DOMINICAN
REPUBLIC

HAITI

MAURITANIA

MALI

NIGE

BELIZE
GUATEMALA   HONDURAS

JAMAICA

CAPE VERDE

SENEGAL

BURKINA
FASO

EL SALVADOR   NICARAGUA

Caribbean Sea

DOMINICA

THE GAMBIA
GUINEA-BISSAU

BENIN

COSTA RICA

TRINIDAD AND TOBAGO

GUINEA

TOGO

NIGERI

PANAMA

VENEZUELA

SIERRA LEONE

IVORY
COAST

P A C I F I C

GUYANA
SURINAM

COLOMBIA

LIBERIA

GHANA

FRENCH GUIANA
(France)

EQUATORIA
GUINE

Galapagos Islands
(Ecuador)

SAO TOME AND
PRINCIPE

O C E A N

ECUADOR

A T L A N T I C

Equator

KIRIBATI

O C E A N

PERU

B R A Z I L

Cook
Islands
(New Zealand)

French
Polynesia
(France)

BOLIVIA

20°
S

Tropic of Capricorn

Pitcairn
Islands
(U.K.)

PARAGUAY

CHILE

URUGUAY

ARGENTINA

1:72,700,000

0   1,000   2,000   3,000   4,000   5,000km

0   1,000   2,000   3,000 miles

Falkland Islands
(U.K.)

South Georgia
(U.K.)

Antarctic Circle

Weddell
Sea

18

ARCTIC OCEAN

20° E 40° 60° 80° 100° 120° 140° 160° 180°

Arctic Circle

Svalbard
(Norway)

RUSSIA

60°

WEDEN FINLAND

ESTONIA
LATVIA
RUSSIA LITHUANIA
ERMANY BELARUS
POLAND
ZECH REP.
JST. SLOVAKIA UKRAINE
HUNGARY MOLDOVA
O ROMANIA
B.H. YUG BULGARIA
ALY ALBANIA MAC.
GREECE TURKEY
Mediterranean Sea CYPRUS
LEB.
ISRAEL SYRIA
JORDAN
LIBYA EGYPT
SAUDI
ARABIA
OMAN

KAZAKHSTAN

MONGOLIA

NORTH
KOREA
SOUTH
KOREA

JAPAN

40°

Black Sea
Caspian
Sea
GEORGIA
ARM.
AZER.
TURKMENISTAN
IRAQ
IRAN
KUWAIT
BAHRAIN
QATAR
U.A.E
UZBEKISTAN
KYRGYZSTAN
TAJIKISTAN
AFGHANISTAN
PAKISTAN

CHINA

PACIFIC

OCEAN

NEPAL
BHUTAN
BANGLA-
DESH
BURMA
(MYANMAR)
TAIWAN

Tropic of Cancer

20°
N

CHAD
SUDAN
ERITREA
YEMEN
DJIBOUTI
ETHIOPIA
CENTRAL
AFRICAN
REPUBLIC
AMEROON
SOMALIA
UGANDA
KENYA
ABON CONGO
ONGO (DEMOCRATIC
REPUBLIC)
RWANDA
BURUNDI
TANZANIA
ANGOLA
ZAMBIA
MALAWI
ZIMBABWE
AMIBIA BOTSWANA MOZAMBIQUE
SWAZILAND
LESOTHO
SOUTH AFRICA

INDIA

LAOS
THAILAND
VIETNAM
CAMBODIA

PHILIPPINES

Northern
Mariana
Islands
(U.S.A.)

MARSHALL
ISLANDS

SRI LANKA

MALDIVES

MALAYSIA
SINGAPORE

BRUNEI

PALAU

FEDERATED STATES
OF MICRONESIA

Equator

SEYCHELLES

INDIAN

OCEAN

INDONESIA

PAPUA
NEW GUINEA

NAURU

KIRIBATI

SOLOMON
ISLANDS

TUVALU

COMOROS

MADAGASCAR
MAURITIUS

Coral Sea
Islands
Territory
(Australia)
New
Caledonia
(France)

VANUATU

SAMOA

FIJI TONGA

Tropic of Capricorn

20°
S

Reunion
(France)

AUSTRALIA

40°

Kerguelen Islands
(France)

NEW
ZEALAND

60°

SOUTHERN OCEAN

Antarctic Circle

The shading on this map is there to help
you see the different countries clearly.

ANTARCTICA

80°

20° E 40° 60° 80° 100° 120° 140° 160° 180°

Copyright © Usborne Publishing Ltd.

19

Abbreviations used on map:

ARM.	ARMENIA
AUST.	AUSTRIA
AZER.	AZERBAIJAN
BELG.	BELGIUM
B.H.	BOSNIA AND HERZEGOVINA
CRO.	CROATIA
CZECH REP.	CZECH REPUBLIC
LEB.	LEBANON
LUX.	LUXEMBOURG
MAC.	MACEDONIA
NETH.	NETHERLANDS
SLOV.	SLOVENIA
SWITZ.	SWITZERLAND
U.A.E.	UNITED ARAB EMIRATES
YUG.	YUGOSLAVIA

Beaufort
Sea

80°

160°   140°   120°   100°   80°   60°   40°   20° W   0°

Victoria
Island

Queen
Elizabeth
Islands

Ellesmere
Island

Greenland

Greenland
Sea

Baffin
Bay

Baffin
Island

Iceland

Arctic Circle

Alaska

Mount McKinley
▲
6,194m
(20,321ft)

Yukon

60°

Hudson
Bay

Labrador
Sea

British
Isles

North
Sea

Gulf of Alaska

Aleutian Islands

Rocky Mountains

Great Plains

**NORTH
AMERICA**

Great
Lakes

Newfoundland

40°

Appalachian Mountains

Azores

Canary
Islands

Atlas Mountains

Mississippi

Tropic of Cancer

Gulf of
Mexico

Cuba

West Indies

S

20°
N

Hawaiian
Islands

Greater Antilles

Caribbean
Sea

Lesser
Antilles

Cape Verde
Islands

S

Galapagos
Islands

Guiana
Highlands

P o l y n e s i a

PACIFIC

Equator   0°

Amazon
Basin

Amazon

ATLANTIC

Tahiti

OCEAN

Selvas

Easter Island

A n d e s

**SOUTH
AMERICA**

OCEAN

20°
S

Tropic of Capricorn

Atacama Desert

Aconcagua
▲
6,959m
(22,831ft)

Pampas

40°

1:72,700,000

0   1,000   2,000   3,000   4,000   5,000km

0   1,000   2,000   3,000 miles

Patagonia

Falkland Islands

South Georgia

Cape Horn

60°

Antarctic Circle

Antarctic
Peninsula

Weddell
Sea

80°

160°   140°   120°   100°   80°   60°   40°   20° W   0°

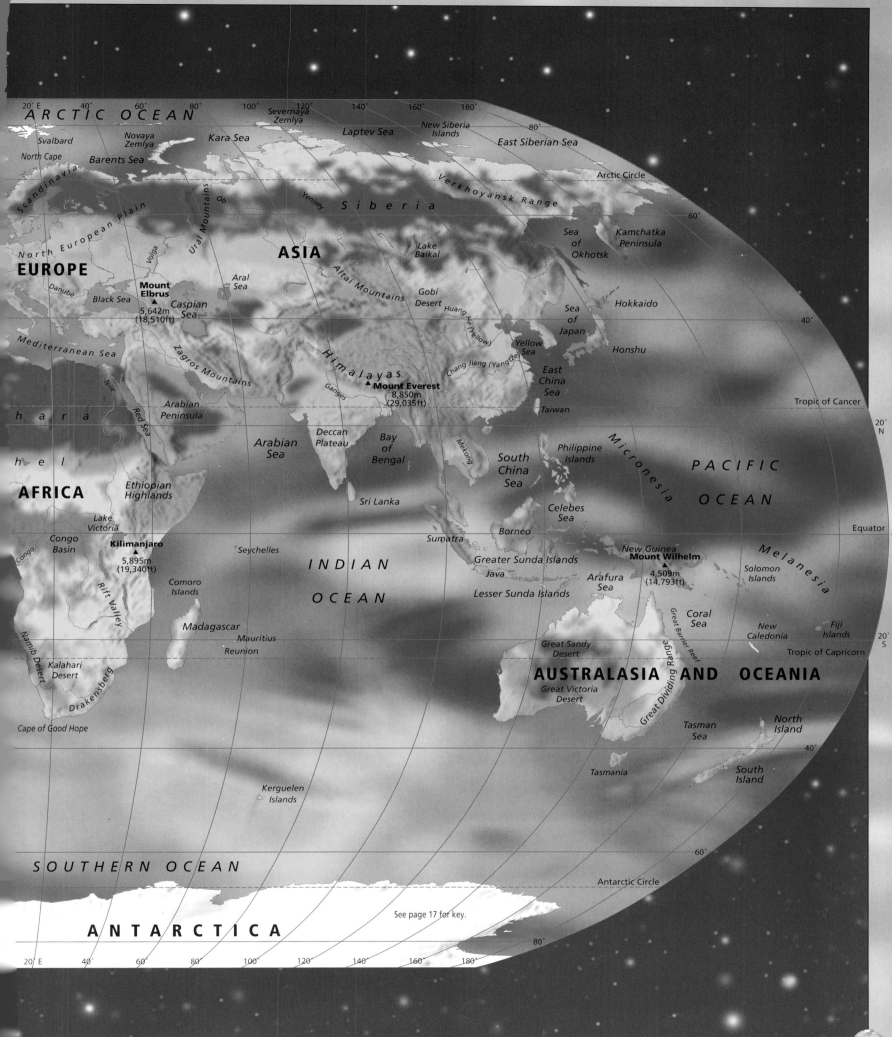

ARCTIC OCEAN

20° E 40° 60° 80° 100° 120° 140° 160° 180°

Svalbard

Severnaya
Zemlya

Novaya
Zemlya

Kara Sea

Laptev Sea

New Siberia
Islands

East Siberian Sea

80°

North Cape

Barents Sea

Arctic Circle

Scandinavia

North European plain

Ob

Yenisey

Siberia

Verkhoyansk Range

60°

Sea
of
Okhotsk

Kamchatka
Peninsula

EUROPE

Volga

Ural Mountains

ASIA

Lake
Baikal

ASIA

Altai Mountains

Mount
Elbrus
▲
5,642m
(18,510ft)

Aral
Sea

Caspian
Sea

Gobi
Desert

Huang He (Yellow)

Sea
of
Japan

Hokkaido

40°

Danube

Black Sea

Honshu

Mediterranean Sea

Zagros Mountains

Himalayas

Chang Jiang (Yangtze)

Yellow
Sea

East
China
Sea

h a r a

Arabian
Peninsula

Red Sea

Ganges

▲ Mount Everest
8,850m
(29,035ft)

Taiwan

Tropic of Cancer

20°
N

h e l

Arabian
Sea

Deccan
Plateau

Bay
of
Bengal

Mekong

South
China
Sea

Philippine
Islands

Micronesia

PACIFIC

AFRICA

Ethiopian
Highlands

OCEAN

Lake
Victoria

Sri Lanka

Celebes
Sea

Congo
Basin

Kilimanjaro
▲
5,895m
(19,340ft)

Seychelles

INDIAN

Sumatra

Borneo

New Guinea
Mount Wilhelm
▲
4,509m
(14,793ft)

Melanesia

Equator

0°

Congo

Comoro
Islands

OCEAN

Greater Sunda Islands

Java

Arafura
Sea

Solomon
Islands

Rift Valley

Madagascar

Lesser Sunda Islands

Coral
Sea

New
Caledonia

Fiji
Islands

Namib Desert

Mauritius

Great Barrier Reef

20°
S

Kalahari
Desert

Reunion

Great Sandy
Desert

Tropic of Capricorn

Drakensberg

AUSTRALASIA AND OCEANIA

Cape of Good Hope

Great Victoria
Desert

Great Dividing Range

Tasman
Sea

North
Island

40°

Kerguelen
Islands

Tasmania

South
Island

60°

SOUTHERN OCEAN

Antarctic Circle

See page 17 for key.

ANTARCTICA

80°

20° E 40° 60° 80° 100° 120° 140° 160° 180°

Copyright © Usborne Publishing Ltd.

NORTH AMERICA

The name "North America" can be used to mean several different things. In this atlas, North America includes Greenland, Canada, the U.S.A., the Caribbean, and the countries of Central America, which run along the narrow strip of land between the U.S.A. and South America. The continent has over 20 countries, including Canada, the second-largest country in the world.

These are columns of rock called hoodoos in Bryce Canyon National Park, U.S.A.

Arctic Circle

ARCTIC OCEAN

Beaufort Sea

Bering Sea

Yukon

Victoria Island

ALASKA (U.S.A.)

Anchorage

CANADA

Vancouver

Columbia

Missouri

PACIFIC OCEAN

Hawaiian Islands (U.S.A.)

UNITED STATES

Colorado

Los Angeles

Rio Grande

Tropic of Cancer

MEXICO

Mexico City

Copyright © Usborne Publishing Ltd.

The shading on this map is there to help you see clearly the different countries that make up the continent.

Ellesmere Island

Queen Elizabeth Islands

Arctic Circle

GREENLAND
(Denmark)

Baffin Island

Godthab ■

Hudson Bay

Newfoundland

St. Lawrence

Montreal
Ottawa ■ ⊙

Great Lakes

Chicago ⊙

New York ⊙

Washington D.C. ■

Mississippi

OF AMERICA

ATLANTIC

OCEAN

Tropic of Cancer

⊙ Houston

THE BAHAMAS

Gulf of Mexico

Havana ■
CUBA

Puerto Rico (U.S.A.)

Guadeloupe (France)

HAITI **DOMINICAN REPUBLIC**

DOMINICA
Martinique (France)

JAMAICA

BARBADOS

BELIZE

Caribbean Sea

TRINIDAD AND TOBAGO

GUATEMALA

HONDURAS

EL SALVADOR

NICARAGUA

COSTA RICA **PANAMA**

Facts

Total land area 22,656,190 sq km (8,745,289 sq miles)

Total population 487 million

Biggest city Mexico City, Mexico

Biggest country Canada 9,970,610 sq km (3,849,653 sq miles)

Smallest country Saint Kitts and Nevis 269 sq km (104 sq miles)

Highest mountain Mount McKinley, Alaska, U.S.A. 6,194m (20,321ft)

Longest river Mississippi/Missouri, U.S.A. 6,019km (3,741 miles)

Biggest lake Lake Superior, between the U.S.A. and Canada 82,414 sq km (31,820 sq miles)

Highest waterfall Yosemite Falls, on the Yosemite Creek, California, U.S.A. 739m (2,425ft)

Biggest desert Great Basin Desert, U.S.A. 492,000 sq km (190,000 sq miles)

Biggest island Greenland 2,175,600 sq km (840,000 sq miles)

Main mineral deposits Silver, gold, copper, lead, zinc, graphite, molybdenum, nickel

Main fuel deposits Oil, coal, natural gas, uranium

The bald eagle is the national bird of the U.S.A. It is not really bald, but has white feathers on its head.

North America covers a huge area, from just south of the North Pole to just north of the Equator. The land in the far north is icy and barren, while southern areas are lush and tropical. The west is dominated by the snow-capped Rocky Mountains.

Enormous parks

North America has many vast national parks. These are specially-protected natural areas where all kinds of animals live. One of the most famous parks is Yellowstone Park in Wyoming, U.S.A., which is home to wolves, black bears and many other animals. The park also has natural hot springs and geysers.

This satellite image of North America shows dry areas in brown, vegetation in green and icy regions in white.

Erupting island

Half of the island of Hawaii is covered by Mauna Loa, the biggest volcano on Earth, and one of the most active. The volcano is monitored constantly to check for impending eruptions. Its biggest eruption was in 1950, when a wide river of red-hot lava flowed 24km (15 miles) to the sea, destroying roads and houses in its path.

This satellite image shows part of Mauna Loa volcano. The dark, round hole at the top is one of the volcano's craters, out of which lava and gases regularly explode.

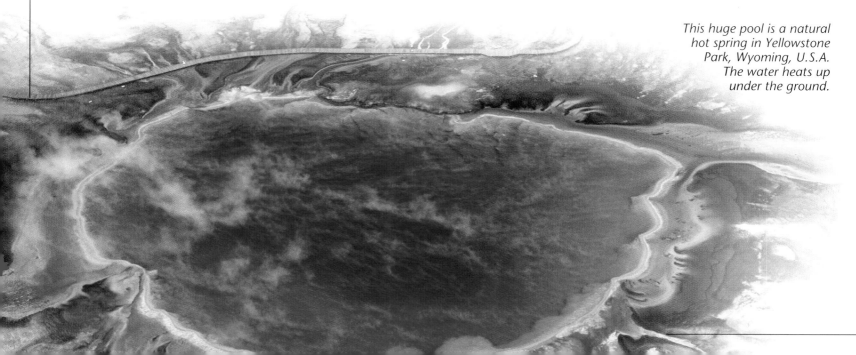

This huge pool is a natural hot spring in Yellowstone Park, Wyoming, U.S.A. The water heats up under the ground.

Internet links

For a link to a Web site where you can take an interactive tour of Yellowstone National Park, which includes videos and photographs of the park's geysers and wildlife, go to **www.usborne-quicklinks.com**

This is the most southerly section of the Mississippi River, where it splits into several small channels before running into the sea.

Mighty Mississippi

The Mississippi/Missouri River is the longest river system in North America and the fourth-longest in the world. The Mississippi flows from Minnesota in northern U.S.A. to the Gulf of Mexico in the south. The Missouri begins in Montana, in the west, and joins the Mississippi in the state of Missouri. The river system is a busy shipping route, and is also vital for wildlife – migratory birds follow it as they fly south in the winter.

The deepest valley

The Grand Canyon, in Arizona, U.S.A., is the world's largest gorge, a deep valley that stretches over 400km (250 miles). In some parts it is 1.6km (1 mile) deep, and up to 29km (18 miles) wide.

The Grand Canyon was carved out by the Colorado River, which eroded the rocky land over many thousands of years. It is possible to hike down the sides of the Canyon, but they are so steep that it takes a whole day to get to the bottom.

Running from top left to bottom right of this satellite image is the jagged Grand Canyon, in the flat, dry state of Arizona, U.S.A. Smaller valleys join the main canyon.

The northern part of North America consists mainly of Canada and the U.S.A. and has many large, dynamic cities as well as forests, deserts and other vast natural spaces.

Huge clouds of spray and mist rise from Horseshoe Falls, one of the two spectacular waterfalls that form Niagara Falls. The falls divide the U.S.A. (left) and Canada (right).

Cold country

Canada has extremely cold, snowy winters, especially in northern and eastern areas. In the city of Montreal, an amazing 1m (40in) of snow once fell in a single day. Not surprisingly, Canada is famous for its many winter sports, such as skiing, ice-skating and ice hockey.

On the border

The border between Canada and the U.S.A. is the longest in the world, covering 6,416km (3,987 miles). In the east, the border runs through several huge lakes, known as the Great Lakes. This section of the border includes Niagara Falls, where water from Lake Erie crashes over two enormous waterfalls.

Big cities

The largest city in the U.S.A. is New York, which is also the country's financial capital. Other big cities include Los Angeles, home of the movie-making area Hollywood, and Las Vegas, which boasts the largest number of hotel rooms of any U.S. city.

At night, the casinos and hotels of Las Vegas are lit up in a blaze of neon lights.

Desert heat

Death Valley in California is the driest place in the U.S.A., and one of the hottest places in the world. The temperature in this vast wilderness has been known to reach a sweltering 57°C (134°F). The desert is generally barren, though when rain does occasionally fall, beautiful wild flowers spring up between the rocks.

In the foreground of this Las Vegas skyline is a replica of the Chrysler Building, a New York skyscraper. It is part of an extravagant hotel that has 12 towers, each in the shape of a famous New York building.

An American alligator lazes in one of Florida's coastal swamps. Alligators eat birds, frogs and other animals – sometimes even small alligators.

The sunshine state

Florida, in southeastern U.S.A., has a hot, tropical climate and is nicknamed "the sunshine state". Southern Florida is covered in swampy wetlands called the Everglades. All kinds of wildlife live there, including Florida panthers and American alligators.

Internet links

For a link to a Web site where you can read profiles of the animals that live in Florida's Everglades National Park and also learn why some of them are in danger of becoming extinct, go to
www.usborne-quicklinks.com

Central America is dominated by the country of Mexico, with its ancient ruins and crowded cities. Farther south, the countries near the border with South America have beautiful beaches, tropical rainforests and fiery volcanoes.

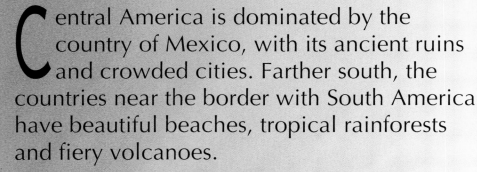

Here a bright wall mural is being painted in the coastal town of Cancun, one of Mexico's lively tourist spots.

City living

Mexico has a huge population, and also has millions of visitors every year. Its biggest city is the capital, Mexico City, where almost a quarter of Mexico's total population lives. The city is so overcrowded that the air is heavily polluted, and many people have poor living conditions and inadequate water supplies.

These statues are in Tula, Mexico. They were built by the ancient Toltec people, and were probably columns that held up a roof.

Ancient remains

In Mexico and nearby areas there are many remains of ancient cities. These were built by people from ancient civilizations, such as the Maya and the Toltec. The Maya had a powerful empire around AD200–900, while the Toltec ruled from about 900 to 1200. These peoples were excellent builders, and created many impressive temples and elaborately carved statues.

Land of volcanoes

Along the Pacific coast of Central America are more than 40 volcanoes. Lava from volcanic eruptions helps make the soil fertile, which is good for growing crops such as bananas and coffee. The volcanoes erupt regularly, and can be very dangerous. For example, the Arenal volcano in Costa Rica wiped out a whole town in a 1963 eruption, and has produced frequent lava flows ever since.

A white-nosed coati raids a banana tree in Costa Rica. These Central American mammals eat all kinds of fruit.

This is the Arenal volcano during a recent eruption. Lava can flow more than 2km (1.5 miles) from the volcano's base.

Sun and storms

The Caribbean islands have stunning sandy beaches and a hot climate. But their position in the Atlantic Ocean means that they are often hit by tropical storms and hurricanes. Some hurricanes reach wind speeds of 250kph (155mph).

Internet links

For a link to a Web site where you can find out all about Mexico, including useful information about its main cities and amazing ancient sites, go to **www.usborne-quicklinks.com**

Linking oceans

The Panama Canal is one of the world's busiest shipping routes. It cuts through the country of Panama and is a short cut for ships sailing between the Atlantic and Pacific oceans. Before the canal opened, ships had to sail around South America, an extra 12,500km (7,800 miles).

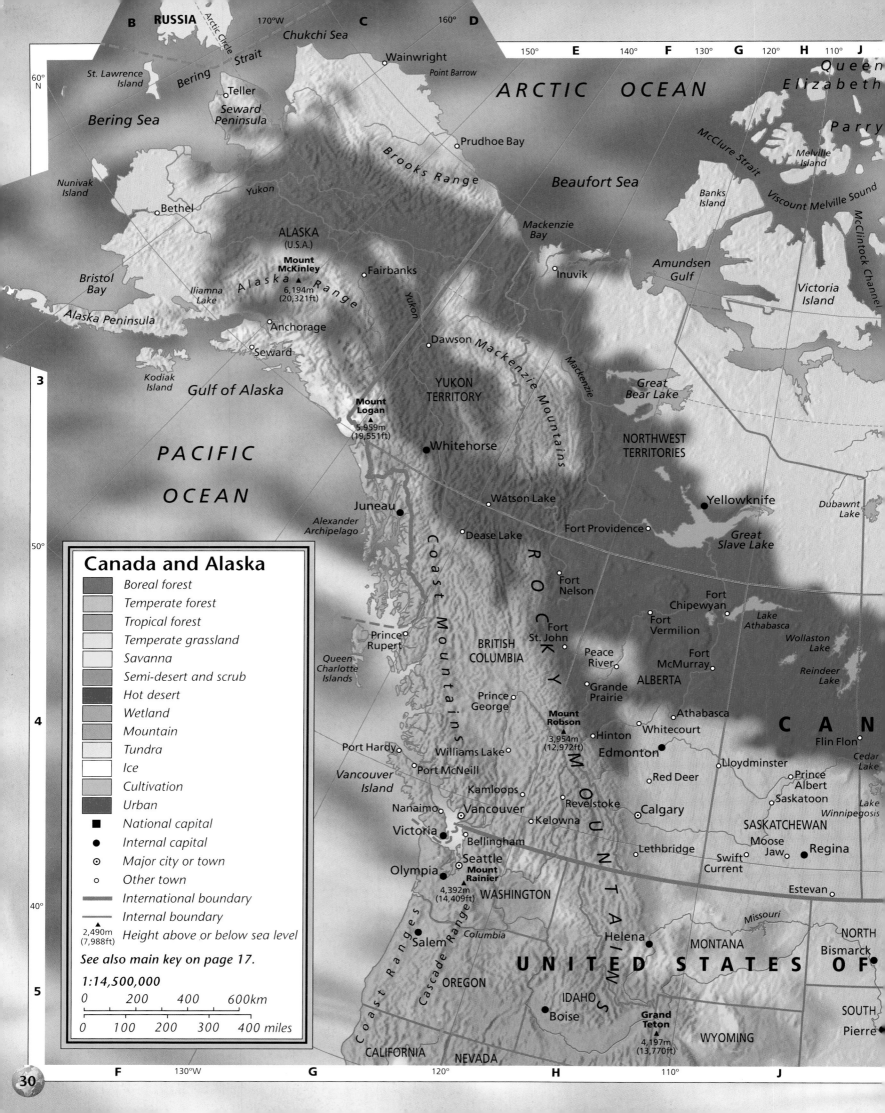

RUSSIA

Arctic Circle

Chukchi Sea

Wainwright

Point Barrow

ARCTIC OCEAN

Queen Elizabeth

60°N

St. Lawrence Island

Bering Strait

Teller

Seward Peninsula

Bering Sea

Prudhoe Bay

Beaufort Sea

McClure Strait

Melville Island

P a r r y

Nunivak Island

Bethel

Yukon

Brooks Range

Mackenzie Bay

Inuvik

Amundsen Gulf

Banks Island

Viscount Melville Sound

McClintock Channel

ALASKA (U.S.A.)

Mount McKinley ▲ 6,194m (20,321ft)

Fairbanks

Victoria Island

Bristol Bay

Iliamna Lake

Alaska Range

Anchorage

Seward

Yukon

Dawson

Mackenzie Mountains

Mackenzie

Great Bear Lake

NORTHWEST TERRITORIES

Dubawnt Lake

Kodiak Island

Gulf of Alaska

Alaska Peninsula

PACIFIC OCEAN

Mount Logan ▲ 5,959m (19,551ft)

YUKON TERRITORY

Whitehorse

Juneau

Alexander Archipelago

Watson Lake

Fort Providence

Yellowknife

Great Slave Lake

50°

Dease Lake

R O C K Y

Fort Nelson

Fort Chipewyan

Lake Athabasca

Wollaston Lake

Prince Rupert

Queen Charlotte Islands

Coast Mountains

BRITISH COLUMBIA

Fort St. John

Peace River

Fort Vermilion

Fort McMurray

ALBERTA

Reindeer Lake

C A N

Prince George

Grande Prairie

Athabasca

Flin Flon

Cedar Lake

Mount Robson ▲ 3,954m (12,972ft)

Hinton

Whitecourt

Port Hardy

Williams Lake

M

Edmonton

Lloydminster

Prince Albert

Vancouver Island

Port McNeill

Kamloops

O

Red Deer

Saskatoon

Lake Winnipegosis

Nanaimo

Vancouver

Revelstoke

U

Calgary

SASKATCHEWAN

Victoria

Kelowna

N

Moose Jaw

Regina

Bellingham

Seattle

Lethbridge

Swift Current

Olympia

Mount Rainier ▲ 4,392m (14,409ft)

WASHINGTON

T

Estevan

40°

Coast Ranges

Cascade Range

Columbia

OREGON

Missouri

A

Helena

MONTANA

NORTH

Bismarck

Salem

2,490m (7,988ft)

I

U N I T E D   S T A T E S   O F

CALIFORNIA

NEVADA

IDAHO

Boise

N

Grand Teton ▲ 4,197m (13,770ft)

WYOMING

SOUTH

Pierre

Canada and Alaska

- Boreal forest
- Temperate forest
- Tropical forest
- Temperate grassland
- Savanna
- Semi-desert and scrub
- Hot desert
- Wetland
- Mountain
- Tundra
- Ice
- Cultivation
- Urban
- ■ National capital
- ● Internal capital
- ⊙ Major city or town
- ○ Other town
- —— International boundary
- —— Internal boundary
- ▲ 2,490m (7,988ft) Height above or below sea level

See also main key on page 17.

1:14,500,000

0   200   400   600km

0   100   200   300   400 miles

B   170°W   C   160°   D   150°   E   140°   F   130°   G   120°   H   110°   J

3

4

5

F   130°W   G   120°   H   110°   J

K 90° L 80° M 70° N 60° P 50° Q 40° R 30° S 60°

Ellesmere Island

Islands

Islands

Baffin

Bay

A 180° B 170°W C

Bering Sea 55°N 55°N

Shishaldin Volcano ▲

Devon Island

Lancaster Sound

1

2,857m (9,372ft) *Unimak Island*

Somerset Island

3 *Attu Island*

Near Islands

Aleutian Islands

Fox Islands

Unalaska Island

3

les

nd

Boothia Peninsula

Gulf of Boothia

70° N

Baffin Island

Rat Islands

Andreanof Islands

Umnak Island

Same scale as main map

A 180° B 170°W C

2

GREENLAND (Denmark) *Cape Farewell*

ing lliam nd

Melville Peninsula

Foxe Basin

Cumberland Peninsula

Nettilling Lake

Davis Strait

Labrador Sea

3

Foxe Peninsula

Amadjuak Lake

Iqaluit •

Atka Island

NUNAVUT

Southampton Island

Hudson Strait

ATLANTIC

OCEAN

Cape Chidley

• Ivujivik

Ungava Peninsula

Ungava Bay

Nain •

Makkovik •

All islands within Hudson Bay, James Bay and Ungava Bay lie within Nunavut.

Kuujjuaq •

• Cartwright

50°

NEWFOUNDLAND

• Inukjuak

Happy Valley- Goose Bay

• Churchill

Hudson Bay

Smallwood Reservoir

• Churchill Falls

Gander •

St. John's •

Labrador City

Newfoundland

Belcher Islands

La Grande Reservoir

• Corner Brook

MANITOBA

• Fort Severn

QUEBEC

Manicouagan Reservoir

Anticosti Island

• Thompson

James Bay

Radisson •

St. Pierre and Miquelon (France)

4

Lake Winnipeg

Fort Albany •

Baie- Comeau •

Gaspe •

Gulf of St. Lawrence

Sydney •

rand apids

Waskaganish •

Lake Mistassini

Bathurst •

PRINCE EDWARD ISLAND

Charlottetown •

ke anitoba

Chicoutimi •

Edmundston •

NEW BRUNSWICK

Moncton •

Halifax •

innipeg

Lake of the Woods

Dryden •

Lake Nipigon

Kirkland Lake •

Val-d'Or •

ONTARIO

Quebec •

Trois-Rivieres •

Fredericton •

St. Lawrence

Saint John •

NOVA SCOTIA

andon

Kenora •

Marathon •

MAINE

Yarmouth •

Montreal •

Augusta •

Thunder Bay •

Lake Superior

Ottawa ■

Montpelier •

40°

Sudbury •

North Bay •

VERMONT

Concord •

KOTA

MINNESOTA

Sault Ste. Marie •

Huntsville •

Kingston •

NEW HAMPSHIRE

Boston •

MERICA

Owen Sound

Lake Ontario

Albany •

MASSACHUSETTS

Providence •

KOTA

MICHIGAN

Lake Huron

Toronto •

NEW YORK

RHODE ISLAND

St. Paul •

Hamilton •

Niagara Falls

Hartford •

Minneapolis •

WISCONSIN

Mississippi

London •

Detroit •

Buffalo •

CONNECTICUT

New York •

Lake Michigan

Lansing •

Lake Erie

Erie •

Trenton •

NEW JERSEY

5

Madison •

Windsor •

Cleveland •

PENNSYLVANIA

Philadelphia •

Chicago •

Harrisburg •

Dover •

ILLINOIS

INDIANA

Pittsburgh •

OHIO

Annapolis •

DELAWARE

70°

N

31

K 90° 80°

Columbus •

Washington D.C. ■

Copyright © Usborne Publishing Ltd.

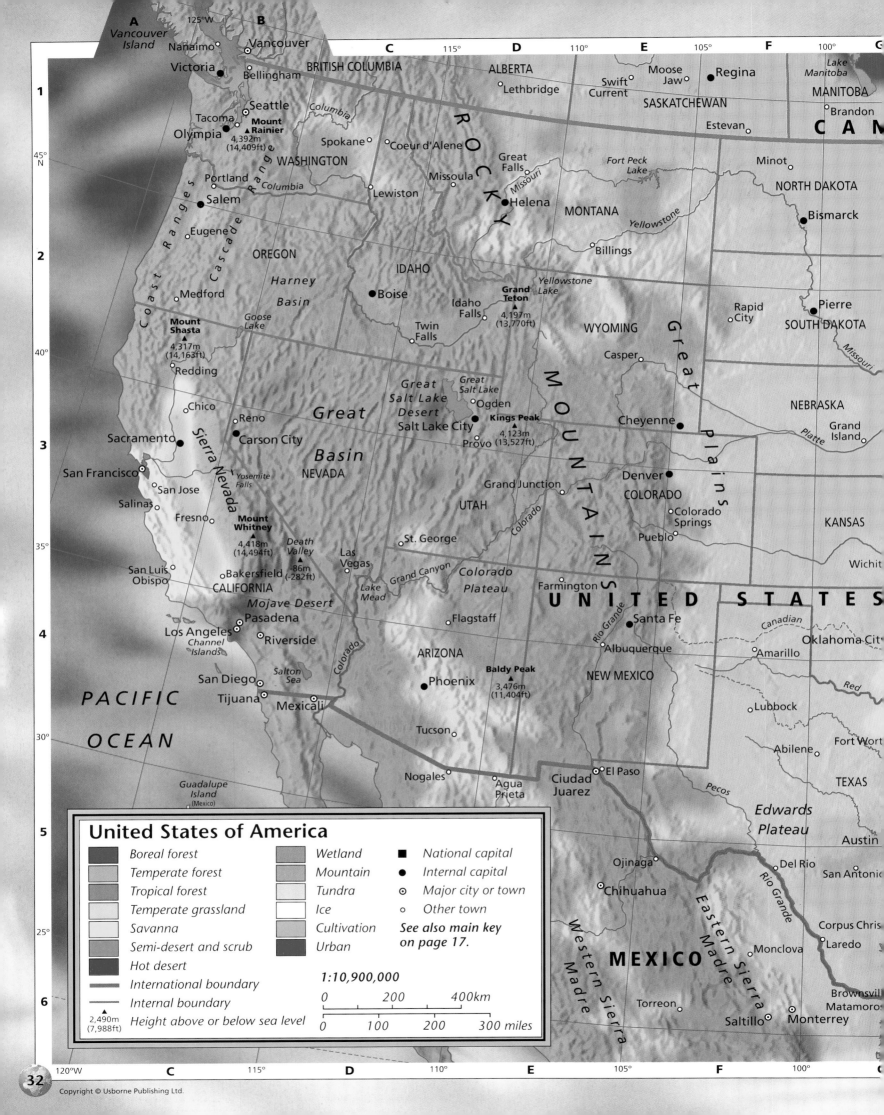

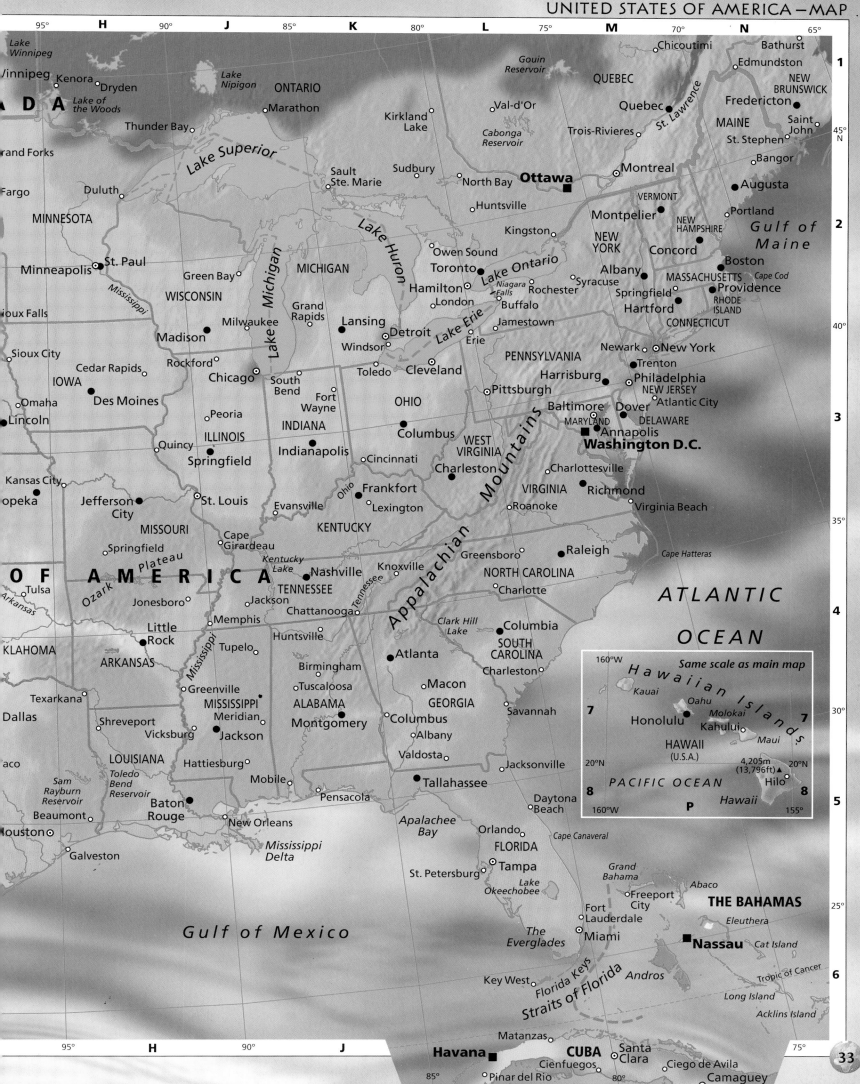

95°   H   90°   J   85°   K   80°   L   75°   M   70°   N   65°

CANADA

Lake Winnipeg

Winnipeg   Kenora   Dryden

Lake of the Woods

Lake Nipigon

Lake Nipigon

ONTARIO

Marathon

Gouin Reservoir

QUEBEC

Chicoutimi   Bathurst

Edmundston

NEW BRUNSWICK

Grand Forks

Thunder Bay

Kirkland Lake

Val-d'Or

Cabonga Reservoir

Quebec

St. Lawrence

Fredericton

Saint John

St. Stephen

MAINE

Fargo

Duluth

Lake Superior

Sault Ste. Marie

Sudbury

North Bay   **Ottawa**

Trois-Rivieres

Montreal

Bangor

45°N

MINNESOTA

Huntsville

Montpelier

VERMONT

Augusta

2

Kingston

NEW HAMPSHIRE

Portland

Gulf of Maine

Minneapolis   St. Paul

Green Bay

Owen Sound

MICHIGAN

Toronto

Lake Ontario

Hamilton

Niagara Falls

Rochester

NEW YORK

Concord

Albany

Syracuse

Springfield

Boston

MASSACHUSETTS

Cape Cod

Providence

40°

Sioux Falls

WISCONSIN

Mississippi

Milwaukee

Madison

Lake Michigan

Grand Rapids

Lansing

Detroit

Windsor

Lake Erie

London

Buffalo

Erie

Jamestown

Hartford

RHODE ISLAND

CONNECTICUT

Sioux City

Cedar Rapids

Rockford

Chicago

South Bend

Fort Wayne

Toledo

Cleveland

OHIO

PENNSYLVANIA

Pittsburgh

Harrisburg

Newark   New York

Trenton

Philadelphia

NEW JERSEY

Atlantic City

IOWA

Omaha

Des Moines

Peoria

INDIANA

Columbus

WEST VIRGINIA

Baltimore

MARYLAND

Dover   **DELAWARE**

Annapolis

3

Lincoln

ILLINOIS

Quincy

Springfield

Indianapolis

Cincinnati

Charleston

Washington D.C.

Kansas City

Topeka

Jefferson City

St. Louis

Evansville

Frankfort

Lexington

Ohio

KENTUCKY

Charlottesville

VIRGINIA

Richmond

Roanoke

Virginia Beach

35°

MISSOURI

Springfield

Cape Girardeau

Ozark Plateau

Kentucky Lake

Nashville

Knoxville

Tennessee

Greensboro

Raleigh

Cape Hatteras

OF   AMERICA

Tulsa

Jonesboro

TENNESSEE

Jackson

Chattanooga

Appalachian Mountains

NORTH CAROLINA

Charlotte

ATLANTIC

4

Arkansas

OKLAHOMA

Little Rock

ARKANSAS

Memphis

Tupelo

Mississippi

Huntsville

Clark Hill Lake

Columbia

SOUTH CAROLINA

Charleston

OCEAN

Texarkana

Greenville

MISSISSIPPI

Meridian

Birmingham

Tuscaloosa

ALABAMA

Atlanta

Macon

GEORGIA

Savannah

160°W   Same scale as main map

Kauai

Hawaiian Islands

Oahu

Molokai

Dallas

Shreveport

Vicksburg

Jackson

Montgomery

Columbus

Albany

7   Honolulu   Kahului   Maui   7   30°

Waco

LOUISIANA

Toledo Bend Reservoir

Hattiesburg

Mobile

Valdosta

Jacksonville

HAWAII (U.S.A.)

4,205m (13,796ft) ▲

20°N

Houston

Sam Rayburn Reservoir

Beaumont

Baton Rouge

Pensacola

FLORIDA

Daytona Beach

20°N   **PACIFIC OCEAN**   Hilo

8   P   Hawaii   8

160°W   155°   5

Galveston

New Orleans

Mississippi Delta

Apalachee Bay

Orlando

Cape Canaveral

Gulf of Mexico

St. Petersburg   Tampa

Lake Okeechobee

Grand Bahama

Abaco

25°

Fort Lauderdale

The Everglades

Miami

Freeport City

Eleuthera

THE BAHAMAS

Nassau

Cat Island

Key West

Florida Keys

Straits of Florida

Andros

Tropic of Cancer

Long Island

Acklins Island

6

95°   H   90°   J

Matanzas

Havana

85°

CUBA

Santa Clara

80°

75°

33

Cienfuegos

Pinar del Rio

Ciego de Avila

Camaguey

120°W A 115° B 110° C 105° D 100° E 95° F 90°

CALIFORNIA
San Diego
Tijuana
Mexicali
Phoenix
ARIZONA
Tucson
NEW MEXICO
OKLAHOMA
Little Rock
ARKANSAS
Tupelo
MISSISSIPPI

UNITED STATES OF AMERICA
Lubbock
Texarkana
Fort Worth
Dallas
Shreveport
Jackson

Nogales
Agua Prieta
Ciudad Juarez
El Paso
Abilene
TEXAS
Waco
Hattiesburg

Guadalupe Island (Mexico)
Hermosillo
Ojinaga
Edwards Plateau
Austin
LOUISIANA
Baton Rouge
New Orleans

Cedros Island
Ciudad Obregon
Chihuahua
Houston
San Antonio
Galveston
Mississippi Delta

Point Eugenia
Rio Grande
Corpus Christi

Tropic of Cancer
Los Mochis
Monclova
Laredo

La Paz
Culiacan
Torreon
Monterrey
Brownsville
Matamoros
Saltillo

Cape San Lucas
Durango
Plateau of Mexico
4,054m (13,300ft)
Ciudad Victoria
Gulf of Mexico

Mazatlan
MEXICO
Matehuala
San Luis Potosi
Tampico

Aguascalientes
Leon
Merida
Yucatan Peninsula

Puerto Vallarta
Guadalajara
Celaya
Bay of Campeche

Colima
Morelia
Teotihuacan
Campeche

Uruapan
Mexico City
Puebla
Veracruz
Ciudad del Carmen

Orizaba 5,610m (18,405ft)
Tehuacan
Coatzacoalcos
Villahermosa

Southern Sierra Madre
Oaxaca
Isthmus of Tehuantepec
Belmopan

Acapulco
Tuxtla Gutierrez
Tikal
BELIZE

Gulf of Tehuantepec
Juchitan
Tajumulco 4,220m (13,845ft)
GUATEMALA

Tapachula
Quezaltenango
Guatemala City
San Salvador
EL SALVADOR

PACIFIC OCEAN

Galapagos Islands (Ecuador)

Puerto Ayora

Inset Map

L 65°W M 60° N

Virgin Islands (U.K.)
Anguilla (U.K.)
ATLANTIC OCEAN

Leeward Islands

San Juan
Virgin Islands (U.S.A.)
St. Martin (France and Netherlands)
ANTIGUA AND BARBUDA
St. John's

Puerto Rico (U.S.A.)
Basseterre
ST. KITTS AND NEVIS
Montserrat (U.K.)

1:7,300,000
Guadeloupe (France)
Windward Islands

0 100 200km
0 50 100 miles
Basse-Terre

Roseau
DOMINICA
15° N

15° N
Martinique (France)
Fort-de-France

Caribbean Sea
Castries
ST. LUCIA

5° N
Kingstown
ST. VINCENT AND THE GRENADINES
BARBADOS
Bridgetown

Lesser Antilles
St. George's
GRENADA

0°
Margarita Island
Porlamar
Tobago

Cumana
Port-of-Spain
TRINIDAD AND TOBAGO
VENEZUELA
Trinidad 60°

L 65°W M N

115°W B 110° C 105° D 100° E 95°

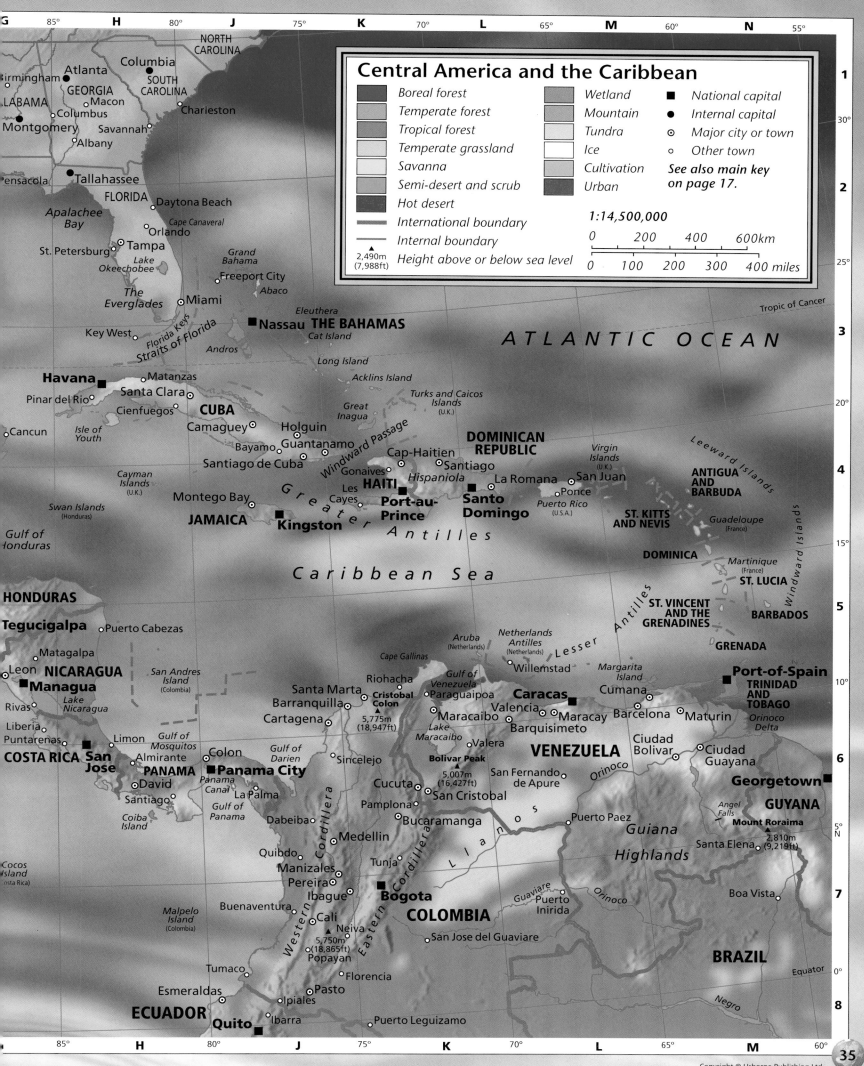

Central America and the Caribbean

Boreal forest
Temperate forest
Tropical forest
Temperate grassland
Savanna
Semi-desert and scrub
Hot desert

Wetland
Mountain
Tundra
Ice
Cultivation
Urban

■ National capital
● Internal capital
⊙ Major city or town
○ Other town

See also main key on page 17.

International boundary
Internal boundary
▲ 2,490m (7,988ft) Height above or below sea level

1:14,500,000

0   200   400   600km

0   100   200   300   400 miles

Birmingham
Atlanta
Columbia
NORTH CAROLINA
GEORGIA
SOUTH CAROLINA
Macon
Columbus
ALABAMA
Montgomery
Savannah
Albany
Charleston
Pensacola
Tallahassee
FLORIDA
Daytona Beach
Apalachee Bay
Cape Canaveral
Orlando
St. Petersburg
Tampa
Lake Okeechobee
Grand Bahama
The Everglades
Miami
Freeport City
Abaco
Key West
Florida Keys
Straits of Florida
■ Nassau   THE BAHAMAS
Eleuthera
Cat Island

ATLANTIC OCEAN

Tropic of Cancer

Havana ■
Matanzas
Pinar del Rio
Santa Clara
Long Island
Acklins Island
Cienfuegos
CUBA
Holguin
Great Inagua
Turks and Caicos Islands (U.K.)
Cancun
Isle of Youth
Camaguey
Bayamo
Guantanamo
DOMINICAN REPUBLIC
Virgin Islands (U.K.)
Leeward Islands
Santiago de Cuba
Windward Passage
Cap-Haitien
Santiago
San Juan
ANTIGUA AND BARBUDA
Cayman Islands (U.K.)
Gonaives
Hispaniola
La Romana
Ponce
Swan Islands (Honduras)
Montego Bay
Greater
Les Cayes
HAITI
Santo Domingo
Puerto Rico (U.S.A.)
ST. KITTS AND NEVIS
Guadeloupe (France)
JAMAICA
Port-au-Prince
DOMINICA
Gulf of Honduras
Kingston ■
Antilles
Windward Islands
Martinique (France)
ST. LUCIA

Caribbean Sea

HONDURAS
Tegucigalpa ●
Puerto Cabezas
Lesser Antilles
ST. VINCENT AND THE GRENADINES
BARBADOS
Matagalpa
Aruba (Netherlands)
Netherlands Antilles (Netherlands)
GRENADA
Leon
NICARAGUA
San Andres Island (Colombia)
Cape Gallinas
Willemstad
Margarita Island
Port-of-Spain ■
Managua ■
Riohacha
Gulf of Venezuela
Cumana
TRINIDAD AND TOBAGO
Lake Nicaragua
Santa Marta
Cristobal Colon
Paraguaipoa
Caracas ■
Rivas
Barranquilla
5,775m (18,947ft)
Maracaibo
Valencia
Maracay
Barcelona
Maturin
Liberia
Cartagena
Valera
Barquisimeto
Orinoco Delta
Puntarenas
Gulf of Mosquitos
Lake Maracaibo
COSTA RICA
Limon
Colon
Gulf of Darien
VENEZUELA
Ciudad Bolivar
Ciudad Guayana
San Jose ■
Sincelejo
Bolivar Peak
PANAMA
Almirante
5,007m (16,427ft)
San Fernando de Apure
Georgetown ■
David
Panama City ■
Orinoco
GUYANA
Panama Canal
La Palma
Cucuta
San Cristobal
Angel Falls
Santiago
Gulf of Panama
Pamplona
Puerto Paez
Coiba Island
Dabeiba
Bucaramanga
Mount Roraima
Cocos Island (Costa Rica)
Medellin
Llanos
Santa Elena
2,810m (9,219ft)
Quibdo
Tunja
Guiana Highlands
Manizales
Puerto Inirida
Guaviare
Boa Vista
Pereira
Orinoco
Ibague
Bogota ■
Malpelo Island (Colombia)
Buenaventura
Western Cordillera
Cali
COLOMBIA
San Jose del Guaviare
Neiva
5,750m (18,865ft)
Popayan
Eastern Cordillera
Tumaco
Florencia
BRAZIL
Esmeraldas
Pasto
Equator
ECUADOR
Ipiales
Puerto Leguizamo
Negro
Quito ■
Ibarra

Copyright © Usborne Publishing Ltd.

SOUTH AMERICA

South America is made up
of 12 independent countries,
along with French Guiana,
which belongs to France.
The continent's biggest and
most industrialized country
is Brazil, which covers about
half of the total land. Brazil
is also home to half of South
America's population.

*This is a guanaco. Guanacos are
members of the camel family that
live in South America. Guanaco
hair is used to make textiles.*

Caribbean Sea

Caracas

VENEZUELA

Medellin°   ■ Bogota

COLOMBIA   Orinoco

Quito ■
          ECUADOR   Manau
Guayaquil°

Equator

Galapagos
Islands
(Ecuador)

PERU

Lima ■

BOLIVIA

■ La Paz

■ Sucre

Tropic of Capricorn

CHILE

PACIFIC

OCEAN

Santiago ■   °Mendoza

ARGENTINA

Cape Horn

Drake Passage

The shading on this map is there to help you see clearly the different countries that make up the continent.

Georgetown
Paramaribo
ịUYANA **Cayenne**
SURINAM **FRENCH GUIANA**
(France)

Amazon

Equator

Recife

B R A Z I L

Brasilia

Parana

Belo Horizonte

PARAGUAY   Sao Paulo   Rio de Janeiro

Tropic of Capricorn

Asuncion

Porto Alegre

A T L A N T I C

O C E A N

URUGUAY
Montevideo
Buenos Aires

Falkland Islands
(U.K.)

This is a red-eyed tree frog. These frogs live in rainforests in South and Central America.

Facts

Total land area 17,866,130 sq km (6,898,113 sq miles)

Total population 346 million

Biggest city Sao Paulo, Brazil

Biggest country Brazil *8,547,400 sq km (3,300,151 sq miles)*

Smallest country Surinam *163,270 sq km (63,039 sq miles)*

Highest mountain Aconcagua, Argentina *6,959m (22,831ft)*

Longest river Amazon, mainly in Brazil *6,440km (4,000 miles)*

Biggest lake Lake Maracaibo, Venezuela *13,312 sq km (5,140 sq miles)*

Highest waterfall Angel Falls, on the Churun River, Venezuela *979m (3,212ft)*

Biggest desert Patagonian Desert, Argentina *673,000 sq km (260,000 sq miles)*

Biggest island Tierra del Fuego *46,360 sq km (17,900 sq miles)*

Main mineral deposits Copper, tin, molybdenum, bauxite, emeralds

Main fuel deposits Oil, coal

Copyright © Usborne Publishing Ltd.

South America has a varied and dramatic landscape. In the north there are lush, tropical rainforests, and in central areas are grassy plains, called pampas. In the far south there are glaciers, which are huge, slow-moving masses of ice.

The big picture

The Andes mountain range stretches more than 7,250km (4,500 miles) down the whole length of western South America. It is the longest chain of mountains on Earth.

South America also has the second-longest river in the world, the Amazon. It snakes through the northern half of the continent, from the Andes in Peru to the coast of Brazil, and carries around one-fifth of the world's fresh water.

On this satellite image of South America the Andes mountains are clearly visible in the west. The range contains many active volcanoes.

This flock of large birds, called scarlet ibises, is flying over lush forest in Venezuela.

Icy lands

The southern tip of South America is near Antarctica, which means that the climate is extremely cold. There are glaciers in the mountainous regions, and icebergs in the area's many lakes. South America's most southerly point is Cape Horn. The seas around it are rough and stormy, which can make sailing around Cape Horn very dangerous.

The bluish-white shape in the middle of this image is part of a huge glacier. Melting ice gradually flows into Lake Viedma, shown in the bottom right.

Internet links

For a link to a Web site where you can test your knowledge of the world's deserts, including the Atacama Desert of South America, go to **www.usborne-quicklinks.com**

38

Water source

On the border of Brazil and Paraguay is a vast expanse of water, about 1,350 sq km (520 sq miles) in size. This is the Itaipu reservoir, a man-made water source which provides water for homes, farms and factories in many areas of Brazil and Paraguay. In the past there had been many droughts, so the reservoir was built to provide a reliable supply of water.

This large blue area is part of the huge Itaipu reservoir, which forms part of the border between Paraguay (left) and Brazil (right).

The river running down the lower part of this image is the Parana River. It flows southward on the eastern side of South America.

This is a mountainous part of the Atacama Desert. In the middle are two snow-capped volcanoes, and on the right are white areas of salt from evaporated salt lakes.

The driest desert

Running down the western coast of Chile is the Atacama Desert, the driest place on Earth. Many areas of the desert go for decades without rain and in some parts rainfall has never been recorded.

Vast areas of the desert are covered in salt, which is all that is left of evaporated saltwater lakes. The rocky landscape looks like the Moon's surface, and NASA vehicles have been tested there in preparation for crossing the Moon's rugged terrain.

One of South America's main features is the Amazon rainforest. This is the largest rainforest in the world, covering an area nearly the size of Europe. The continent also has fascinating cities, both ancient and modern.

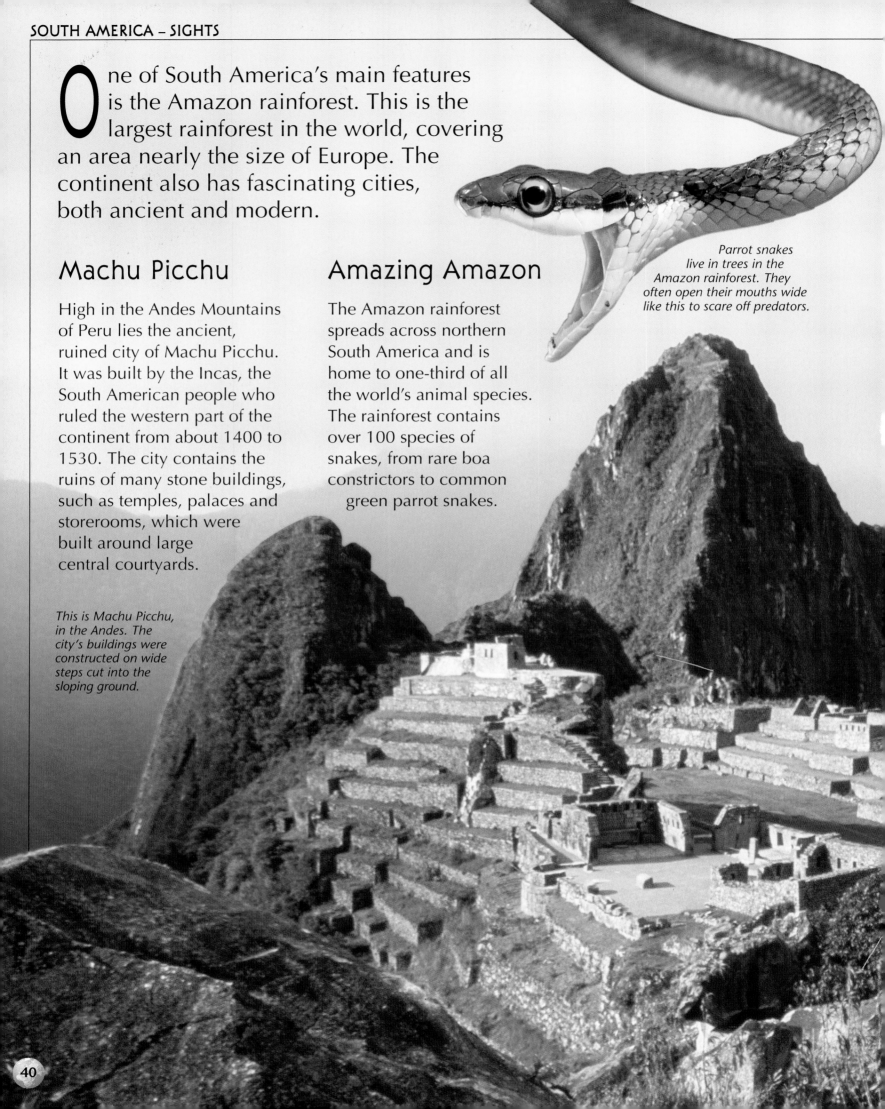

Parrot snakes live in trees in the Amazon rainforest. They often open their mouths wide like this to scare off predators.

Machu Picchu

High in the Andes Mountains of Peru lies the ancient, ruined city of Machu Picchu. It was built by the Incas, the South American people who ruled the western part of the continent from about 1400 to 1530. The city contains the ruins of many stone buildings, such as temples, palaces and storerooms, which were built around large central courtyards.

This is Machu Picchu, in the Andes. The city's buildings were constructed on wide steps cut into the sloping ground.

Amazing Amazon

The Amazon rainforest spreads across northern South America and is home to one-third of all the world's animal species. The rainforest contains over 100 species of snakes, from rare boa constrictors to common green parrot snakes.

Here is part of the wealthy, crowded financial district in Santiago, Chile.

City sprawl

South America has many huge cities, such as Sao Paulo in Brazil and Santiago in Chile. The growth of business and industry in these cities has led to the creation of towering skyscrapers, but also causes extra traffic and pollution. The cities are so overcrowded that many people live in poor, run-down suburbs.

Island animals

The Galapagos Islands are a cluster of small, rocky islands that lie in the Pacific Ocean, about 1,000km (600 miles) off the coast of Ecuador.

The islands are home to all kinds of unusual animals, such as giant tortoises. These enormous creatures weigh up to 250kg (550lb), and can live for more than a hundred years. Many tropical birds live on the islands too, including Galapagos penguins and frigate birds.

Fantastic falls

South America's mountainous landscape has led to the formation of many waterfalls, including Angel Falls in Venezuela, which is the world's biggest waterfall. It is 979m (3,212ft) high, more than twice the height of the tallest building in the world.

A male frigate bird puffs out his bright red pouch to attract females. Frigate birds live on many of the Galapagos Islands.

Internet links

For a link to a Web site where you can discover the sights and sounds of the Amazon rainforest, including howling monkeys and squawking macaws, go to **www.usborne-quicklinks.com**

41

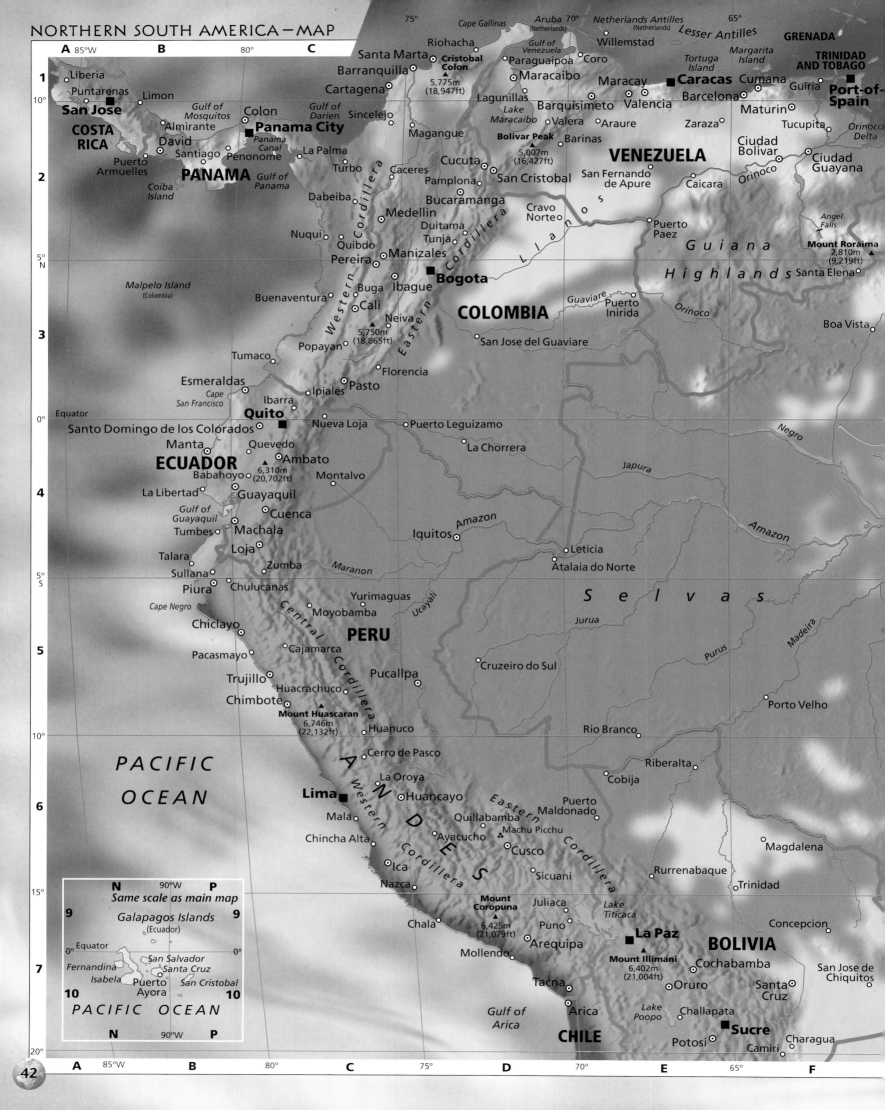

A 85°W   B   80°   C

Liberia
Puntarenas
Limon
San Jose
COSTA
RICA
Gulf of
Mosquitos
Colon
Panama City
Almirante
David
Santiago
Penonome
Panama
Canal
PANAMA
Puerto
Armuelles
Gulf of
Panama
Coiba
Island
Malpelo Island
(Colombia)

Riohacha
Cape Gallinas
Aruba 70°
(Netherlands)
Netherlands Antilles
(Netherlands)
Lesser Antilles
65°
GRENADA
Santa Marta
Cristobal
Colon
5,775m
(18,947ft)
Gulf of
Venezuela
Willemstad
Coro
Paraguaipoa
Margarita
Island
TRINIDAD
AND TOBAGO
Barranquilla
Maracaibo
Maracay
Tortuga
Island
Caracas
Cumana
Guiria
Cartagena
Gulf of
Darien
Sincelejo
Lagunillas
Valencia
Barcelona
Maturin
Port-of-
Spain
Colon
Magangue
Lake
Maracaibo
Barquisimeto
Araure
Zaraza
Tucupita
La Palma
Turbo
Caceres
Cucuta
Valera
San Fernando
de Apure
Ciudad
Bolivar
Orinoco
Delta
Dabeiba
Pamplona
Bolivar Peak
5,007m
(16,427ft)
Barinas
VENEZUELA
Caicara
Orinoco
Ciudad
Guayana
Medellin
Bucaramanga
San Cristobal
Cravo
Norte
Nuqui
Duitama
Llanos
Puerto
Paez
Guiana
Angel
Falls
Quibdo
Tunja
Mount Roraima
2,810m
(9,219ft)
Pereira
Manizales
Highlands
Santa Elena
Buenaventura
Buga
Ibague
Bogota
Guaviare
Puerto
Inirida
Boa Vista
Cali
COLOMBIA
Neiva
5,750m
(18,865ft)
San Jose del Guaviare
Orinoco
Popayan
Tumaco
Florencia
Esmeraldas
Ipiales
Pasto
Cape
San Francisco
Ibarra
Equator
Quito
Nueva Loja
Puerto Leguizamo
Negro
Santo Domingo de los Colorados
La Chorrera
Manta
Quevedo
Ambato
Japura
ECUADOR
6,310m
(20,702ft)
Montalvo
Babahoyo
La Libertad
Guayaquil
Amazon
Gulf of
Guayaquil
Cuenca
Iquitos
Amazon
Tumbes
Machala
Leticia
Talara
Loja
Atalaia do Norte
Sullana
Zumba
Maranon
Selvas
Piura
Chulucanas
Cape Negro
Central
Cordillera
Yurimaguas
Ucayali
Jurua
Purus
Madeira
Chiclayo
Moyobamba
PERU
Cajamarca
Pacasmayo
Cruzeiro do Sul
Trujillo
Pucallpa
Chimbote
Huacrachuco
Porto Velho
Mount Huascaran
6,746m
(22,132ft)
Huanuco
Rio Branco
Cerro de Pasco
Riberalta
PACIFIC
La Oroya
Cobija
OCEAN
Lima
Huancayo
Puerto
Maldonado
ANDES
Mala
Quillabamba
Eastern
Chincha Alta
Western
Ayacucho
Machu Picchu
Cordillera
Ica
Cordillera
Cusco
Rurrenabaque
Magdalena
Nazca
Sicuani
Mount
Coropuna
Juliaca
Lake
Titicaca
Trinidad
Chala
6,425m
(21,079ft)
Puno
Concepcion
Arequipa
La Paz
Mollendo
Mount Illimani
BOLIVIA
Tacna
6,402m
(21,004ft)
Cochabamba
Oruro
Santa
Cruz
San Jose de
Chiquitos
Arica
Lake
Poopo
Challapata
Charagua
CHILE
Sucre
Potosi
Camiri

Inset:
N   90°W   P
Same scale as main map
9   9
Galapagos Islands
(Ecuador)
0° Equator   0°
Fernandina
Isabela
San Salvador
Santa Cruz
San Cristobal
Puerto
Ayora
10   10
PACIFIC OCEAN
N   90°W   P

A 85°W   B   80°   C   75°   D   70°   E   65°   F

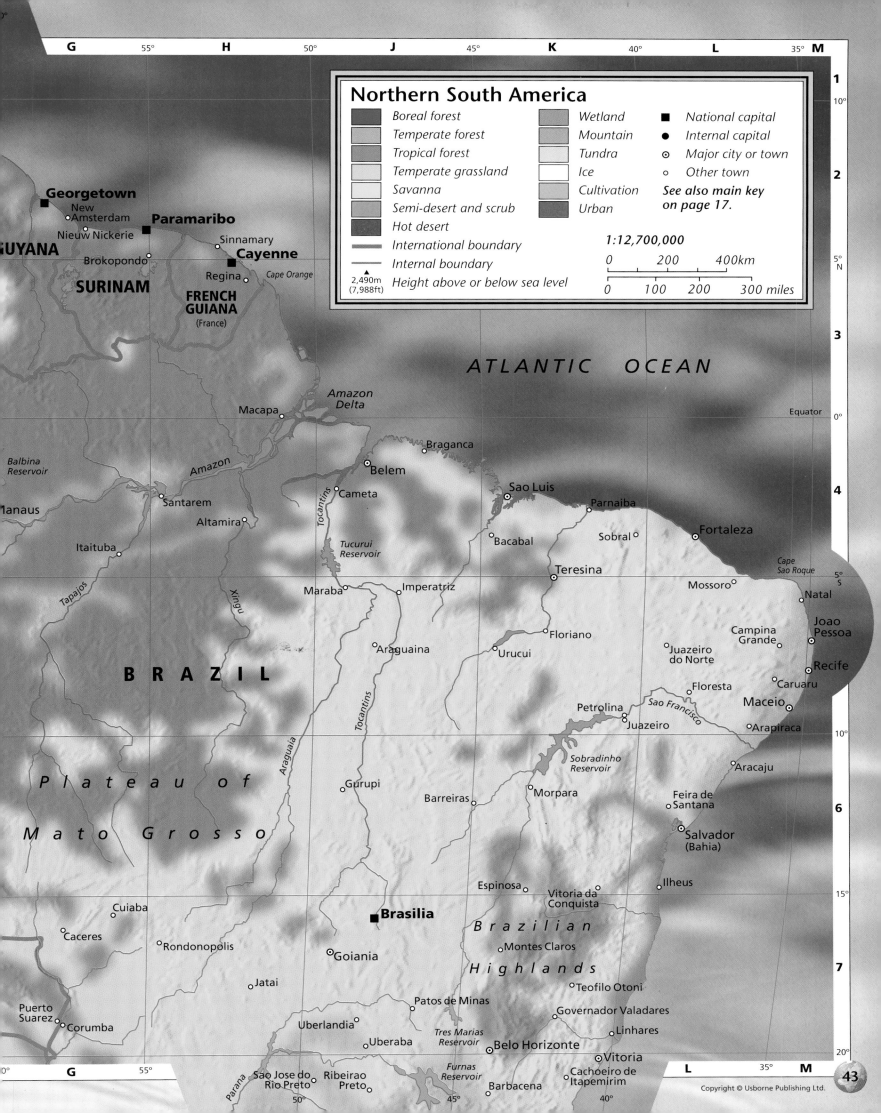

Northern South America

Boreal forest	Wetland	■ National capital
Temperate forest	Mountain	● Internal capital
Tropical forest	Tundra	⊙ Major city or town
Temperate grassland	Ice	○ Other town
Savanna	Cultivation	
Semi-desert and scrub	Urban	**See also main key on page 17.**
Hot desert		

International boundary
Internal boundary
▲ 2,490m (7,988ft) Height above or below sea level

1:12,700,000

0 200 400km
0 100 200 300 miles

Georgetown
New Amsterdam
Nieuw Nickerie
GUYANA
Brokopondo
SURINAM
Paramaribo
Sinnamary
Cayenne
Regina
Cape Orange
FRENCH GUIANA
(France)

ATLANTIC OCEAN
Equator 0°

Amazon Delta
Macapa
Balbina Reservoir
Amazon
Manaus
Santarem
Altamira
Itaituba
Tapajos
Xingu

Braganca
Belem
Cameta
Tocantins
Tucurui Reservoir

Sao Luis
Parnaiba
Bacabal
Sobral
Fortaleza
Cape Sao Roque
Mossoro
Natal
Teresina
5°S
Maraba
Imperatriz
Floriano
Campina Grande
Joao Pessoa
Juazeiro do Norte
Recife
Araguaina
Urucui
Floresta
Caruaru
BRAZIL
Petrolina
Sao Francisco
Maceio
Juazeiro
Arapiraca
10°
Tocantins
Sobradinho Reservoir
Aracaju
Plateau of
Gurupi
Barreiras
Morpara
Feira de Santana
6
Mato Grosso
Araguaia
Salvador (Bahia)
Espinosa
Vitoria da Conquista
Ilheus
15°
Cuiaba
Brasilia
Brazilian
Caceres
Montes Claros
Rondonopolis
Goiania
Highlands
7
Jatai
Teofilo Otoni
Puerto Suarez
Patos de Minas
Governador Valadares
Corumba
Uberlandia
Linhares
20°
Uberaba
Tres Marias Reservoir
Belo Horizonte
Vitoria
Parana
Sao Jose do Rio Preto
Ribeirao Preto
Furnas Reservoir
Cachoeiro de Itapemirim
Barbacena

Copyright © Usborne Publishing Ltd.

PERU
BOLIVIA
BRAZIL
PARAGUAY
URUGUAY
Plateau of Mato Grosso
Brazilian Highlands
Gran Chaco
ANDES
CHILE
Atacama Desert
Tropic of Capricorn
Rio Branco
Puerto Maldonado
Cobija
Riberalta
Rurrenabaque
Trinidad
Magdalena
Juliaca
Puno
Lake Titicaca
La Paz
Mount Illimani 6,402m (21,004ft)
Oruro
Lake Poopo
Challapata
Cochabamba
Sucre
Potosi
Uyuni
Ollague
Tupiza
Tarija
Charagua
Camiri
Santa Cruz
Concepcion
San Jose de Chiquitos
Puerto Suarez
Corumba
Caceres
Cuiaba
Rondonopolis
Campo Grande
Tacna
Arica
Iquique
Pica
Calama
San Pedro de Atacama
Antofagasta
Taltal
Chanaral
Copiapo
Vallenar
Coquimbo
Ovalle
Illapel
Valparaiso
Santiago
Rancagua
San Fernando
Mount Ojos del Salado 6,908m (22,664ft)
Aconcagua 6,959m (22,831ft)
San Juan
Mendoza
San Rafael
Merlo
San Luis
Villa Mercedes
La Rioja
Catamarca
Salta
San Salvador de Jujuy
Tartagal
Pilcomayo
San Miguel de Tucuman
Santiago del Estero
Salado
Cordoba
San Francisco
Villa Maria
Rio Cuarto
Rufino
Venado Tuerto
Chacabuco
Rosario
Santa Fe
Parana
Reconquista
Corrientes
Formosa
Asuncion
Villarrica
Concepcion
Pedro Juan Caballero
Ponta Pora
Paraguay
Encarnacion
Posadas
Ciudad del Este
Foz do Iguacu
Iguacu Falls
Eldorado
Cascavel
Uruguaiana
Concordia
Salto
Paysandu
Gualeguaychu
Gualeguay
San Nicolas de los Arroyos
Buenos Aires
La Plata
Rivera
Tacuarembo
Durazno
Minas
Montevideo
Bage
Melo
Pelotas
Rio Grande
Mirim Lake
Patos Lagoon
Porto Alegre
Santa Maria
Passo Fundo
Caxias do Sul
Criciuma
Florianopolis
Itajai
Guarapuava
Curitiba
Paranagua
Londrina
Itapetininga
Dourados
Presidente Prudente
Sao Jose do Rio Preto
Marilia
Araraquara
Campinas
Sao Paulo
Ribeirao Preto
Pocos de Caldas
Uberlandia
Uberaba
Jatai
Goiania
Brasilia
Gurupi
Tocantins
Araguaia
Barreiras
Patos de Minas
Tres Marias Reservoir
Furnas Reservoir
Mount Agulhas Negras 2,787m (9,144ft)
Belo Horizonte
Barbacena
Juiz de Fora
Nova Iguacu
Rio de Janeiro
Macae
Campos
Cachoeiro de Itapemirim
Vitoria
Governador Valadares
Teofilo Otoni
Linhares
Montes Claros
Espinosa
Vitoria da Conquista
Ilheus
Feira de Santana
Morpara
Sobradinho Reservoir
70°W
65°
60°
55°
50°
45°
40°
10° S
15°
20°
25°
30°
35°
D
E
F
G
H
J
K
L
1
2
3
4
5
6

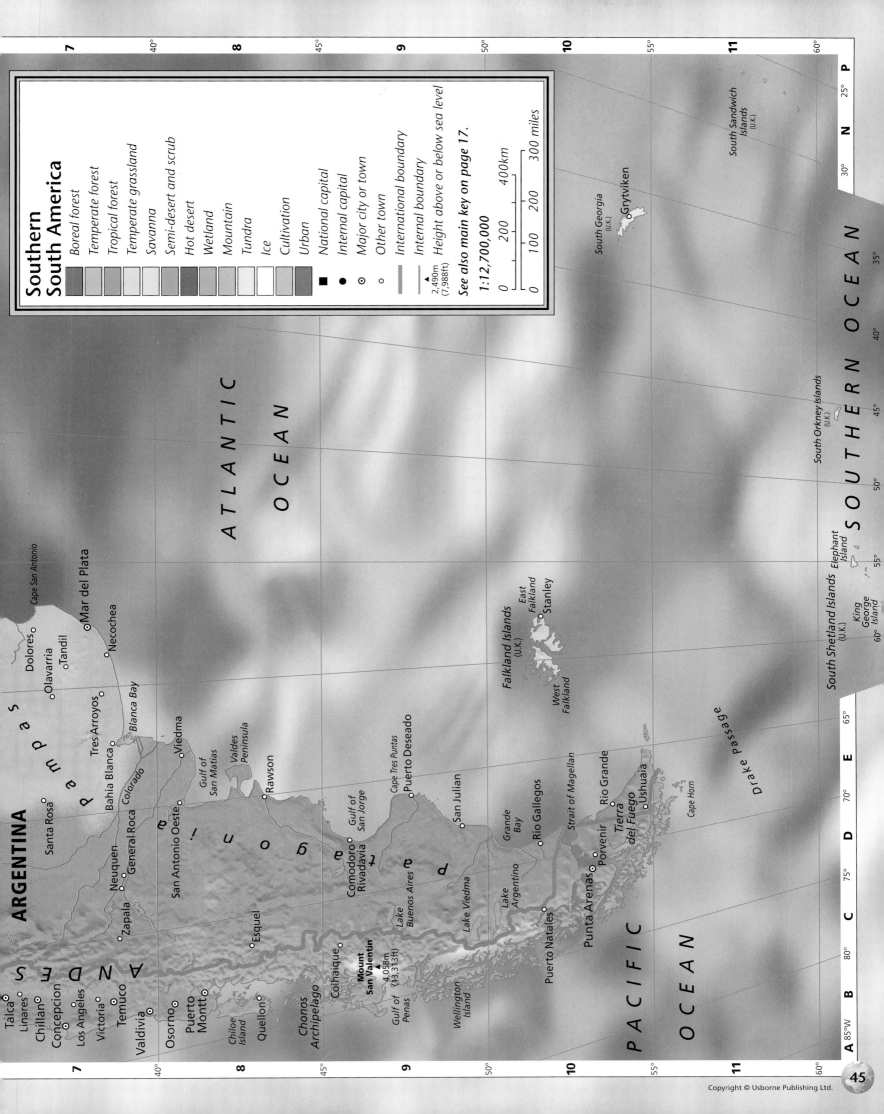

Southern South America

Boreal forest
Temperate forest
Tropical forest
Temperate grassland
Savanna
Semi-desert and scrub
Hot desert
Wetland
Mountain
Tundra
Ice
Cultivation
Urban

■ National capital
● Internal capital
⊙ Major city or town
○ Other town

—— International boundary
—— Internal boundary

▲ 2,490m (7,988ft) Height above or below sea level

See also main key on page 17.

1:12,700,000

0   100   200   300 miles
0   200   400km

ARGENTINA

ANDES

Pampas

Patagonia

ATLANTIC OCEAN

PACIFIC OCEAN

SOUTHERN OCEAN

Talca
Linares
Chillan
Concepcion
Los Angeles
Victoria
Temuco
Valdivia
Osorno
Puerto Montt
Chiloe Island
Quellon
Chonos Archipelago
Coihaique
Esquel
Zapala
Neuquen
Santa Rosa
General Roca
San Antonio Oeste
Bahia Blanca
Tres Arroyos
Olavarria
Tandil
Dolores
Necochea
Mar del Plata
Cape San Antonio
Blanca Bay
Colorado
Viedma
Gulf of San Matias
Valdes Peninsula
Rawson
Comodoro Rivadavia
Gulf of San Jorge
Cape Tres Puntas
Puerto Deseado
San Julian
Lake Buenos Aires
Lake Viedma
Lake Argentino
Grande Bay
Rio Gallegos
Puerto Natales
Punta Arenas
Porvenir
Rio Grande
Tierra del Fuego
Ushuaia
Cape Horn
Strait of Magellan
Drake Passage

Mount San Valentin
▲ 4,058m (13,313ft)

Gulf of Penas
Wellington Island

Falkland Islands (U.K.)
West Falkland
East Falkland
Stanley

South Georgia (U.K.)
Grytviken

South Sandwich Islands (U.K.)

South Orkney Islands (U.K.)

South Shetland Islands (U.K.)
Elephant Island
King George Island

Copyright © Usborne Publishing Ltd.

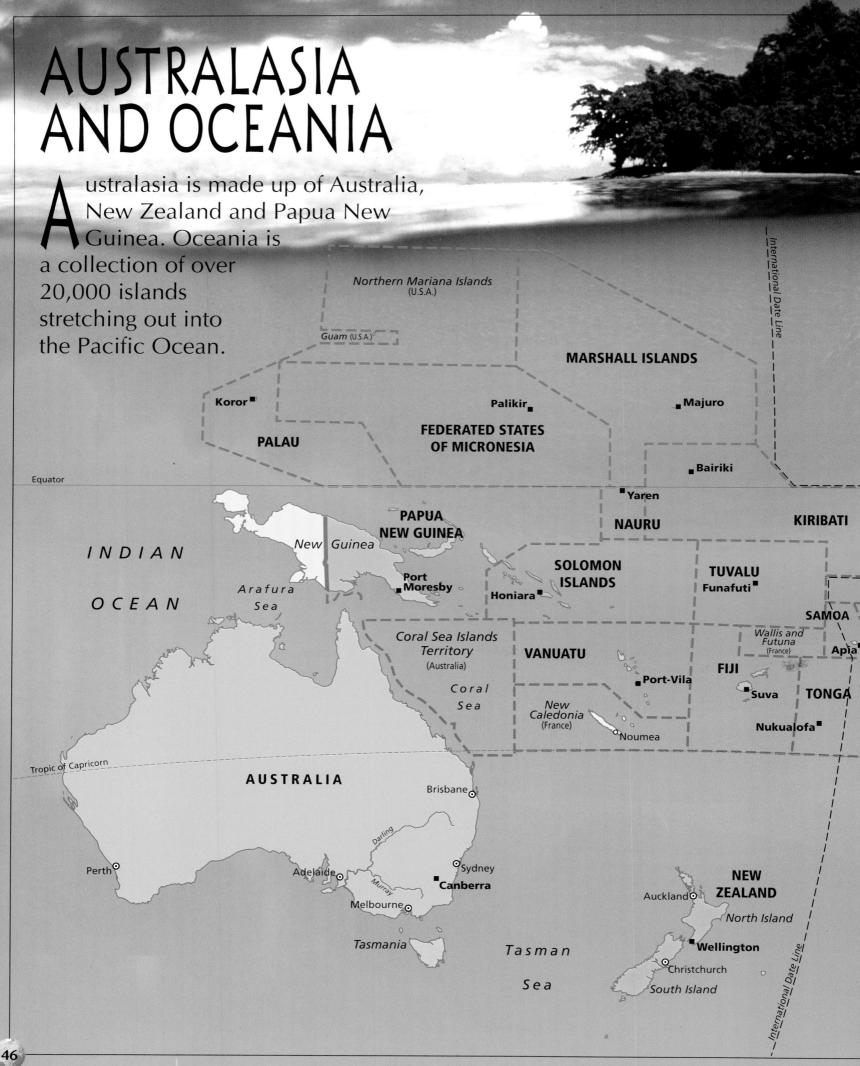

AUSTRALASIA AND OCEANIA

Australasia is made up of Australia, New Zealand and Papua New Guinea. Oceania is a collection of over 20,000 islands stretching out into the Pacific Ocean.

International Date Line

Northern Mariana Islands (U.S.A.)

Guam (U.S.A.)

Koror ■

PALAU

Palikir ■

FEDERATED STATES OF MICRONESIA

MARSHALL ISLANDS

■ Majuro

■ Bairiki

Equator

■ Yaren

NAURU

KIRIBATI

INDIAN

PAPUA NEW GUINEA

New Guinea

Arafura Sea

OCEAN

Port Moresby ■

SOLOMON ISLANDS

Honiara ■

TUVALU
Funafuti ■

SAMOA

Wallis and Futuna (France)

■ Apia

Coral Sea Islands Territory (Australia)

VANUATU

FIJI

Coral Sea

Port-Vila ■

■ Suva

TONGA

New Caledonia (France)

Noumea ○

Nukualofa ■

Tropic of Capricorn

AUSTRALIA

Brisbane ○

Darling

Perth ○

Adelaide ○

Murray

Sydney ○
■ **Canberra**

NEW ZEALAND

Auckland ○

North Island

Melbourne ○

Tasmania

Tasman Sea

■ **Wellington**

Christchurch ○

South Island

International Date Line

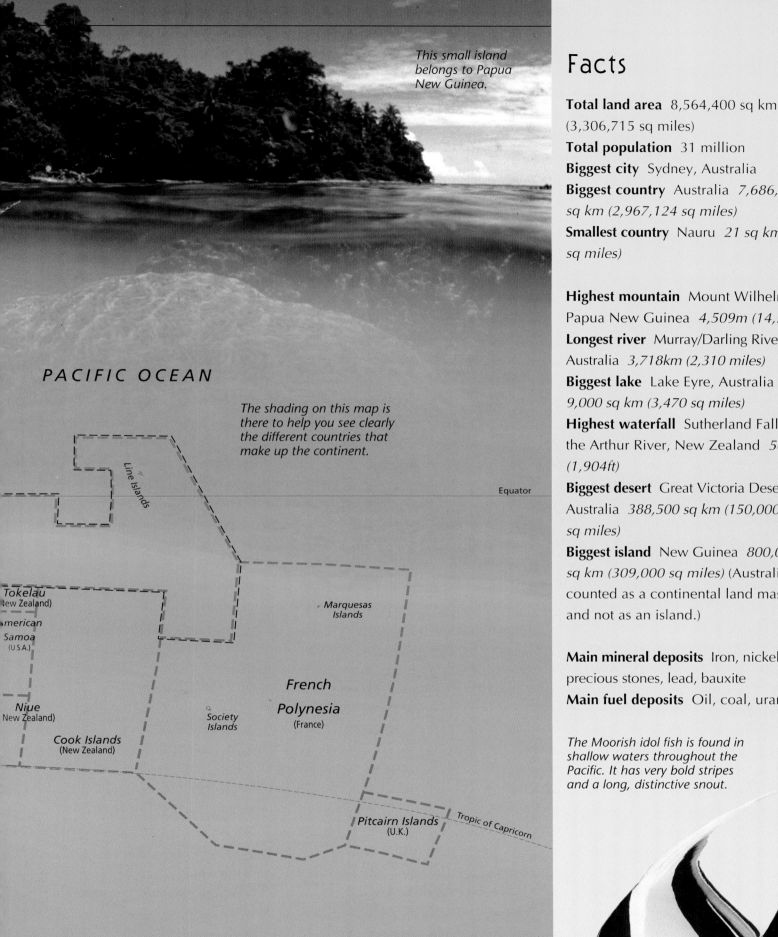

This small island belongs to Papua New Guinea.

PACIFIC OCEAN

The shading on this map is there to help you see clearly the different countries that make up the continent.

Line Islands

Equator

Tokelau
(New Zealand)

American
Samoa
(U.S.A.)

Marquesas
Islands

Niue
(New Zealand)

Society
Islands

French
Polynesia
(France)

Cook Islands
(New Zealand)

Pitcairn Islands
(U.K.)

Tropic of Capricorn

Facts

Total land area 8,564,400 sq km (3,306,715 sq miles)

Total population 31 million

Biggest city Sydney, Australia

Biggest country Australia 7,686,850 sq km (2,967,124 sq miles)

Smallest country Nauru 21 sq km (8 sq miles)

Highest mountain Mount Wilhelm, Papua New Guinea 4,509m (14,793ft)

Longest river Murray/Darling River, Australia 3,718km (2,310 miles)

Biggest lake Lake Eyre, Australia 9,000 sq km (3,470 sq miles)

Highest waterfall Sutherland Falls, on the Arthur River, New Zealand 580m (1,904ft)

Biggest desert Great Victoria Desert, Australia 388,500 sq km (150,000 sq miles)

Biggest island New Guinea 800,000 sq km (309,000 sq miles) (Australia is counted as a continental land mass and not as an island.)

Main mineral deposits Iron, nickel, precious stones, lead, bauxite

Main fuel deposits Oil, coal, uranium

The Moorish idol fish is found in shallow waters throughout the Pacific. It has very bold stripes and a long, distinctive snout.

Copyright © Usborne Publishing Ltd.

Australasia and Oceania's climate is generally very hot. New Zealand and Papua New Guinea are both lush, while Australia is mostly barren. The tiny tropical islands that make up Oceania are surrounded by vast areas of open sea.

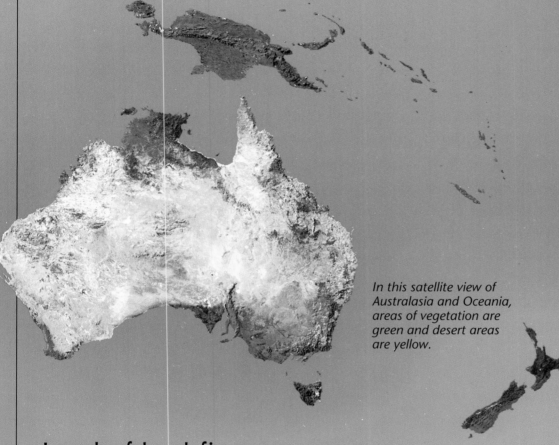

In this satellite view of Australasia and Oceania, areas of vegetation are green and desert areas are yellow.

This image shows a section of the Southern Alps of South Island, New Zealand. The two turquoise patches are Lake Pukaki and Lake Tekapo.

Milky waters

New Zealand has two main islands, North Island and South Island, and several smaller ones. On South Island there is a mountain range called the Southern Alps, which has some dramatic milky-turquoise lakes. Their cloudy appearance is caused by rock dust, which is collected, finely ground and then deposited in the lake by glaciers. The rock dust is so fine, it stays suspended in the water, instead of sinking.

Land of bushfires

Most of Australia is hot, dry desert and the country suffers badly from bushfires almost every year. The fires are usually caused by lightning striking dry vegetation. Some species of trees found in Australia have adapted to cope with the constant outbreaks of fire. Eucalyptus trees can withstand fire, and some types of banksia trees actually need fire to open their seed pods.

Internet links

For a link to a Web site where you can find out how eucalyptus trees have become fire resistant, go to
www.usborne-quicklinks.com

These are the Palau Rock Islands of Micronesia, Oceania. There are over 200 rock islands in total. Each one is made of limestone rock and covered with thick forest.

Tropical islands

Lots of the small islands in the South Pacific are volcanoes. Coral reefs (dense colonies of tentacled sea animals) often grow in shallow waters around the islands. They form barriers which trap water between the reef and the island's coast. The trapped water is known as a lagoon.

Many of the volcanoes are inactive, and are slowly sinking back into the sea. Sometimes, a volcano sinks entirely into the sea, leaving behind a shallow lagoon surrounded by a coral reef. This is called an atoll.

This is Bora Bora Island, a volcanic island in the South Pacific. Vegetation is green, deep water is black and shallow water is pale blue.

The coral reef is the thin, white line around the edge.

This is Lake Eyre in Australia. It wasn't completely dry when this picture was taken – dry areas are pale pink and wet areas are dark pink.

A vanishing lake

Australia's largest salt lake, Lake Eyre, is in the dry, central part of the country. Most of the year it is virtually dry, and you can see a glistening sheet of white salt on the lake bed. When the lake fills, it spreads out over 9,500 sq km (3,670 sq miles), but this usually only happens about once every eight years. The lake has two main sections, Lake Eyre North and Lake Eyre South, which are joined by a channel called the Goyder Channel.

Australasia and Oceania's attractions include a group of huge stone carvings, a strange tree formation and animals equipped with their own baby-carriers.

Great Barrier Reef

Around the coast of Queensland, Australia, lies the Great Barrier Reef, an enormous coral reef structure. It is made up of over 2,800 coral reefs, covering 345,000 sq km (133,200 sq miles) and is home to more than 1,500 species of fish.

Coral reefs are very fragile. They are found in clear, shallow waters with a constant, warm temperature. Global warming might make the sea too hot for coral reefs to survive, and the Great Barrier Reef could die out.

Easter Island

Easter Island is a remote island, far east of Australia, famous for its large stone carvings of human figures with large heads. The carvings are thought to be between 400 and 1,000 years old, and are believed to represent the spirits of important chiefs and ancestors of the island. A Dutch navigator named Jacob Roggeveen gave Easter Island its name when he first visited it on Easter day in 1722.

These sculptures on Easter Island were carved out of volcanic rock. They are about 4m (13ft) tall, and some are partly buried.

Internet links

For a link to a Web site where you can explore interactive pictures of Easter Island go to **www.usborne-quicklinks.com**

The Olgas

In Uluru National Park, in Australia's Northern Territory, there is a group of 36 enormous rocks known as the Olgas. The rocks are a type of sandstone, which means they were formed by loose sand that has become hardened and folded by the Earth's movements to produce layered rocks. The rocks were gradually eroded by wind and rain into the rounded hills we see today. The sand grains that make up the sandstone are mostly made of a pink mineral called feldspar.

These rounded rocks are the Olgas. The aboriginals, who were the first people to settle in Australia, named the site "Kata Tjunta" meaning "many heads".

The seven-in-one tree

On the island of Rarotonga, in the Cook Islands, there is a group of seven coconut trees which have grown naturally in a perfect circle. A legend tells that the seven trees grew from one seed, so they are known as the "seven-in-one tree", but they probably grew from seven separate seeds.

This is a tree kangaroo, a type of animal only found in Queensland, Australia, and Papua New Guinea. Tree kangaroos can leap great distances from tree to tree.

Marsupials

Australasia and Oceania are home to lots of unusual animals, including a group of mammals called marsupials. As soon as marsupials are born, they crawl into a pouch of skin on their mother's tummy. They stay inside the pouch for the first few months of their lives. Kangaroos, koalas, wombats and possums are all marsupials.

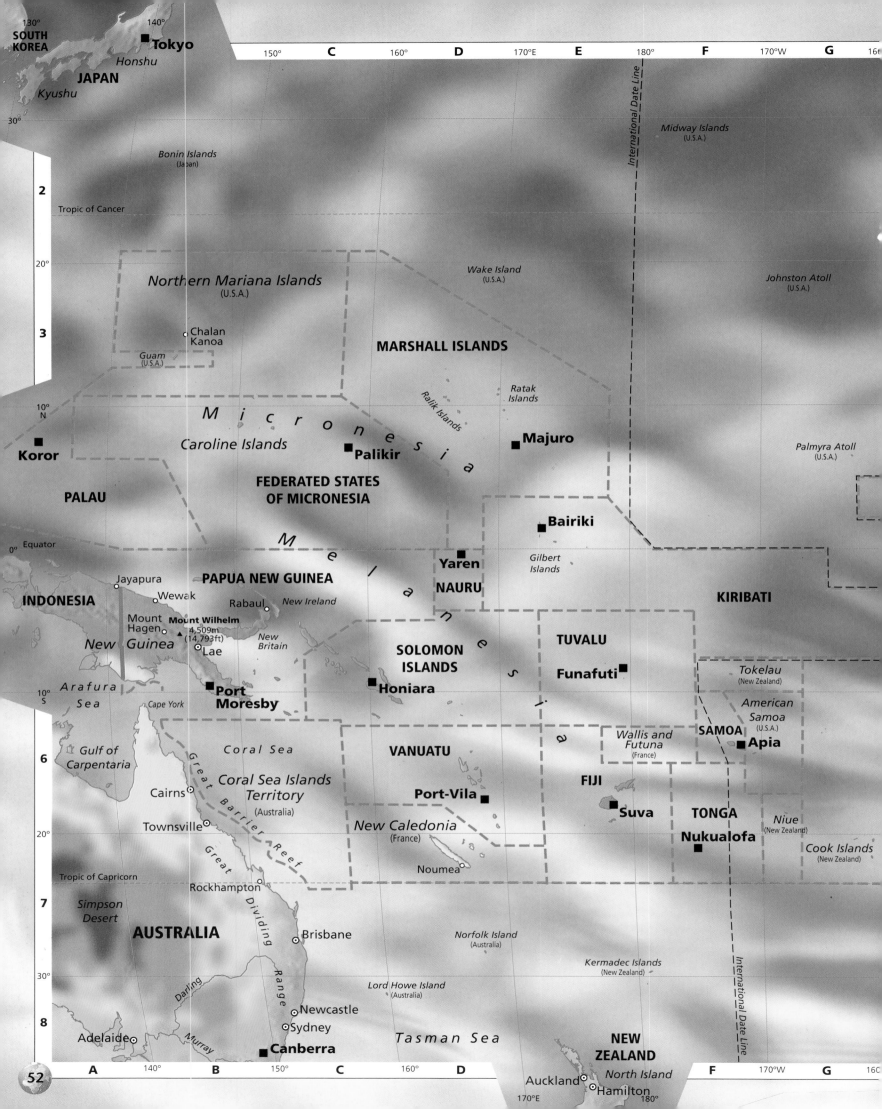

SOUTH
KOREA
Tokyo
Honshu
JAPAN
Kyushu
30°

Bonin Islands
(Japan)

Midway Islands
(U.S.A.)

2

Tropic of Cancer

Northern Mariana Islands
(U.S.A.)

Wake Island
(U.S.A.)

Johnston Atoll
(U.S.A.)

3

Chalan
Kanoa

Guam
(U.S.A.)

MARSHALL ISLANDS

Ratak
Islands

10°
N

M i c r o n e s i a

Ralik Islands

Palmyra Atoll
(U.S.A.)

Caroline Islands

Palikir

Majuro

Koror

PALAU

FEDERATED STATES
OF MICRONESIA

Bairiki

0° Equator

M
e
l
a

INDONESIA

Jayapura

PAPUA NEW GUINEA

Yaren

NAURU

Gilbert
Islands

KIRIBATI

Wewak

Rabaul

New Ireland

Mount
Hagen

Mount Wilhelm
▲ 4,509m
(14,793ft)

New
Britain

n
e

TUVALU

New Guinea

Lae

s
i
a

Arafura

SOLOMON
ISLANDS

Funafuti

Tokelau
(New Zealand)

10°
S

Sea

Port
Moresby

Cape York

Honiara

American
Samoa
(U.S.A.)

Gulf of
Carpentaria

Coral Sea

Wallis and
Futuna
(France)

SAMOA

Apia

6

Cairns

Coral Sea Islands
Territory
(Australia)

VANUATU

FIJI

Port-Vila

Suva

Townsville

Great Barrier Reef

New Caledonia
(France)

TONGA

Niue
(New Zealand)

20°

Nukualofa

Cook Islands
(New Zealand)

Tropic of Capricorn

Rockhampton

Noumea

7

Simpson
Desert

Great Dividing Range

AUSTRALIA

Brisbane

Norfolk Island
(Australia)

Kermadec Islands
(New Zealand)

30°

Darling

Lord Howe Island
(Australia)

8

Adelaide

Newcastle

Sydney

Murray

Canberra

Tasman Sea

NEW
ZEALAND

Auckland

North Island

Hamilton

International Date Line

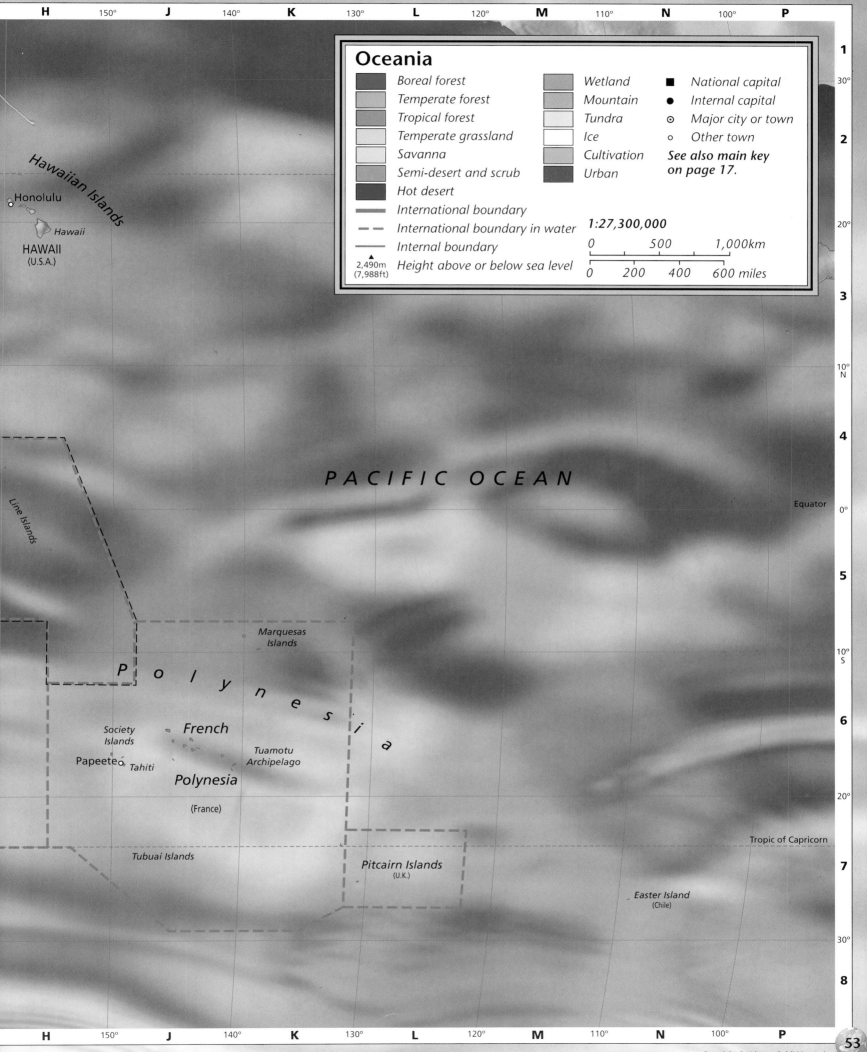

H 150° **J** 140° **K** 130° **L** 120° **M** 110° **N** 100° **P**

Oceania

Boreal forest		Wetland	■	National capital
Temperate forest		Mountain	●	Internal capital
Tropical forest		Tundra	⊙	Major city or town
Temperate grassland		Ice	○	Other town
Savanna		Cultivation		
Semi-desert and scrub		Urban		**See also main key**
Hot desert				**on page 17.**

International boundary
International boundary in water
Internal boundary

▲ 2,490m (7,988ft) Height above or below sea level

1:27,300,000

0   500   1,000km
0   200   400   600 miles

Hawaiian Islands

○ Honolulu

Hawaii

HAWAII
(U.S.A.)

Line Islands

PACIFIC OCEAN

Equator   0°

P o l y n e s i a

Marquesas
Islands

P

French

Society
Islands

Papeete○ ○ Tahiti

Tuamotu
Archipelago

Polynesia

(France)

Tubuai Islands

Pitcairn Islands
(U.K.)

Tropic of Capricorn

Easter Island
(Chile)

H 150° **J** 140° **K** 130° **L** 120° **M** 110° **N** 100° **P**

53

Copyright © Usborne Publishing Ltd.

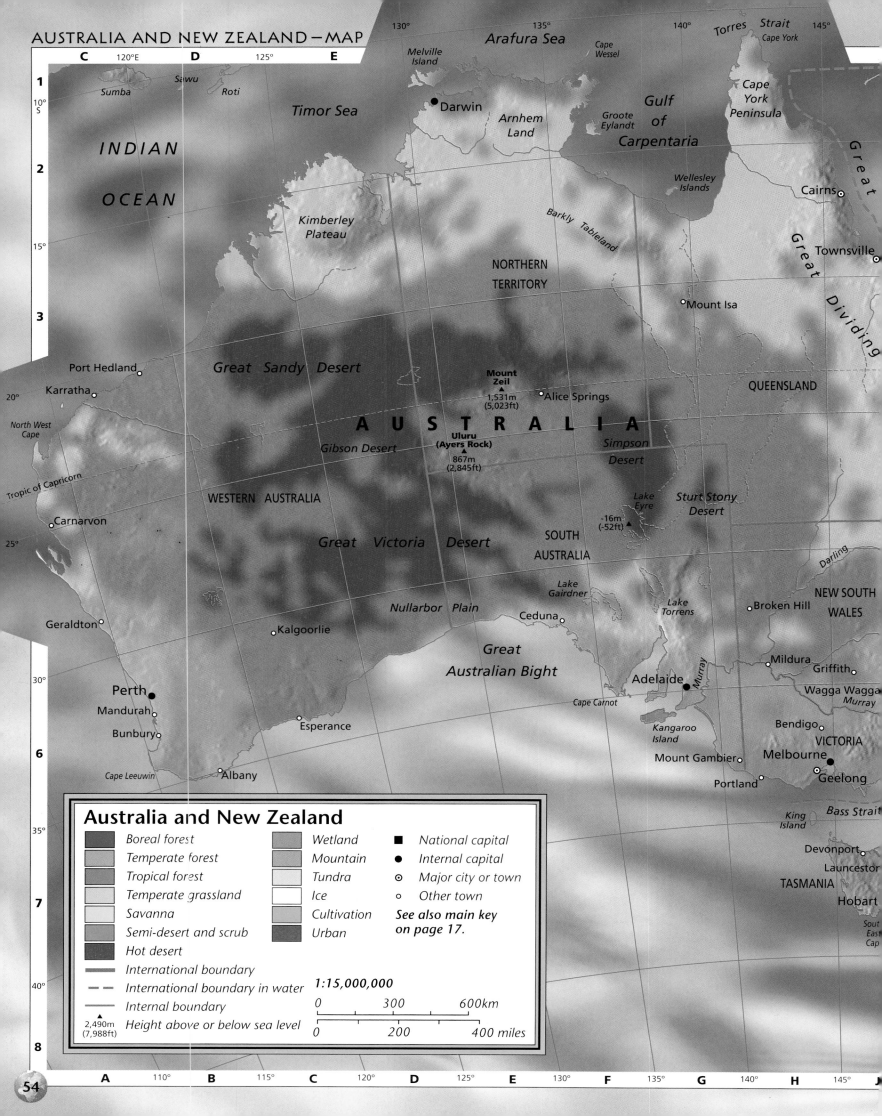

Australia and New Zealand

▨	Boreal forest
▨	Temperate forest
▨	Tropical forest
▨	Temperate grassland
▨	Savanna
▨	Semi-desert and scrub
▨	Hot desert
▨	Wetland
▨	Mountain
▨	Tundra
▨	Ice
▨	Cultivation
▨	Urban
■	National capital
●	Internal capital
⊙	Major city or town
○	Other town

See also main key on page 17.

― International boundary
- - - International boundary in water
— Internal boundary
▲ 2,490m (7,988ft) Height above or below sea level

1:15,000,000

0   300   600km
0   200   400 miles

Map labels:

Arafura Sea · Torres Strait · Cape York · Timor Sea · Melville Island · Darwin · Arnhem Land · Cape Wessel · Gulf of Carpentaria · Groote Eylandt · Cape York Peninsula · INDIAN OCEAN · Sumba · Sawu · Roti · Kimberley Plateau · NORTHERN TERRITORY · Wellesley Islands · Barkly Tableland · Cairns · Townsville · Great Dividing · Mount Isa · QUEENSLAND · Port Hedland · Great Sandy Desert · Mount Zeil 1,531m (5,023ft) · Alice Springs · Karratha · North West Cape · AUSTRALIA · Gibson Desert · Uluru (Ayers Rock) 867m (2,845ft) · Simpson Desert · WESTERN AUSTRALIA · Carnarvon · Lake Eyre · Sturt Stony Desert · -16m (-52ft) · Great Victoria Desert · SOUTH AUSTRALIA · Lake Gairdner · Darling · NEW SOUTH WALES · Broken Hill · Lake Torrens · Nullarbor Plain · Ceduna · Geraldton · Kalgoorlie · Mildura · Griffith · Great Australian Bight · Murray · Wagga Wagga · Murray · Adelaide · Perth · Mandurah · Bunbury · Esperance · Cape Carnot · Kangaroo Island · Bendigo · VICTORIA · Mount Gambier · Melbourne · Geelong · Cape Leeuwin · Albany · Portland · King Island · Bass Strait · Devonport · Launceston · TASMANIA · Hobart · South East Cape

Tropic of Capricorn

Grid labels: C 120°E D 125° E · 10°S · 1 · 15° · 2 · 20° · 25° · 3 · 30° · 6 · 35° · 7 · 40° · 8 · A 110° B 115° C 120° D 125° E 130° F 135° G 140° H 145° · 130° 135° 140° 145°

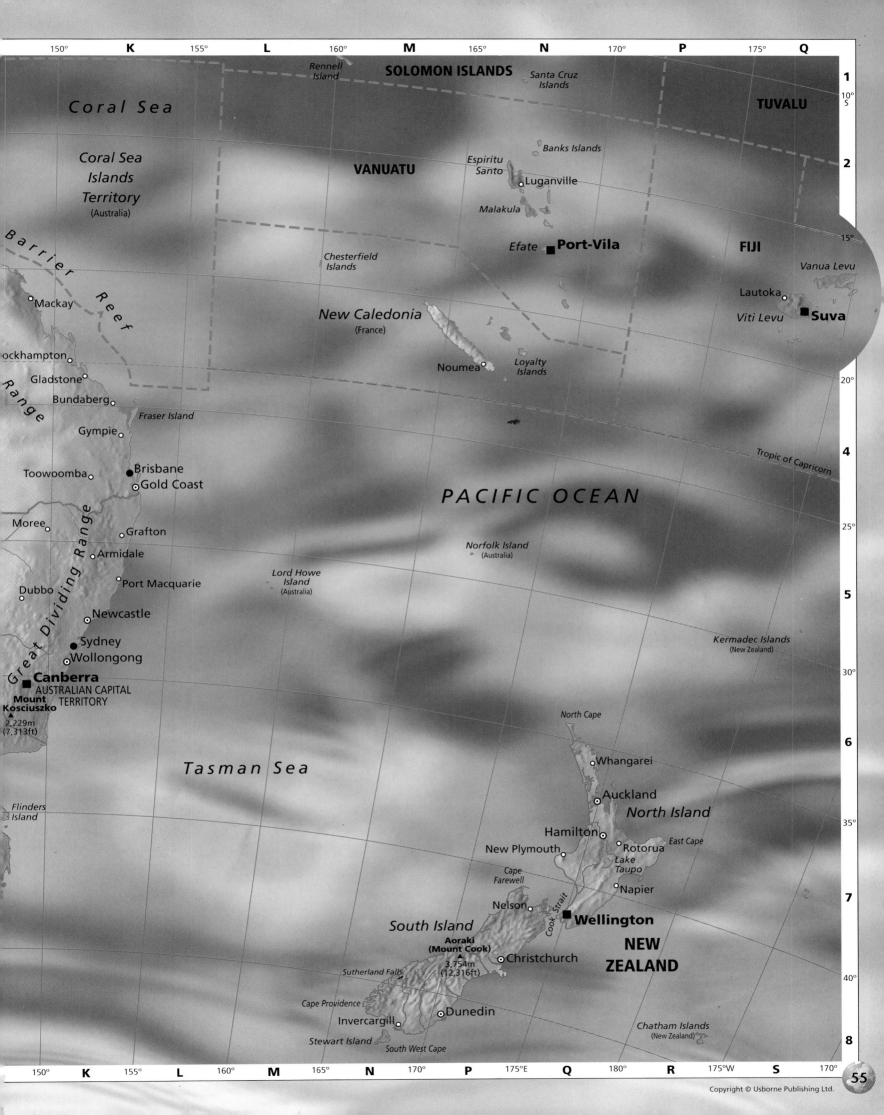

1

10°
S

2

SOLOMON ISLANDS

*Rennell
Island*

*Santa Cruz
Islands*

TUVALU

Coral Sea

*Coral Sea
Islands
Territory*
(Australia)

Banks Islands

VANUATU

*Espiritu
Santo*

Luganville

15°

Barrier Reef

Malakula

Efate ■ **Port-Vila**

FIJI

*Chesterfield
Islands*

Vanua Levu

Lautoka

■ **Suva**

Mackay

New Caledonia
(France)

Viti Levu

ockhampton

Gladstone

Bundaberg

Noumea

*Loyalty
Islands*

20°

Range

Fraser Island

Gympie

PACIFIC OCEAN

Tropic of Capricorn

4

Toowoomba

● **Brisbane**
◉ **Gold Coast**

Moree

Grafton

Norfolk Island
(Australia)

25°

Great Dividing Range

Armidale

Dubbo

Port Macquarie

*Lord Howe
Island*
(Australia)

5

Newcastle

● **Sydney**
◉ **Wollongong**

Kermadec Islands
(New Zealand)

30°

■ **Canberra**
AUSTRALIAN CAPITAL
TERRITORY
▲ **Mount
Kosciuszko**
2,229m
(7,313ft)

North Cape

Tasman Sea

Whangarei

6

*Flinders
Island*

Auckland

North Island

35°

Hamilton

East Cape

New Plymouth

Rotorua
*Lake
Taupo*

*Cape
Farewell*

Napier

Nelson

Cook Strait

■ **Wellington**

7

South Island

**NEW
ZEALAND**

▲ **Aoraki
(Mount Cook)**
3,754m
(12,316ft)

Christchurch

Sutherland Falls

40°

Cape Providence

Dunedin

Invercargill

Chatham Islands
(New Zealand)

Stewart Island

South West Cape

8

Copyright © Usborne Publishing Ltd.

ASIA

Asia is the largest continent and has over 40 countries, including Russia, the biggest country in the world. As well as large land masses, it has thousands of islands and inlets, giving it over 160,000km (100,000 miles) of coastline. Turkey and Russia are partly in Europe and partly in Asia, but both are shown in full on the map on the right.

The shading on this map is there to help you see clearly the different countries that make up the continent.

This is a type of Chinese boat called a junk, sailing in the sea off Singapore.

ARCTIC OCEAN

Franz Josef Land

Novaya Zemlya

Barents Sea

Kara Sea

■ Moscow

R U S S

Ob

Yenisey

Volga

Black Sea

■ Ankara

TURKEY

GEORGIA

Caspian Sea

Astana ■

KAZAKHSTAN

Aral Sea

CYPRUS

ARMENIA

AZERBAIJAN

UZBEKISTAN

■ Bishkek

LEBANON

Beirut ■

SYRIA

■ Damascus

TURKMENISTAN

Tashkent ■

KYRGYZSTAN

Jerusalem

■ Amman

Ashgabat ■

Dushanbe ■

ISRAEL

JORDAN

■ Baghdad

■ Tehran

TAJIKISTAN

IRAQ

IRAN

Kabul ■

■ Islamabad

Tropic of Cancer

KUWAIT

AFGHANISTAN

SAUDI ARABIA

Riyadh ■

BAHRAIN

■ Doha

QATAR

■ Abu Dhabi

PAKISTAN

Indus

New Delhi ■

NEPAL

Kathmandu ■

UNITED ARAB EMIRATES

■ Muscat

Ganges

■ Thimphu

BANGLADESH

■ Sana

OMAN

Arabian Sea

I N D I A

YEMEN

Bay of Bengal

Socotra (Yemen)

INDIAN OCEAN

Equator

Sri Jayewardenepura Kotte

SRI LANKA

■ Colombo

MALDIVES

■ Male

56

Copyright © Usborne Publishing Ltd.

Wrangel Island

New Siberia Islands

Bering Sea

Severnaya Zemlya

East Siberian Sea

Laptev Sea

Lena

I A

Sea of Okhotsk

Lake Baikal

Ulan Bator ■

MONGOLIA

Hokkaido

Sea of Japan

NORTH KOREA

JAPAN

Pyongyang ■

Seoul ■

Tokyo ■

Beijing ■

SOUTH KOREA

C H I N A

Huang He (Yellow)

East China Sea

Honshu

Chang Jiang (Yangtze)

Tropic of Cancer

Taipei ■

TAIWAN

PACIFIC

BHUTAN

Irrawaddy

Dhaka ■

BURMA (MYANMAR)

Hanoi ■

LAOS

PHILIPPINES

OCEAN

Vientiane ■

Mekong

South China Sea

Rangoon ■

THAILAND

VIETNAM

Manila ■

Philippine Sea

Bangkok ■

CAMBODIA

Andaman Islands (India)

Phnom Penh ■

Nicobar Islands (India)

BRUNEI

Equator

MALAYSIA

New Guinea

Kuala Lumpur ■

SINGAPORE

Borneo

Celebes

Sumatra

INDONESIA

Arafura Sea

Dili ■

EAST TIMOR

Jakarta ■

Java

Facts

Total land area 44,537,920 sq km (17,196,090 sq miles)

Total population 3.8 billion (including all of Russia)

Biggest city Tokyo, Japan

Biggest country Russia *Total area: 17,075,200 sq km (6,592,735 sq miles) Area of Asiatic Russia: 12,780,800 sq km (4,934,667 sq miles)*

Smallest country Maldives *300 sq km (116 sq miles)*

Highest mountain Mount Everest, Nepal/China border *8,850m (29,035ft)*

Longest river Chang Jiang (Yangtze), China *6,380km (3,964 miles)*

Biggest lake Caspian Sea, western Asia *370,999 sq km (143,243 sq miles)*

Highest waterfall Jog Falls, on the Sharavati River, India *253m (830ft)*

Biggest desert Arabian Desert, in and around Saudi Arabia *2,230,000 sq km (900,000 sq miles)*

Biggest island Borneo *751,100 sq km (290,000 sq miles)*

Main mineral deposits Zinc, mica, tin, chromium, iron, nickel

Main fuel deposits Oil, coal, uranium, natural gas

These are lotus flowers, a type of water lily. In China they are associated with purity and for Buddhists they are sacred.

57

Asia is made up of all kinds of rugged terrain. In the far north are vast, frozen plains, and farther south are dry deserts. Asia also has enormous mountain ranges, including the Himalayas, the world's highest range. Most of Asia's population lives in the far south, which is hot and humid, with lush rainforests.

Empty land

Southern Saudi Arabia has a sandy desert that covers an area about the size of France. It is called Rub al Khali, and is often nicknamed the Empty Quarter as it has hardly any plants or animals and no permanent human settlements. Strong winds blow the sand into mounds that can be more than 330m (1,000ft) high, taller than the Eiffel Tower in Paris.

The white areas in the middle of this satellite image of Asia are mountain ranges, which include the Himalayas.

This view of Rub al Khali in Saudi Arabia shows how the wind has blown sand into long, high ridges.

This photograph shows a section of the Great Wall of China, which winds across northern China. The wall can be seen from space as a long, thin line.

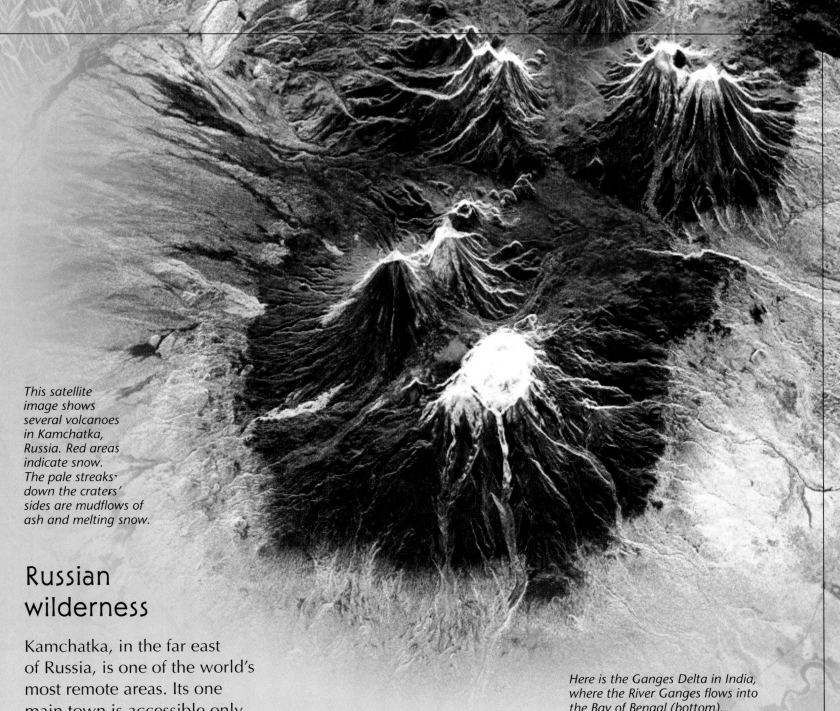

This satellite image shows several volcanoes in Kamchatka, Russia. Red areas indicate snow. The pale streaks down the craters' sides are mudflows of ash and melting snow.

Russian wilderness

Kamchatka, in the far east of Russia, is one of the world's most remote areas. Its one main town is accessible only by air or sea. Much of the land is mountainous, with more than 300 volcanoes. Some of these are active, and they regularly eject boiling rivers of mud and great plumes of steam from their rocky craters.

Internet links

For a link to a Web site where you can discover more about the Great Wall of China and see a photograph of it taken from space, go to **www.usborne-quicklinks.com**

A sacred river

The River Ganges begins in the Himalayas and flows through India and Bangladesh to the Indian Ocean. The river is regarded as holy by followers of the Hindu religion. Every day thousands of Hindus bathe in the Ganges, which they believe washes away their sins. People often worship the river by throwing flowers into it or floating oil lamps on its surface.

Here is the Ganges Delta in India, where the River Ganges flows into the Bay of Bengal (bottom).

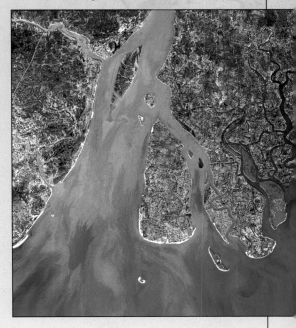

Much of central and southern Asia is densely populated, so there are many large cities, including Tokyo, the world's most populous city. There are beautiful natural areas too, such as the forests and mountain ranges of China.

A panda climbs a tree in China. Pandas are good climbers, and often rest or sleep high in trees.

Pandas of China

Wild pandas live in the mountainous forests of China. Pandas depend on the bamboo that grows there, as their diet consists almost exclusively of bamboo shoots. But forests are being cut down, so pandas are losing their habitat and food source. There may be as few as 1,000 wild pandas left.

A floating market

Near Bangkok, in Thailand, there is a famous floating market which is held on a canal. Farmers go there daily with fresh fruit and vegetables piled high on narrow boats. Customers weave their way along the busy canal in similar boats, looking for bargains. They must come early, though, as the market begins at about 8 a.m., and everything is sold by 11 a.m.

These women have brought fruit and vegetables to sell at Bangkok's floating market.

Enormous department stores with glaring neon signs line a street in central Tokyo.

Japanese capital

One of Asia's most vibrant cities is Tokyo, the capital of Japan. This big, sprawling city has been rebuilt twice, first in the 1920s when an earthquake destroyed vast areas, and then after the Second World War, when bombs devastated the city. Modern Tokyo is a mixture of a few old streets and many new, towering skyscrapers.

Forbidden City

In the middle of the city of Beijing, in China, is an ancient, walled city. For hundreds of years it was the palace of China's kings, or emperors. It was known as the Forbidden City because no one but the emperor, his family and guests was allowed in its grounds.

China no longer has a royal family, and the Forbidden City is a popular tourist attraction. The city has 800 buildings, including huge temples and elaborate arches, decorated with ornate carvings and grand bronze statues.

Internet links

For a link to a Web site where you can take a tour of the Forbidden City's most famous buildings, go to
www.usborne-quicklinks.com

This bronze tortoise stands in Beijing's Forbidden City. According to ancient Chinese beliefs, tortoises were divine animals, and tortoise statues were said to bring good luck.

The countries of western Asia are full of important cultural and historical sights, such as places of worship and the remains of ancient civilizations. The Asian part of Russia stretches far across the continent. It is dominated by the region of Siberia, where the climate is so harsh that most of the land is uninhabited.

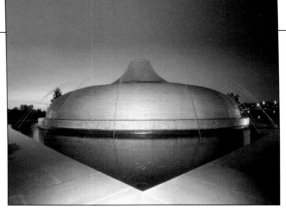

This museum in Jerusalem, Israel, houses ancient manuscripts known as the Dead Sea Scrolls.

The Dead Sea

The Dead Sea, in Israel, gets its name because it is so salty that nothing can live in it. However, many people swim in the sea, as its water contains health-giving minerals.

The Dead Sea is also famous for the Dead Sea Scrolls. These are 2,000-year-old Jewish handwritten papers that were discovered in caves by the sea. The scrolls cover mainly religious topics, and have helped historians to learn what life was like in ancient times.

Homes of rock

The region of Cappadocia, near Ankara in central Turkey, has a strange landscape of rocky cones, made of soft volcanic rock. Many hundreds of years ago, people carved caves in the rock, creating whole towns and villages that included houses, stables and even churches. They also built an amazing network of underground tunnels that linked the houses.

These rocky peaks in Cappadocia, Turkey, were carved out to create rock houses. Today, they are crumbling away.

Holy places

Many different religions are followed in Asia, and their various places of worship and study, such as Muslim mosques and Hindu temples, are found in towns and cities all over the continent. Many of these buildings are intricately decorated, for example with huge domes covered in thousands of patterned tiles.

This is the Trans-Siberian Express in Siberia. The train runs from Moscow to Vladivostok, stopping at other stations on the way.

This elaborate, domed building in Esfahan, Iran, is a school for Muslim students.

Russian train trip

Crossing the enormous country of Russia is the Trans-Siberian rail line. This is the longest rail line in the world, running more than 9,000km (5,600 miles) between Moscow in the west and Vladivostok in the east. The line passes through the plains of Siberia, which freeze over in winter. The fastest train trip along the line takes about seven days.

Reindeers

Siberia is home to many reindeers. They have thick fur that keeps them warm in winter, and also have such a good sense of smell that they can sniff out plants to eat that are buried deep under the snow.

Internet links

For a link to a Web site where you can read a fascinating account of a reindeer-herding journey in Siberia, go to **www.usborne-quicklinks.com**

These reindeers are being driven by Siberian herders through western Siberia. Reindeers can easily pull heavy, loaded sleds.

A   100°E   B   105°   C   110°   D   115°

Southern Southeast Asia

- Boreal forest
- Temperate forest
- Tropical forest
- Temperate grassland
- Savanna
- Semi-desert and scrub
- Hot desert
- International boundary
- Internal boundary
- ▲ 2,490m (7,988ft) Height above or below sea level

- Wetland
- Mountain
- Tundra
- Ice
- Cultivation
- Urban

- ■ National capital
- ● Internal capital
- ⊙ Major city or town
- ○ Other town

See also main key on page 17.

1:10,900,000

0   200   400km
0   100   200   300 miles

VIETNAM

⊙ Qui Nhon

⊙ Nha Trang

South China Sea

Spratly Islands

THAILAND

Andaman Sea

⊙ Hat Yai
○ Yala
⊙ Kota Bharu
○ Alor Setar
⊙ Kuala Terengganu

Kota Kinabalu ⊙

⊙ Banda Aceh
○ Lhokseumawe
George Town ⊙ (Penang)
○ Taiping
Gunung Tahan ▲ 2,187m (7,175ft)
○ Ipoh
○ Kuantan

M A L A Y S I A

Bandar Seri Begawan ■
BRUNEI
○ Miri

○ Langsa
⊙ Medan
Natuna Islands
Bintulu ○
Tarakan ○

○ Pematangsiantar
Lake Toba
■ **Kuala Lumpur**
Anambas Islands
○ Sibu
▲ 2,988m (9,803ft)
○ Tanjungredeb

Simeulue
○ Seremban
⊙ Melaka
○ Kuching

○ Sibolga
Strait of Malacca
Johor Bahru
⊙ **Singapore**
SINGAPORE

Nias

Sumatra

○ Pekanbaru
Riau Islands
○ Pontianak
Borneo
Samarinda ○

5° N
Equator 0°

○ Padang
Gunung Kerinci ▲ 3,805m (12,483ft)
Karimata Strait
Balikpapan ○

Mentawai Islands
○ Jambi
Bangka
Palangkaraya ○

4
○ Pangkalpinang
Banjarmasin ○

⊙ Palembang
Belitung
Martapura ○

○ Bengkulu
Lahat ○
○ Baturaja
G r e a t e r   S u n d a   I s l a n d s
I N D O N E S I A

5° S
Tanjungkarang-Telukbetung
Java Sea

Krakatoa ▲ 813m (2,667ft)
○ Serang
Jakarta ■
Tegal ○
⊙ Semarang
Lesser

○ Bandung
⊙ Bogor
J a v a
⊙ Surakarta
Surabaya ⊙

5
Cilacap ○
Yogyakarta ⊙
○ Jember
Lombok

INDIAN
Malang ○
Bali
○ Mataram

Denpasar ○
Sumbawa

OCEAN

10°

◁ Christmas Island (Australia)

6

A   100°E   B   105°   C   110°   D   115°   E

120°
Luzon Cabanatuan
Olongapo
⊙ Quezon City
Manila ■
125°
G
130°
H
135°
J
140°

° Lucena
° Naga
Legaspi
Mindoro
Calamian Group
Masbate
Masbate
° Calbayog
Samar
PHILIPPINES

Panay
° Roxas
Taytay
Iloilo ⊙ Bacolod
⊙ Cebu
° Tacloban
Philippine Sea

Negros
Bohol
° Surigao
Puerto Princesa °
Dumaguete ⊙
Butuan °
Palawan
⊙ Cagayan de Oro
Pagadian °
⊙ Iligan
Mindanao
Sulu Sea
⊙ Davao
Zamboanga ⊙
° Jolo
⊙ General Santos
Sandakan °
Sulu Archipelago

Tawau °
5°N

Celebes Sea
Talaud Islands

Sangihe Islands

Manado ⊙
Morotai
° Gorontalo
Halmahera
Ternate °

Molucca Sea
PACIFIC OCEAN
PALAU

Peleng
Obi
Sorong °
Biak
Palu °
Misool
Yapen
Celebes
Sula Islands
Ceram Sea
Jayapura °
Palopo °
Buru
Ceram
Fakfak °
Parepare °
Kendari °
Ambon °
Maoke Range
Watampone °
Puncak Jaya ▲
5,030m
(16,502ft)
New Guinea
Ujung Pandang ⊙
Buton
Banda Sea
Equator 0°

Flores Sea
Aru Islands

Sunda Islands
Wetar
Tanimbar Islands
Dolak
Flores
■ **Dili**
Ende °
EAST TIMOR
Sawu Sea
Timor
Arafura Sea
Sumba
Sawu
Kupang °
Torres Strait
Roti
Timor Sea
AUSTRALIA

120°
F
125°
G
130°
H
135°
J
140°
● Darwin NORTHERN TERRITORY

Inset map:
J 140°E
K
145°
L
150°
M Equator 155° N
0°

Admiralty Islands
PACIFIC OCEAN
Jayapura °
° Wewak
Bismarck Sea
New Ireland
Mount Wilhelm
4,509m
(14,793ft)
Madang °
Rabaul °
Mount Hagen ° ▲
New Britain
New Guinea
Lae °
PAPUA NEW GUINEA
Kerema °
Solomon Sea
Gulf of Papua
D'Entrecasteaux Islands
■ **Port Moresby**
Torres Strait
1:16,400,000
Cape York
0 — 400km
Cape York Peninsula
AUSTRALIA
0 — 200 miles
J 140°E
K
145°
L
150°
M
155° N

Copyright © Usborne Publishing Ltd.

A 90°E B 95° C 100° D 105° E

Brahmaputra Lhasa *Mekong* *Chang Jiang (Yangtze)* Chengdu Wanxian Enshi

H i m a l a y a s Gongga Shan Leshan Chongqing

Mount Everest 7,556m Neijiang Luzhou
8,850m (24,790ft)
(29,035ft) Xichang Yibin Zunyi Huaihu

Thimphu Zhaotong
NEPAL Darjeeling **BHUTAN** **INDIA** C H I N

Biratnagar Panzhihua Guiyang

Darbhanga *Brahmaputra* Dibrugarh Kunming Anshun

Rangpur Jorhat

Bhagalpur Guwahati Dali Liuzhou

Rajshahi Sylhet Shillong Baoshan

BANGLADESH Imphal *Red* Kaiyuan Nannin

Dhaka Myitkyina Gejiu

Jamshedpur Aizawl Simao Ha Giang

Kolkata Khulna Lashio Lao Cai Qinzhou
(Calcutta)
Chittagong Monywa Mandalay Phongsali Thai Nguyen

Mouths of the Ganges Mount **BURMA** Son La **Hanoi**
Victoria **(MYANMAR)**
3,053m Meiktila Hai Phong
(10,016ft)
Sittwe Taunggyi Thanh Hoa *Gulf of*

Bay of Bengal Pyinmana *Mekong* Louangphrabang *Tonkin*

Salween **LAOS** Vinh

Sandoway Pye Chiang Mai Sanya

Henzada *Irrawaddy* **Vientiane**

Pathein Pegu Udon Thani Savannakhet Hue

Rangoon Thaton Phitsanulok Da Nang

Moulmein Khon **THAILAND**
Kaen
Mouths of the Nakhon Sawan Ubon Pakxe
Irrawaddy Ratchathani
THAILAND Attapu

I N D I A N Tavoy Nakhon Ratchasima **VIETNAM**

O C E A N **Bangkok** Qui Nhon
Stoeng Treng
Andaman *Andaman* Pattaya Angkor *Tonle Sap* **CAMBODIA** Buon Me
Islands *Sea* Batdambang Thuot
(India) Mergui Kampong Kampong Da Lat Nha
Chhnang Cham Trang
Port Blair Krong **Phnom**
Prachuap Kaoh Kong **Penh** Bien Hoa
Little Khiri Khan
Andaman *Mergui* Kampong Saom Ho Chi Minh City
Archipelago Long Xuyen (Saigon)
Chumphon *Mekong*
Ten Degree Channel *Gulf of Thailand* Can Tho

Bac Lieu

Con Son
Nicobar Islands Nakhon Si
(India) Thammarat

Hat Yai

Yala
Banda Aceh Alor Setar Kota Bharu *Natuna*
Islands
Lhokseumawe George Town Kuala Terengganu (Indonesia)
(Penang) Gunung
Sumatra Tahan
Langsa Taiping Ipoh 2,187m **MALAYSIA**
(7,175ft)
INDONESIA

A 90°E B 95° C 100° D 105° E 110

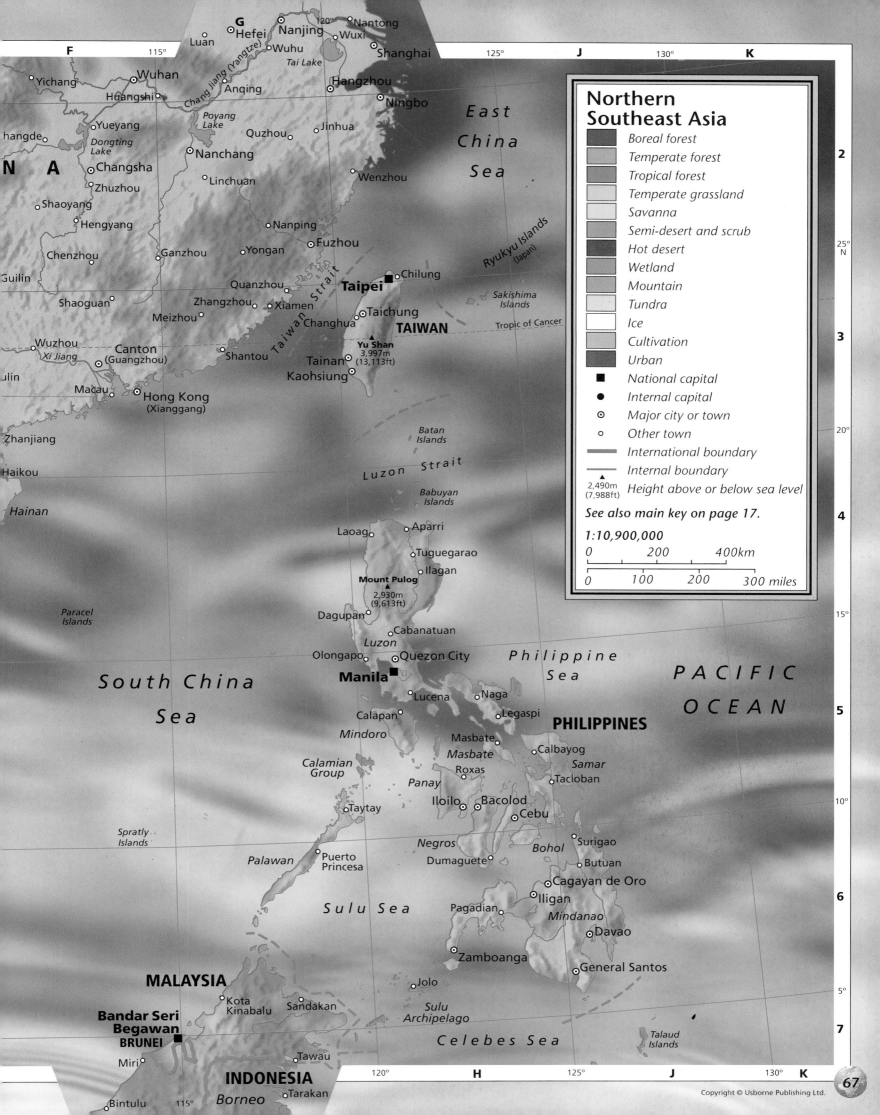

F   115°   125°   J   130°   K

Luan
G
Hefei
Nanjing
Nantong
Wuxi
Shanghai
Wuhu

Yichang
Wuhan
Hangzhou
East
China
Sea

Huangshi
Anqing
Chang Jiang (Yangtze)
Ningbo

hangde
Yueyang
Poyang
Lake
Quzhou
Jinhua

N
A
Dongting
Lake
Nanchang
Changsha
Linchuan
Wenzhou

Zhuzhou

Shaoyang
Hengyang
Nanping

Chenzhou
Ganzhou
Yongan
Fuzhou
Ryukyu Islands
(Japan)
25°
N

Guilin
Quanzhou
Taipei ■
Chilung

Shaoguan
Zhangzhou
Xiamen
Taichung
Sakishima
Islands

ulin
Wuzhou
Canton
(Guangzhou)
Changhua
TAIWAN
Tropic of Cancer
3

Xi Jiang
Shantou
Tainan
Yu Shan
3,997m
(13,113ft)

Macau
Kaohsiung
Taiwan Strait

Hong Kong
(Xianggang)

Zhanjiang
Batan
Islands
20°

Haikou

Luzon Strait

Hainan
Babuyan
Islands
4

Paracel
Islands
Laoag
Aparri

Tuguegarao

Ilagan

Mount Pulog
2,930m
(9,613ft)
15°

Dagupan

South China
Sea
Cabanatuan
Luzon

Olongapo
Quezon City
Philippine
Sea
PACIFIC

Manila ■
OCEAN

Lucena
Naga

Calapan
Legaspi
5

Mindoro
PHILIPPINES

Masbate
Calbayog

Masbate
Samar

Calamian
Group
Roxas
Tacloban

Panay

Taytay
Iloilo
Bacolod
Cebu
10°

Spratly
Islands
Negros
Bohol
Surigao

Palawan
Puerto
Princesa
Dumaguete
Butuan

Cagayan de Oro

Sulu Sea
Pagadian
Iligan
6

Mindanao
Davao

Zamboanga
General Santos

MALAYSIA
Jolo
5°

Bandar Seri
Begawan
Kota
Kinabalu
Sandakan
Sulu
Archipelago
Talaud
Islands

BRUNEI
Celebes Sea
7

Miri
Tawau

INDONESIA
120°
H
125°
J
130°
K

Bintulu
115°
Borneo
Tarakan

Copyright © Usborne Publishing Ltd.

Northern Southeast Asia

- Boreal forest
- Temperate forest
- Tropical forest
- Temperate grassland
- Savanna
- Semi-desert and scrub
- Hot desert
- Wetland
- Mountain
- Tundra
- Ice
- Cultivation
- Urban
- ■ National capital
- ● Internal capital
- ⊙ Major city or town
- ○ Other town
- ▬ International boundary
- — Internal boundary
- ▲ 2,490m (7,988ft) Height above or below sea level

See also main key on page 17.

1:10,900,000

0   200   400km

0   100   200   300 miles

A 80°E B 85° C 90° D 95° E 100° F 105° G 110°

KAZAKHSTAN

2 Almaty Karamay

Yining *Dzungarian Basin* Altay

Lake Issyk Kuytun Shihezi **Ulan Bator**

Urumqi **MONGOLIA**

KYRGYZSTAN Pik Pobedy
7,439m
(24,406ft) *T i e n S h a n* Erenhot

Aksu Turpan Hami

40°N Korla *Bosten Lake* -154m
(-505ft) *Turpan Depression* *G o b i D e s e r t*

3 Hotan *Tarim Basin* Lop Lake Mogao Caves Baotou Hohhot

Taklimakan Desert Yumen *The Great Wall of China* Wuhai

35° *Altun Mountains* 5,547m
(18,199ft) Yinchuan

Kunlun Mountains *Qaidam Basin* Golmud *Qinghai Lake* Xining Taiyua

Lanzhou

4 *Plateau of Tibet* **C H I N A** *Huang He (Yellow)*

Mount Li
(Terracotta Arm
Baoji
Siling Lake Xian

30° *Himalayas* **TIBET** Yushu Shiyan

Nam Lake *Chang Jiang (Yangtze)* Xiangfan

Brahmaputra Lhasa *Salween* *Mekong* Chengdu

5 **NEPAL** **Kathmandu** Gongga Shan
7,556m
(24,790ft) Yichang

Mount Everest
8,850m
(29,035ft) **Thimphu** Leshan Chongqing

Darbhanga Darjeeling **BHUTAN** *Brahmaputra* Dibrugarh *Chang Jiang (Yangtze)* Luzhou Changde

25° Patna Biratnagar Xichang

Ganges Bhagalpur Rangpur Guwahati Zunyi Huaihua

INDIA Shillong Panzhihua

Ranchi Asansol Rajshahi Sylhet Hengyan

Tropic of Cancer **BANGLADESH** Imphal Myitkyina Dali Guiyang

6 **Dhaka** Aizawl Kunming

Kolkata
(Calcutta) Khulna Guilin

Chittagong Liuzhou

Cuttack *Mouths of the Ganges* Lashio Red Wuzhou

Monywa Mandalay Simao Gejiu Nanning Xi

20° **Mount Victoria**
3,053m
(10,016ft) **BURMA
(MYANMAR)** Lao Cai Yulin

Bay of Bengal Sittwe Taunggyi Phongsali Son La Thai
Nguyen Zhanjiang

7 *INDIAN* Pyinmana Mekong **Hanoi** Hai
Phong *Gulf of Tonkin* Haikou

Sandoway Pye Louangphrabang Thanh Hoa

OCEAN *Irrawaddy* Chiang
Mai **LAOS** **VIETNAM** *Hainan*

Henzada **THAILAND** **Vientiane** Vinh

Pathein Pegu Udon Thani Sanya

Rangoon

C 90°E D *Mouths of the Irrawaddy* F 100° G 105° 110°

Moulmein 95°

68

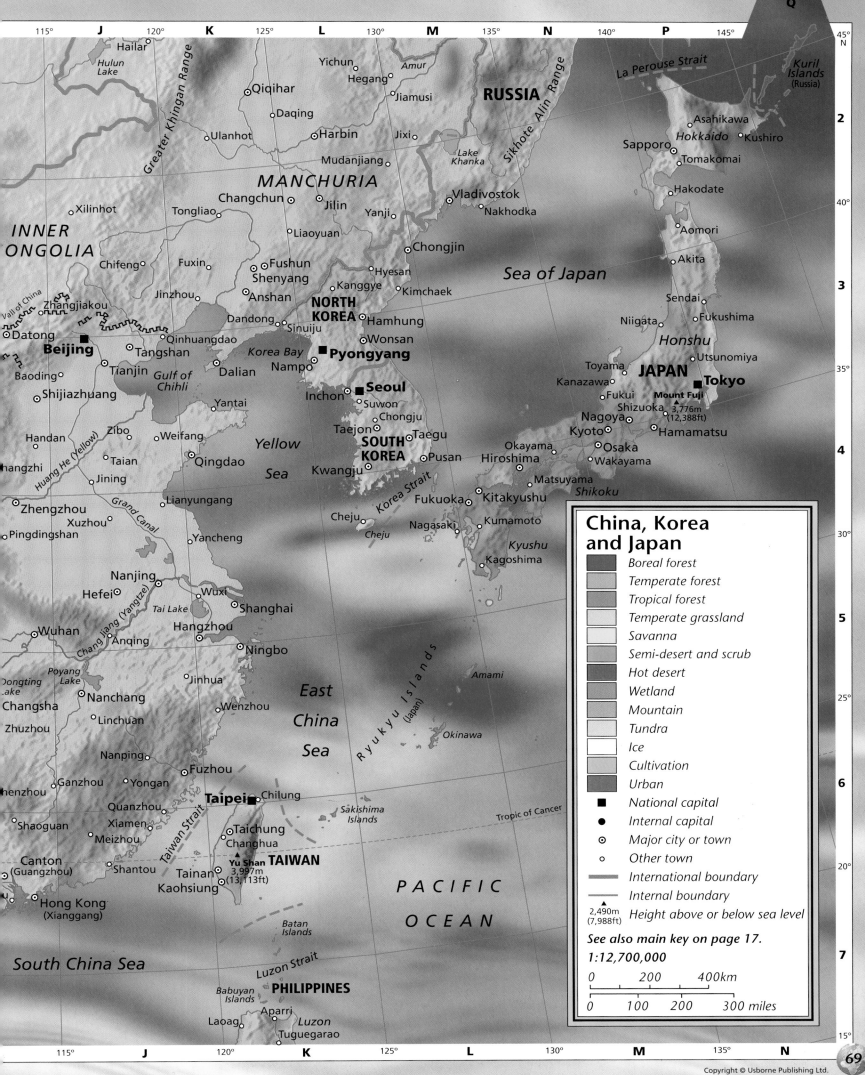

45°
N

115° **J** 120° **K** 125° **L** 130° **M** 135° **N** 140° **P** 145°

Hailar

Hulun
Lake

Qiqihar

Daqing

Ulanhot

Xilinhot

INNER
ONGOLIA

Chifeng

Yichun

Hegang

Jiamusi

Harbin

Jixi

Mudanjiang

MANCHURIA

Changchun

Jilin

Yanji

Liaoyuan

Amur

RUSSIA

La Perouse Strait

Kuril
Islands
(Russia)

Asahikawa

Hokkaido Kushiro

Sapporo

Tomakomai

Hakodate

2

Vladivostok

Nakhodka

Chongjin

Aomori

40°

Tongliao

Fuxin

Fushun
Shenyang

Anshan

Jinzhou

Hyesan

Kanggye

Kimchaek

Akita

Sea of Japan

Sikhote Alin Range

Lake
Khanka

3

Wall of China

Zhangjiakou

Datong

Beijing

Baoding

Tianjin

Qinhuangdao

Tangshan

Dandong

Sinuiju

NORTH
KOREA Hamhung

Wonsan

Korea Bay

Pyongyang

Nampo

Sendai

Niigata

Fukushima

Honshu

Toyama

Utsunomiya

JAPAN Tokyo

35°

Shijiazhuang

Dalian

Kanazawa

Fukui

Shizuoka ▲ Mount Fuji
3,776m
(12,388ft)

Handan

Zibo

Weifang

Yantai

Korea Bay

Seoul

Inchon Suwon

Chongju

Kyoto

Osaka

Nagoya

Hamamatsu

hangzhi

Huang He (Yellow)

Taian

Qingdao

Yellow

Taejon

SOUTH
KOREA Taegu

Kwangju Pusan

Okayama

Hiroshima

Wakayama

4

Jining

Sea

Matsuyama

Shikoku

Zhengzhou

Xuzhou

Pingdingshan

Grand Canal

Lianyungang

Yancheng

Cheju

Cheju

Korea Strait

Fukuoka

Nagasaki

Kitakyushu

Kumamoto

Kyushu

Kagoshima

30°

Nanjing

Hefei

Wuxi

Shanghai

Tai Lake

Hangzhou

Anqing

Chang Jiang (Yangtze)

Wuhan

Ningbo

5

Poyang
Lake

Jinhua

Dongting
Lake

Changsha

Nanchang

Linchuan

Wenzhou

East

China

Zhuzhou

Nanping

Amami

25°

Ryukyu Islands
(Japan)

Okinawa

Sea

China, Korea and Japan

Ganzhou

Yongan

Fuzhou

henzhou

Shaoguan

Quanzhou

Xiamen

Meizhou

Taiwan Strait

Taipei Chilung

Sakishima
Islands

Tropic of Cancer

	Boreal forest
	Temperate forest
	Tropical forest
	Temperate grassland
	Savanna
	Semi-desert and scrub
	Hot desert
	Wetland
	Mountain
	Tundra
	Ice
	Cultivation
	Urban

20°

Canton
(Guangzhou)

Shantou

Taichung

Changhua

▲ Yu Shan
3,997m
(13,113ft)

TAIWAN

Tainan

Kaohsiung

■ National capital
● Internal capital
⊙ Major city or town
○ Other town

International boundary

Internal boundary

▲ 2,490m
(7,988ft) Height above or below sea level

Hong Kong
(Xianggang)

Batan
Islands

PACIFIC

OCEAN

See also main key on page 17.

1:12,700,000

0   200   400km

0   100   200   300 miles

South China Sea

Luzon Strait

Babuyan
Islands

PHILIPPINES

Laoag

Aparri

Luzon

Tuguegarao

15°

115° **J** 120° **K** 125° **L** 130° **M** 135° **N**

Copyright © Usborne Publishing Ltd.

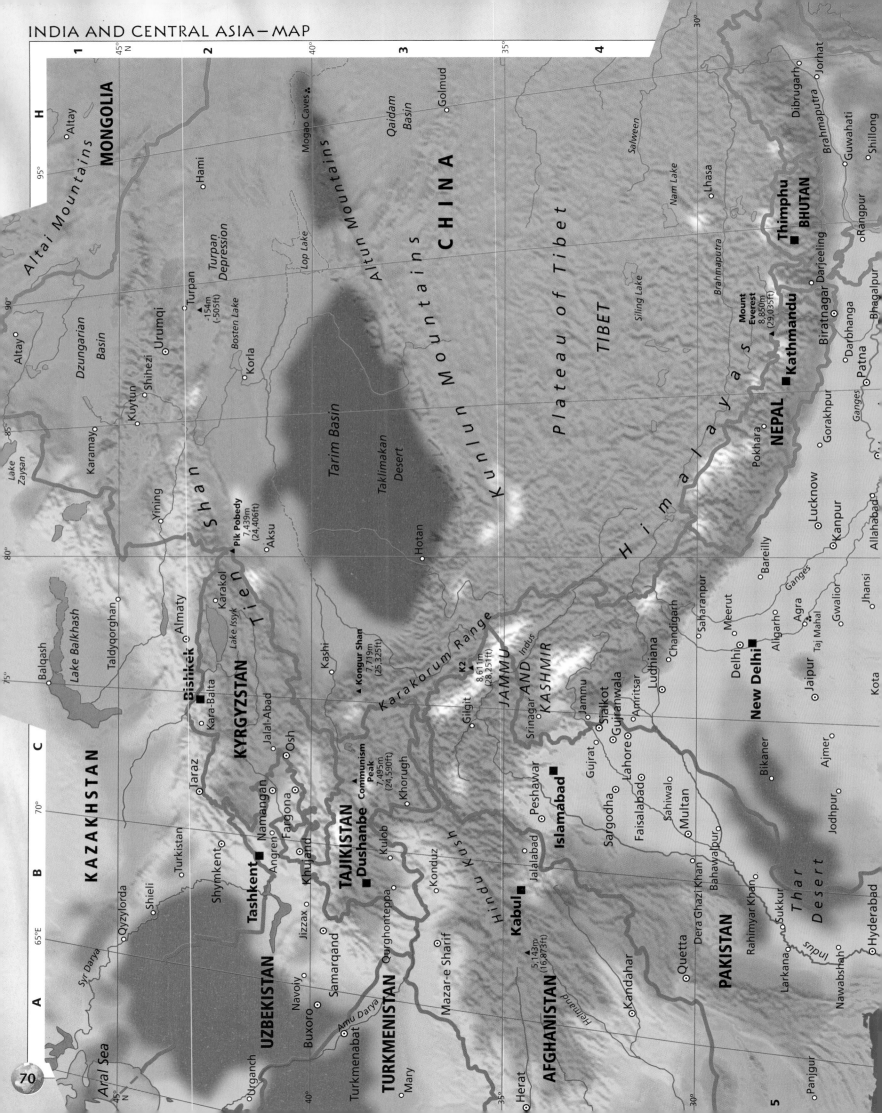

H
95°

MONGOLIA

Altay
Altay

Altai Mountains

Hami

Mogao Caves

Turpan
Turpan
Depression
-154m
(-505ft)

Bosten Lake

Lop Lake

Qaidam
Basin

Golmud

CHINA

Salween

Nam Lake

Lhasa

Dibrugarh
Jorhat

Brahmaputra

Guwahati
Shillong

Thimphu
BHUTAN

Rangpur

90°

Dzungarian
Basin

Urumqi

Shihezi

Kuytun

Karamay

Altun Mountains

Kunlun Mountains

Plateau of Tibet

TIBET

Brahmaputra

Mount
Everest
8,850m
(29,035ft)

Kathmandu

Biratnagar Darjeeling

Brahmaputra

Bhagalpur

85°

Lake
Zaysan

Kara-Balta

Yining

Tarim Basin

Taklimakan
Desert

Silling Lake

NEPAL

Pokhara

Gorakhpur

Ganges

Patna

80°

Balqash

Lake Balkhash

Taldyqorghan

Almaty

Karakol

Lake Issyk

Tien

Shan

Pik Pobedy
7,439m
(24,406ft)

Aksu

Hotan

Himalayas

Lucknow

Kanpur

Allahabad

75°

KAZAKHSTAN

Taldyqorghan

Bishkek

Kara-Balta

KYRGYZSTAN

Jalal-Abad

Osh

Kashi

Kongur Shan
7,719m
(25,325ft)

K2
8,611m
(28,251ft)

JAMMU AND KASHMIR

Indus

Srinagar

Gilgit

Karakorum Range

Jammu

Sialkot

Ludhiana

Chandigarh

Saharanpur

Meerut

Bareilly

Aligarh

Agra

Gwalior

Jhansi

Delhi

New Delhi

Jaipur

Taj Mahal

Kota

C
70°

Taraz

Namangan

Fargona

Jizzax

Khujand

TAJIKISTAN

Dushanbe

Communism
Peak
7,495m
(24,590ft)

Khorugh

Kulob

Hindu Kush

Peshawar

Islamabad

Gujrat

Gujranwala

Amritsar

Lahore

Sargodha

Faisalabad

Sahiwalo

Multan

Bikaner

Ajmer

Jaipur

B
65°E

Turkistan

Shymkent

Angren

Tashkent

Samarqand

Ourghonteppa

Konduz

Kabul

Jalalabad

Dera Ghazi Khan

Bahawalpur

Rahimyar Khan

Thar
Desert

Jodhpur

A

Qyzylorda

Shieli

Navoly

Buxoro

UZBEKISTAN

TURKMENISTAN

Mary

Turkmenabat

Amu Darya

Mazar-e Sharif

AFGHANISTAN

Herat

5,143m
(16,873ft)

Kandahar

Quetta

PAKISTAN

Larkana

Sukkur

Nawabshah

Panjgur

Indus

Hyderabad

Aral Sea

Syr Darya

45°N

40°

35°

30°

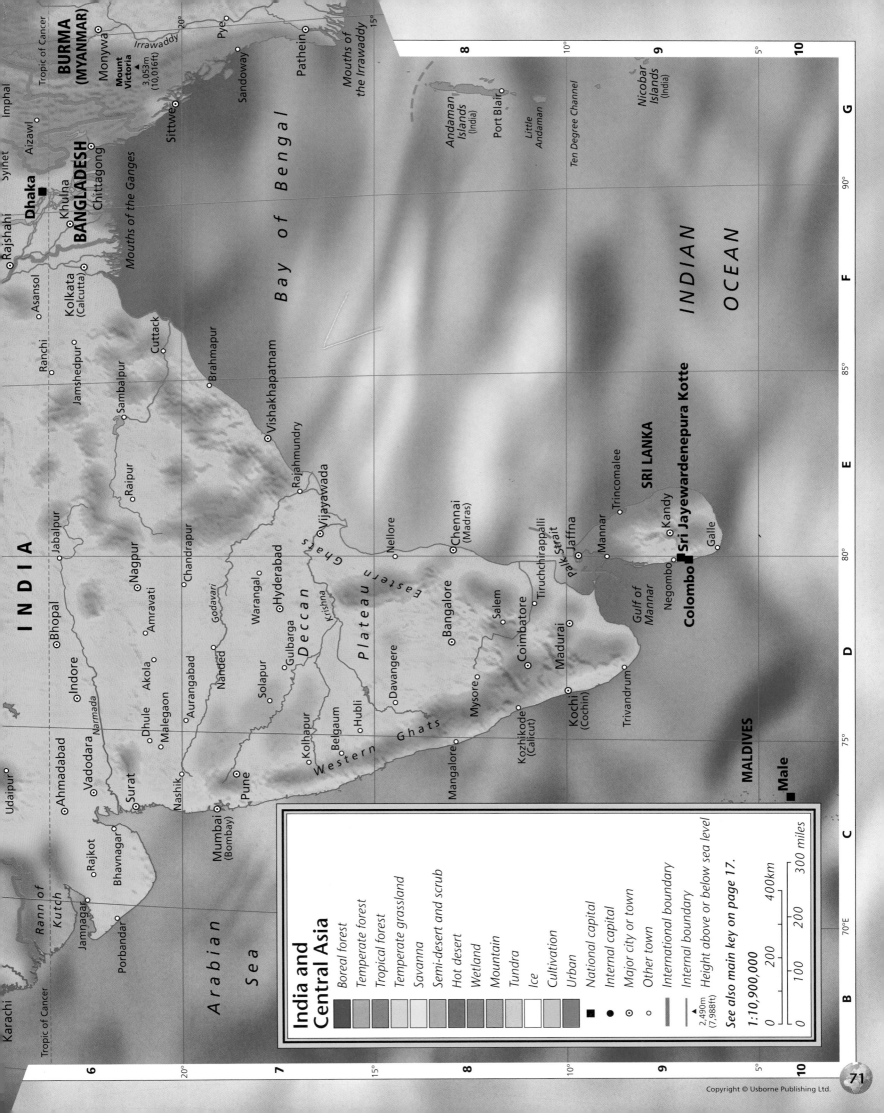

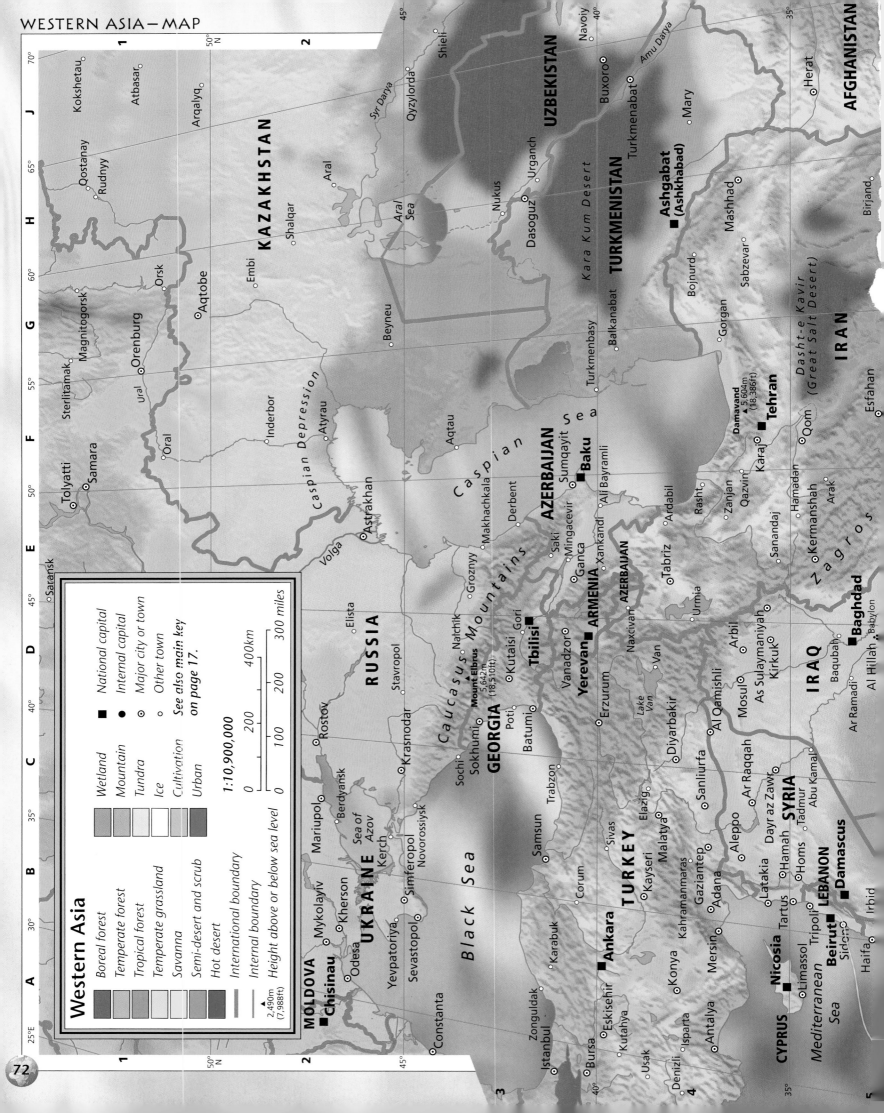

Western Asia

Boreal forest	
Temperate forest	
Tropical forest	
Temperate grassland	
Savanna	
Semi-desert and scrub	
Hot desert	

■ National capital
● Internal capital
⊙ Major city or town
○ Other town

See also main key on page 17.

Wetland
Mountain
Tundra
Ice
Cultivation
Urban

1:10,900,000

0 100 200 400km
0 100 200 300 miles

International boundary
Internal boundary

▲ 2,490m (7,988ft) Height above or below sea level

Countries and places

KAZAKHSTAN
UZBEKISTAN
TURKMENISTAN
Ashgabat (Ashkhabad)
AFGHANISTAN
Herat
Birjand
Mashhad
Sabzevar
Bojnurd
Gorgan
IRAN
Dasht-e Kavir (Great Salt Desert)
Esfahan
Qom
Tehran
Damavand ▲ 5,604m (18,386ft)
Karaj
Qazvin
Zanjan
Hamadan
Arak
Kermanshah
Zagros
Sanandaj
Ardabil
Rasht
Tabriz
Urmia
AZERBAIJAN
Baku
Sumqayit
Ali Bayramli
Ganca
Mingacevir
Xankandi
Naxcivan
ARMENIA
Yerevan
AZERBAIJAN
Van
Lake Van
Erzurum
Diyarbakir
IRAQ
Baghdad
Babylon
Al Hillah
Baqubah
Ar Ramadi
Arbil
Kirkuk
As Sulaymaniyah
Mosul
Al Qamishli
Ar Raqqah
SYRIA
Dayr az Zawr
Abu Kamal
Tadmur
Aleppo
Hamah
Homs
LEBANON
Tripoli
Beirut
Sidon
Damascus
Irbid
Tartus
Latakia
Haifa
Mediterranean Sea
CYPRUS
Nicosia
Limassol
TURKEY
Ankara
Sanliurfa
Gaziantep
Kahramanmaras
Adana
Mersin
Konya
Malatya
Elazig
Sivas
Kayseri
Corum
Eskisehir
Kutahya
Usak
Denizli
Isparta
Antalya
Bursa
Istanbul
Zonguldak
Karabuk
Samsun
Trabzon
GEORGIA
Tbilisi
Poti
Batumi
Sokhumi
Kutaisi
Gori
Mount Elbrus ▲ 5,642m (18,510ft)
Vanadzor
Caucasus Mountains
RUSSIA
Natchik
Grozny
Makhachkala
Derbent
Stavropol
Elista
Krasnodar
Rostov
Sochi
Novorossiysk
Black Sea
Sea of Azov
Kerch
Sevastopol
Simferopol
Yevpatoriya
UKRAINE
Kherson
Mykolayiv
Odesa
Mariupol
Berdyansk
MOLDOVA
Chisinau
Constanta
Caspian Sea
Caspian Depression
Astrakhan
Volga
Ural
Atyrau
Inderbor
Oral
Aqtau
Beyneu
Turkmenbasy
Balkanabat
Kara Kum Desert
Dasoguz
Turkmenabat
Mary
Nukus
Buxoro
Urganch
Navoiy
Amu Darya
Syr Darya
Aral
Aral Sea
Shalqar
Embi
Aqtobe
Orsk
Orenburg
Magnitogorsk
Sterlitamak
Samara
Tolyatti
Saransk
Arqalyq
Qostanay
Rudnyy
Kokshetau
Atbasar
Shieli
Qyzylorda
KAZAKHSTAN

ARCTIC

Svalbard
(Norway)

A

B

Franz Josef
Land

C

D

E

1

2

60°

80°

20°

40°

60°

80°

UNITED
KINGDOM
London

North
Sea

Paris

NETHERLANDS

BELGIUM

LUXEMBOURG

FRANCE

GERMANY

Berlin

Norwegian
Sea

Arctic Circle

NORWAY

Oslo

DENMARK

SWEDEN

Baltic
Sea

Stockholm

FINLAND

Helsinki

North Cape

○ Murmansk

Barents
Sea

Kola
Peninsula

Novaya
Zemlya

Kara
Sea

3

CZECH
REPUBLIC

AUSTRIA

POLAND

Warsaw

LITHUANIA

Vilnius

LATVIA

ESTONIA

Lake
Ladoga

○ St. Petersburg

Lake
Onega

○ Arkhangelsk

○ Vorkuta

○ Norilsk

SLOVAKIA

Budapest

HUNGARY

Minsk

BELARUS

○ Lviv

○ Cherepovets

○ Ukhta

○ Novyy Urengoy

West Siberian

ROMANIA

Kiev

MOLDOVA

Chisinau

UKRAINE

○ Kharkiv

○ Odesa

○ Dnipropetrovsk

○ Simferopol

Moscow

○ Ryazan

○ Nizhniy Novgorod

Volga

○ Voronezh

○ Kazan

○ Perm

Ural Mountains

Ob

Plain

○ Surgut

Yenisey

R U S

40°
N

Black
Sea

○ Rostov

○ Krasnodar

○ Volgograd

Volga

Mount Elbrus
▲
5,642m
(18,510ft)

○ Astrakhan

○ Oral

○ Atyrau

○ Aqtobe

○ Orenburg

○ Yekaterinburg

○ Chelyabinsk

Irtysh

Ob

○ Omsk

○ Tomsk

○ Krasnoyarsk

Ankara

TURKEY

○ Adana

GEORGIA

Tbilisi

ARMENIA

Yerevan

AZERBAIJAN

Baku

Caspian Sea

○ Aqtau

○ Aqtau

KAZAKHSTAN

Astana

○ Pavlodar

○ Novosibirsk

○ Barnaul

○ Abakan

4

○ Aleppo

SYRIA

○ Mosul

Baghdad

IRAQ

Tehran

○ Tabriz

Damavand
▲
5,604m
(18,386ft)

○ Aqtau

Aral
Sea

○ Nukus

○ Dasoguz

TURKMENISTAN

Ashgabat
(Ashkhabad)

○ Turkmenabat

○ Qyzylorda

○ Balqash

Lake
Balkhash

○ Uskemen

○ Kyzyl

○ Altay

Qaraghandy

UZBEKISTAN

Tashkent

○ Shymkent

○ Almaty

Bishkek

KYRGYZSTAN

○ Osh

Tien Shan

○ Urumqi

○ Aksu

○ Ahvaz

○ Esfahan

○ Mashhad

○ Samarqand

Dushanbe

TAJIKISTAN

IRAN

Kuwait City

KUWAIT

○ Shiraz

Persian Gulf (The Gulf)

○ Herat

○ Mazar-e Sharif

Tarim Basin

○ Hotan

Taklimakan Desert

SAUDI
ARABIA

Riyadh

Manama

QATAR

Doha

○ Bandar-e
Abbas

○ Zahedan

○ Kandahar

AFGHANISTAN

Kabul

Islamabad

K2
▲
8,611m
(28,251ft)

○ Srinagar

Plateau of Tibet

Abu Dhabi

Gulf

PAKISTAN

Indus

○ Lahore

INDIA

C

60°E

D

80°

E

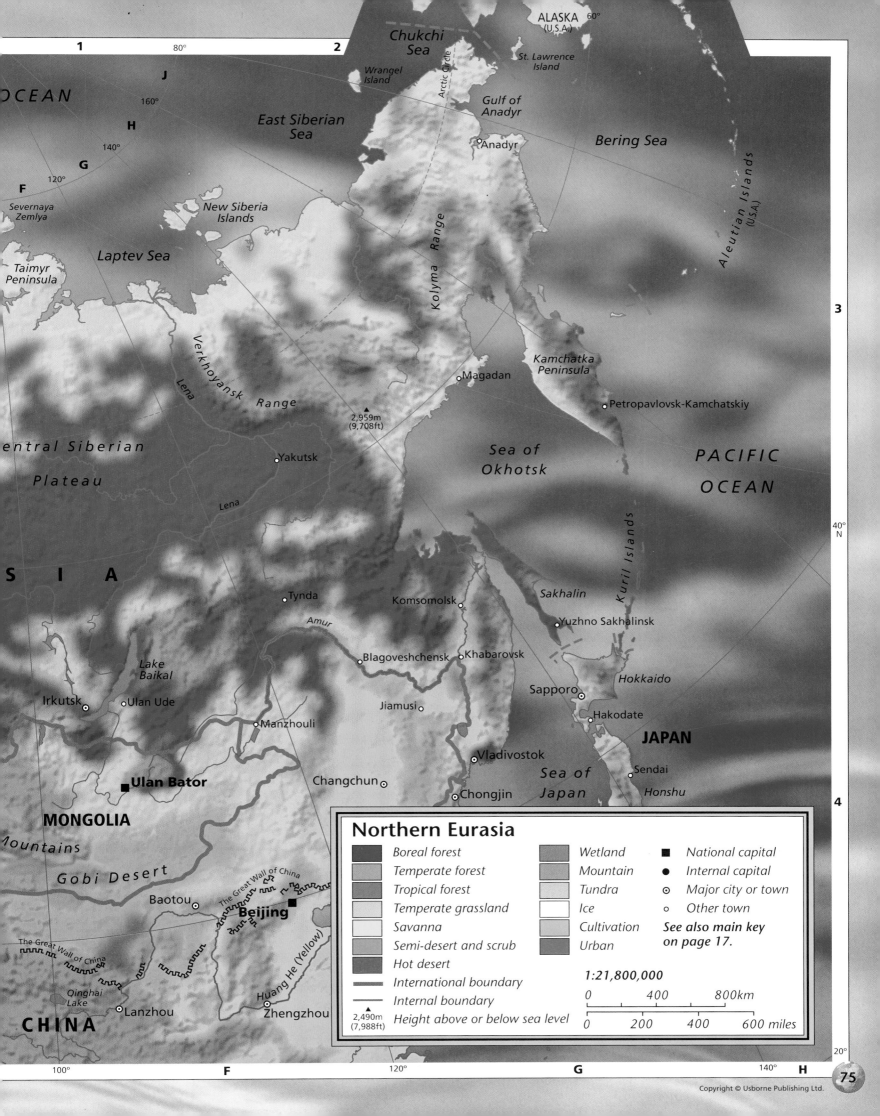

OCEAN

ALASKA 60°
(U.S.A.)

Chukchi
Sea

Wrangel
Island

J

80°

1

2

East Siberian
Sea

Gulf of
Anadyr

Bering Sea

Anadyr

St. Lawrence
Island

160°

H

140°

G

120°

F

Severnaya
Zemlya

New Siberia
Islands

Laptev Sea

Aleutian Islands
(U.S.A.)

Taimyr
Peninsula

3

Verkhoyansk
Range

Kolyma
Range

Magadan

Kamchatka
Peninsula

Petropavlovsk-Kamchatskiy

Lena

2,959m
(9,708ft)

Yakutsk

Central Siberian
Plateau

Sea of
Okhotsk

PACIFIC

OCEAN

Lena

40°
N

S I A

Tynda

Komsomolsk

Amur

Kuril Islands

Sakhalin

Blagoveshchensk

Khabarovsk

Yuzhno Sakhalinsk

Lake
Baikal

Jiamusi

Hokkaido

Irkutsk

Ulan Ude

Sapporo

Hakodate

Manzhouli

JAPAN

Vladivostok

Ulan Bator

Changchun

Sendai

Sea of
Japan

Honshu

MONGOLIA

Chongjin

4

Mountains

Gobi Desert

The Great Wall of China

Baotou

Beijing

The Great Wall of China

Huang He (Yellow)

Qinghai
Lake

Lanzhou

Zhengzhou

CHINA

Northern Eurasia

Boreal forest
Temperate forest
Tropical forest
Temperate grassland
Savanna
Semi-desert and scrub
Hot desert
International boundary
Internal boundary
2,490m (7,988ft) Height above or below sea level

Wetland
Mountain
Tundra
Ice
Cultivation
Urban

National capital
Internal capital
Major city or town
Other town

See also main key on page 17.

1:21,800,000

0   400   800km
0 200 400 600 miles

100°   F   120°   G   140°   H

20°

75

Copyright © Usborne Publishing Ltd.

EUROPE

Europe is a small continent, packed with over 40 countries and more than 700 million people. Russia is an enormous country, spanning two continents. Its western part is in Europe, while its eastern part is in Asia. The European part of Russia is larger than any other country in Europe.

The shading on this map is there to help you see clearly the different countries that make up the continent.

Arctic Circle

ARCTIC OCEAN

Reykjavik
ICELAND

Norwegian Sea

Faroe Islands (Denmark)

SWEDEN

Shetland Islands

NORWAY

Oslo

Stockholm

Orkney Islands

North Sea

DENMARK
Copenhagen

Baltic Sea

IRELAND
Dublin

UNITED KINGDOM

The Hague
London

Amsterdam
NETHERLANDS

Berlin

POLAND

Brussels
BELGIUM

GERMANY

LUXEMBOURG
Luxembourg

Prague

CZECH REPUBLIC

Paris

Rhine

Vienna
Bratislava

ATLANTIC OCEAN

Bay of Biscay

FRANCE

Bern Vaduz
LIECHTENSTEIN
SWITZERLAND

AUSTRIA

Budapest

SLOVENIA
Ljubljana

HUNGARY

Zagreb
CROATIA

MONACO

PORTUGAL

Lisbon

ANDORRA
Andorra la Vella

Madrid

SPAIN

SAN MARINO

BOSNIA AND HERZEGOVINA
Sarajevo

ITALY

Corsica

Rome

VATICAN CITY

ALBANIA
Tirana

Balearic Islands

Sardinia

Mediterranean Sea

Sicily

MALTA
Valletta

Barents Sea

Arctic Circle

⊙ Murmansk

⊙ Arkhangelsk

FINLAND

■ Helsinki

⊙ St. Petersburg

■ Tallinn
ESTONIA

R U S S I A

Nizhniy Novgorod ⊙   Kazan ⊙

■ Riga   LATVIA

■ Moscow

LITHUANIA
Vilnius ■

RUSSIA

Volga

■ Minsk

BELARUS

■ Warsaw

■ Kiev

Volgograd ⊙

UKRAINE

Dnieper

SLOVAKIA

MOLDOVA

■ Chisinau

ROMANIA

Black Sea

■ Belgrade

■ Bucharest

Danube

YUGOSLAVIA

BULGARIA
■ Sofia

■ Skopje
MACEDONIA   TURKEY

GREECE

■ Athens

Crete

Facts

Total land area 10,205,720 sq km
(3,940,428 sq miles) (including
European Russia)

Total population 727 million
(including all of Russia)

Biggest city Moscow, Russia

Biggest country Russia *Total area:
17,075,200 sq km (6,592,735 sq
miles) Area of European Russia:
4,294,400 sq km (1,658,068 sq miles)*

Smallest country Vatican City *0.44
sq km (0.17 sq miles)*

Highest mountain Elbrus, Russia
5,642m (18,510ft)

Longest river Volga *3,700km
(2,298 miles)*

Biggest lake Lake Ladoga, Russia
17,700 sq km (6,834 sq miles)

Highest waterfall Utigard, on the
Jostedal Glacier, Norway *800m
(2,625ft)*

Biggest desert No deserts in Europe

Biggest island Great Britain *234,410
sq km (90,506 sq miles)*

Main mineral deposits Bauxite, zinc,
iron, potash, fluorspar

Main fuel deposits Oil, coal, natural
gas, peat, uranium

*A cow in Devon, in the
south of England*

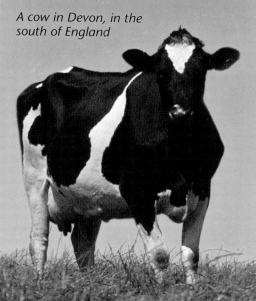

Copyright © Usborne Publishing Ltd.

Europe has lots of islands and many of its countries are largely surrounded by sea. The Alps, one of Europe's principal mountain ranges, lies in the west, and is the source of many of its major rivers, including the Rhine and the Rhone.

Europe by night

Satellite pictures taken at night show how much light is being generated in different areas. Highly populated areas, such as Europe, where there are many big cities, light up brightly at night. This is because when many people live in one area, the combined lights of all the buildings at night are so bright they show up as a dot.

This satellite image of Europe was taken at night, but the land and water have been falsely-shaded, so you can see their outlines clearly. Each blue dot represents a highly populated area that is lit up.

Internet links

For a link to a Web site where you can find out more about Mount Vesuvius' famous eruption, go to **www.usborne-quicklinks.com**

This is a satellite image of Mount Vesuvius, a volcano in southern Italy. The black dot in the middle is the crater.

Mount Vesuvius

Mount Vesuvius is a volcano near the city of Naples in southern Italy. It is famous for its eruption in AD79, which buried the towns of Pompeii and Herculaneum in around 30m (100ft) of ash, mud and stones. The towns remained buried until the 18th century when they were rediscovered.

Vesuvius is monitored very carefully today, as it is close to the city of Naples and more than two million people live nearby. It has had over 50 minor eruptions since the one in AD79.

This area of the Alps is in Switzerland. Over 70% of Switzerland is mountainous.

The Rhine River

The Rhine River carries more traffic than any other river in the world. It is 1,320km (820 miles) long and winds through the west of Europe, flowing from the Alps in Switzerland, along the Swiss-Austrian border, through Germany and France to the Netherlands. Many cities lie along its banks, including Strasbourg, in France, and Cologne, in Germany.

This is a section of the Rhine River running through west Germany. The river is black, vegetation is blue and buildings are brown. The patchwork of rectangles to the east of the river is farmland.

Norwegian fjords

Norway's dramatic coastline is a mixture of steep mountains and long, thin inlets of water, called fjords. The fjords were formed by glaciers. When glacier ice builds up at the top of a mountain, it becomes heavy and starts to slide down the slopes, carving out a deep channel in the rock. When the glacier melts, the water fills the channel, making a fjord.

The satellite image below shows an area of Norway's coastline. The long, thin blue strips are inlets of water, called fjords.

Eastern Europe stretches as far as the Ural Mountains, which separate European Russia from Asian Russia. Northern Europe is made up of Iceland and the Scandinavian countries, including Norway and Sweden.

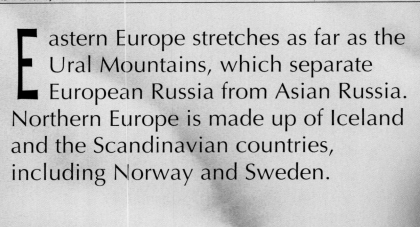

Onion-shaped domes

Early Russian churches have an easily recognizable style, with high walls, very few doors and windows, and steeply-sloped roofs topped with onion-shaped domes. This style became popular during the 11th century. Many of these early churches were built from wood, as it was a building material widely available from Russia's dense forests.

This is the Church of the Intercession on Kizhi Island in northern Russia. It was built almost entirely from wood in 1764.

This is a Viking helmet. It was discovered in a grave in Uppland, Sweden.

Viking lands

During the 9th to the 11th centuries, the Vikings, a group of master ship builders and sea traders from Scandinavia, dominated northern Europe. Viking heritage can still be seen today. The Vikings carved stories and pictures into large stones, called rune stones. Many of these stones have survived and give clues to how they lived. The Viking Ship Museum in Oslo, Norway, has three well-preserved Viking ships, and in Sweden, a Viking festival is held each year in a reconstructed Viking village.

In this dramatic image of Budapest you can see the Chain Bridge, which links Buda and Pest across the Danube River.

Internet links

For a link to a Web site where you can go on a virtual Viking quest, go to **www.usborne-quicklinks.com**

Danube River

The Danube River flows from the west to the east of Europe, through many major cities, including Bratislava, the capital of Slovakia, and Budapest, the capital of Hungary. The river splits Budapest into two parts, Buda and Pest. The Royal Palace, is in Buda, on the west bank, while Hungary's parliament building is in Pest, on the east bank.

Atlantic puffins

One type of bird common throughout northern Europe is the Atlantic puffin. Atlantic puffins are sea birds that live in the cold waters around the coasts of the North Atlantic Ocean.

Atlantic puffins are very skilled at diving underwater to catch fish to eat. They only come ashore once a year to nest on rocky cliff tops and grassy islands. Iceland has the largest puffin population in the world at around nine million.

These are Atlantic puffins. They are about 18cm (10in) tall and have yellow, orange and blue beaks, which is why they are also known as sea parrots.

The west of Europe stretches as far as Portugal on the Atlantic coast, while southern Europe reaches down to the many small islands in the Mediterranean Sea, where the climate is famously sunny, warm and dry.

Sights of London

There are many famous sights in London, from the huge clock tower of Big Ben, to Buckingham Palace, the official residency of the Queen.

One of the city's most recent additions is the London Eye, the world's largest Ferris wheel, which was constructed to mark the millennium. The top of the wheel is 135m (443ft) high, giving an impressive view of the city.

The London Eye sits on the south bank of the River Thames. Big Ben sits on the opposite bank.

Internet links

For a link to a Web site where you can explore the Tower of London, where the Crown Jewels are kept, go to **www.usborne-quicklinks.com**

Eiffel Tower

The Eiffel Tower in Paris, France, was opened in 1889, and has since had over 200 million visitors. It was built for an international exhibition celebrating the scientific and engineering achievements of the time. The iron structure is around 300m (980ft) tall and has three levels with many shops and restaurants.

There are over 350 electric lamps fitted to the outside of the Eiffel Tower, lighting it up dramatically at night.

The Leaning Tower

One of Italy's most famous sights is the Leaning Tower of Pisa. The 55m (180ft) tall bell tower is part of Pisa Cathedral. Building work began on it in 1173, and the tower started to lean while it was being built. It leans because the ground beneath it is a mixture of sand and clay, which are easily compressed. The huge weight of the tower compressed the ground more in some areas than others, so the tower began to lean.

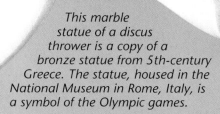

This marble statue of a discus thrower is a copy of a bronze statue from 5th-century Greece. The statue, housed in the National Museum in Rome, Italy, is a symbol of the Olympic games.

Home of the Olympics

Athletes from all over the world compete in the Olympic games every four years. The first Olympic games were held in celebration of the Greek God Zeus in Olympia, Greece, in 776BC. Today, some of the foundations, steps and pillars of the original stadium, which seated around 30,000 spectators, remain. The start and finish lines of the running track, and the judges' seats, have also survived.

F | 50° | G | 55° | H | 60° | J | 65° | K | 70° | L

West Siberian Plain

Kotlas
Syktyvkar
Ivdel
Uray

Solikamsk
Serov
Irtysh
Tobolsk

Berezniki

Kama Reservoir

Kirov
Glazov
Perm
Nizhniy Tagil
Tyumen

R U S S I A

Yekaterinburg

Votkinsk
Izhevsk
Tobol

Yoshkar-Ola
Sarapul
Kurgan
55° N

Cheboksary
Belaya
Zlatoust
Chelyabinsk

Kazan
Naberezhnyye Chelny
Ufa
Uy
Ershovka

Buinsk
Kuybyshev Reservoir
Almetyevsk
▲ Yamantau 1,640m (5,381ft)
Komsomolets
Qostanay

Ulyanovsk
Oktyabrskiy
Beloretsk
Rudnyy

Sterlitamak
Magnitogorsk
Tobyl
Semiozernoe

Volga
Tolyatti
Belaya
3

Syzran
Saratov Reservoir
Samara
Buzuluk
Zhetiqara

Uplands
Zhayylma

Orenburg
Ural
Orsk
Tolybay

Balakovo
50°

Saratov
Engels
Oral
Aqsay
Torghay

Volgograd Reservoir
Aqtobe

K A Z A K H S T A N

Chapaev

Kaztalovka

Zhanibek
Ural
4

Inderbor

Volga

Topoli

Balkuduk

Caspian Depression

Atyrau

Astrakhan
Caspian Sea

Eastern Europe

Boreal forest	Wetland	■ National capital
Temperate forest	Mountain	● Internal capital
Tropical forest	Tundra	⊙ Major city or town
Temperate grassland	Ice	○ Other town
Savanna	Cultivation	**See also main key on page 17.**
Semi-desert and scrub	Urban	
Hot desert		

International boundary

Internal boundary

▲ 2,490m (7,988ft) Height above or below sea level

1:6,400,000

0   100   200   300km

0   100   200 miles

50° | 55° | H | 60° | J | 45°

Copyright © Usborne Publishing Ltd.

Barents Sea

Kola Peninsula

White Sea

RUSSIA

North Cape

Arctic Circle

Severomorsk
Vadso
Kirkenes
Murmansk
Monchegorsk
▲1,191m (3,907ft)
Apatity
Kandalaksha
Belomorsk
Lake Vyg
Lake Onega
Lake Seg
Medvezhyegorsk
Petrozavodsk
Lake Top
Lake Kuyto
Kostomuksha
Lake Pya
Kostomuksha
Lake Ladoga
Volkhov
Tikhvin
Kirishi
Borovichi
Lake Ilmen

Hammerfest
Soroya
Utsjoki
Sevettijarvi
Kaamanen
Alta
Lake Inari
Lokan Reservoir
Sodankyla
Kuusamo
Lieksa
Pielis Lake
Lake Pielis
Kuhmo
Kajaani
Oulu Lake
Vyborg
Zelenogorsk
St. Petersburg
Pushkin
Gatchina
Kingisepp
Novgorod

Tromso
Kiruna
Kebnekaise ▲2,114m (6,935ft)
Narvik
Rovaniemi
Tornio
Raahe
Oulu
Kiuruvesi
Kuopio
Varkaus
Hauki Lake
Pihlaja Lake
Saimaa Lake
Pajanne Lake
Mikkeli
Lappeenranta
Kouvola
Kotka
Narva
Lake Peipus
Lake Pskov

Svolvaer
Stora Lule Lake
Horn Lake
Storavan Lake
Storuman
Skelleftea
Boden
Umea
FINLAND
Kokkola
Saarijarvi
Jyvaskyla
Alavus
Nasi Lake
Tampere
Hameenlinna
Lahti
Helsinki
Espoo
Gulf of Finland
Tallinn
ESTONIA
Haapsalu
Kohtla-Jarve
Tartu
Parnu

Lofoten Vesteralen
Vestfjorden
Bodo
Moi Rana
Ume
Sundsvall
Hudiksvall
Gavle
Vaasa
Kurikka
Pori
Rauma
Turku
Aland Islands
Hiiumaa
Sarremaa
Sea

Namsos
Steinkjer
Stor Lake
Ostersund
Indals
Borlange
Dal
Uppsala
Eskilstuna
Lake Malar
Stockholm
Sodertalje
Norrkoping

Vikna
Froya Hitra
Trondheim
Oppdal
SWEDEN
Lillehammer
Glama
Klar
Karlstad
Orebro
Lake Vaner
Lidkoping
Linkoping

Kristiansund
Smola
Sula
Sotra
Galdhopiggen ▲2,469m (8,100ft)
NORWAY
Honefoss
Drammen
Oslo
Fredrikstad
Larvik
Uddevalla
Arendal

Bergen
Odda
Karmoy
Stavanger
Kristiansand
Varhaug

Norwegian Sea

Gulf of Bothnia

Lapland

ICELAND
Langanes
Seydhisfjordhur
Siglufjordhur
Isafjordhur
Faxafloi
Keflavik
Reykjavik
Vatnajokull
Hvannadalshnukur ▲2,119m (6,952ft)
ATLANTIC OCEAN
Arctic Circle
Same scale as main map

Central and Northern Europe

Key
- Boreal forest
- Temperate forest
- Tropical forest
- Temperate grassland
- Savanna
- Semi-desert and scrub
- Hot desert
- Wetland
- Mountain
- Tundra
- Ice
- Cultivation
- Urban
- ■ National capital
- ● Internal capital
- ⊙ Major city or town
- ○ Other town
- International boundary
- Internal boundary
- ▲ 2,490m (7,988ft) Height above or below sea level

See also main key on page 17.

1:6,400,000

0 100 200 300km
0 100 200 miles

Copyright © Usborne Publishing Ltd.

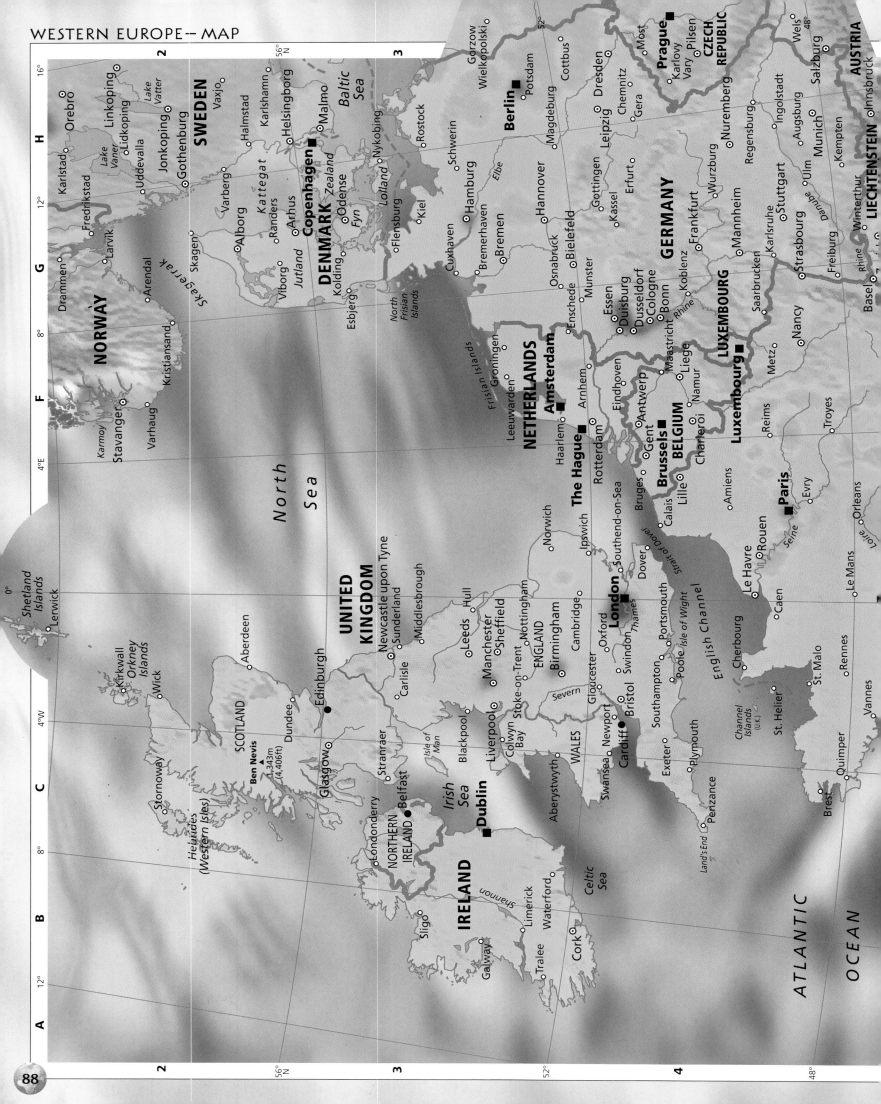

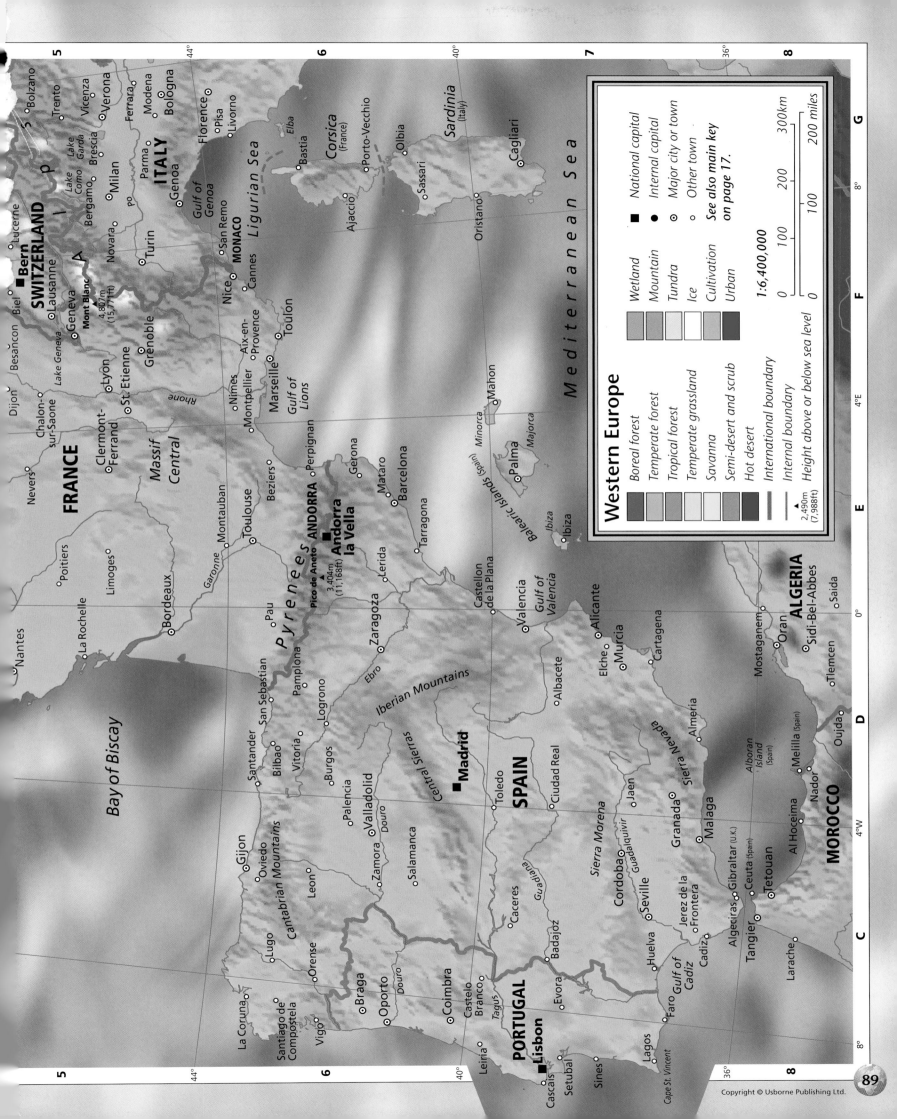

SOUTHERN EUROPE—MAP

Cherbourg, Le Havre, Caen, Amiens, Charleroi, Namur, **BELGIUM**, Koblenz, Erfurt, Gera, Dresden, Wroclaw, Walbrzych, Oder, Opole, Rouen, Frankfurt, **LUXEMBOURG** ■ Luxembourg, Most, Liberec, Hradec Kralove, **Prague**, Paris ■, Reims, Metz, Saarbrucken, Mannheim, Wurzburg, **GERMANY**, Karlovy Vary, Pilsen, **CZECH REPUBLIC**, Evry, Nancy, Karlsruhe, Nuremberg, Regensburg, Olomouc, Brno, Zlin, Le Mans, Orleans, Troyes, Strasbourg, Rhine, Stuttgart, Ingolstadt, Danube, Ceske Budejovice, Angers, Tours, Freiburg, Ulm, Augsburg, Linz, Vienna ■, Trnava, Poitiers, Nevers, Dijon, Basel, Munich, Wels, St. Polten, **Bratislava** ■, Limoges, Besancon, Winterthur, Kempten, Salzburg, **AUSTRIA**, Knittelfeld, Gyor, Szombathely, **FRANCE**, Chalon-sur-Saone, Biel, Zurich, Lucerne, Innsbruck, Grossglockner 3,798m (12,461ft), Graz, Lake Balaton, Clermont-Ferrand, Geneva, Lausanne, **Bern** ■, **SWITZERLAND** ■ **Vaduz**, **LIECHTENSTEIN**, Villach, Klagenfurt, Zalaegerszeg, St. Etienne, Lake Geneva, Mont Blanc 4,807m (15,771ft), Bolzano, Trento, Kranj, **SLOVENIA** ■ **Ljubljana**, Maribor, Grenoble, Lake Como, Bergamo, Brescia, Lake Garda, Vicenza, Trieste, Novo Mesto, **Zagreb** ■, Novara, Milan, Verona, Po, Venice, Rijeka, **CROATIA**, Turin, Parma, Modena, Ferrara, Bologna, Ravenna, Pula, Zadar, Karlovac, Slavonski Brod, Montauban, Genoa, **ITALY**, Rimini, Banja Luka, Toulouse, Nimes, Aix-en-Provence, **MONACO**, Gulf of Genoa, San Remo, Nice, Livorno, Pisa, Florence, **SAN MARINO**, Ancona, **BOSNIA AND HERZEGOVINA**, Zenica, Montpellier, Beziers, Gulf of Lions, Marseille, Cannes, Perugia, Split, Mostar, **Andorra la Vella** ■, Toulon, *Ligurian Sea*, Bastia, Elba, Terni, Pescara, Ajaccio, *Corsica (France)*, **VATICAN CITY** ■ **Rome**, Foggia, Porto-Vecchio, Olbia, Bari, Sassari, Naples, Pompeii, Salerno, Taranto, *Sardinia (Italy)*, *Tyrrhenian Sea*, Oristano, Cosenza, Cagliari, Catanzaro, *Mediterranean Sea*, *Lipari Islands*, Trapani, Palermo, Messina, Annaba, Menzel Bourguiba, Bizerte, *Sicily*, Mount Etna 3,323m (10,902ft), Catania, Guelma, Carthage, Agrigento, Syracuse, Souk Ahras, **Tunis** ■, *Pantelleria (Italy)*, Ragusa, Tebessa, Kairouan, Nabeul, **MALTA** ■ **Valletta**, Sousse, **TUNISIA**, Monastir, *Pelagian Islands (Italy)*, Kasserine, El Jem, Biskra

Southern Europe

- Boreal forest
- Temperate forest
- Tropical forest
- Temperate grassland
- Savanna
- Semi-desert and scrub
- Hot desert
- Wetland
- Mountain
- Tundra
- Ice
- Cultivation
- Urban
- ■ National capital
- ● Internal capital
- ⊙ Major city or town
- ○ Other town
- —— International boundary
- — Internal boundary
- ▲ 2,490m (7,988ft) Height above or below sea level

See also main key on page 17.

1:6,400,000

0 100 200 300km
0 100 200 miles

Apennines, *Dinaric Alps*, *Adriatic Sea*, *Massif Central*, Garonne, Loire, Seine, Rhone, Elbe

Czestochowa
Kielce
Zamosc
Lutsk
Rivne
Zhytomyr
Kiev
Lubny
Poltava
Katowice
417m
(1,368ft)
Bila Tserkva
Slovyansk
Rybnik
Krakow
Tarnow
Lviv
Shepetivka
Cherkasy
Kremenchuk
Kramatorsk
Ostrava
POLAND
Vistula
Rzeszow
Ternopil
Vinnytsya
UKRAINE
Kremenchukske Reservoir
Dnipropetrovsk
Zilina
Banska
Bystrica
Gerlachovsky stit
2,655m
(8,711ft)
Presov
Ivano-Frankivsk
Dniester
Khmelnytskyy
Uman
Dniprodzerzhynsk
Dnieper
Zaporizhzhya
Nitra
SLOVAKIA
Kosice
Uzhhorod
Chernivtsi
Kamyanets-Podilskyy
Oleksandriya
Kirovohrad
Kryvyy Rih
Nikopol
Kakhovske Reservoir
Berdyansk
Miskolc
Satu Mare
Botosani
Balti
Rabnita
Yuzhnoukrayinsk
Melitopol
Budapest
Debrecen
Baia Mare
Suceava
MOLDOVA
Mykolayiv
Szekesfehervar
Oradea
Iasi
Chisinau
Tighina
Kherson
Sea of Azov
HUNGARY
Cluj-Napoca
Targu Mures
Piatra Neamt
Tiraspol
Odesa
Dzhankoy
Kecskemet
ROMANIA
Bacau
Bilhorod-Dnistrovskyy
Crimea
Kerch
Bekescsaba
Arad
Sibiu
Mount Moldoveanu
2,544m
(8,346ft)
Brasov
Focsani
Galati
Yevpatoriya
Feodosiya
Szeged
Timisoara
Transylvanian Alps
Ramnicu Valcea
Braila
Tulcea
Simferopol
Danube
Pecs
Subotica
Novi Sad
Pitesti
Ploiesti
Buzau
Sevastopol
Osijek
Carpathian Mountains
Drobeta-Turnu Severin
Bucharest
Mouths of the Danube
Tuzla
Belgrade
Craiova
Danube
Constanta
YUGOSLAVIA
Kragujevac
Ruse
Black Sea
Sarajevo
Kraljevo
Pleven
Dobrich
Niksic
Nis
Vratsa
Shumen
Varna
Dubrovnik
Leskovac
Balkan Mountains
BULGARIA
Podgorica
Pristina
Vranje
Sofia
Sliven
Stara Zagora
Burgas
Shkoder
Tetovo
Kumanovo
Plovdiv
Zonguldak
Karabuk
Skopje
Blagoevgrad
Corum
Durres
MACEDONIA
Prilep
Edirne
Istanbul
Adapazari
Tirana
Bitola
Serres
Kavala
Tekirdag
Bosporus
Elbasan
ALBANIA
Korce
Thessaloniki
Thasos
Sea of Marmara
Bursa
Ankara
Kirikkale
Vlore
Mount Olympus
2,917m
(9,570ft)
Canakkale
Eskisehir
Pindus Mountains
Larisa
Limnos
Balikesir
Kutahya
Lake Tuz
Corfu
Ioannina
Volos
Aegean Sea
Lesvos
Akhisar
Usak
TURKEY
Aksaray
Corfu
Euboea
Skyros
Manisa
Konya
Preveza
GREECE
Lamia
Izmir
Odemis
Kefallonia
Chalkida
Chios
Ephesus
Aydin
Denizli
Isparta
Beysehir Lake
Karaman
Patra
Peiraias
Athens
Antalya
Pyrgos
Cyclades
Alanya
Ionian Sea
Kalamata
Kythira
Rhodes
Taurus Mountains
Gulf of Antalya
Dodecanese
Rhodes
Kyrenia
Chania
Crete
Irakleio
Karpathos
Nicosia
CYPRUS
Larnaca
Ierapetra
Paphos
Limassol

AFRICA

Africa is the second-biggest continent in the world, and has 53 countries. These range from the vast, dry Sudan, to small, tropical islands such as the Seychelles. More than a quarter of Africa's countries are landlocked, with no access to the sea except through other countries.

Here is a group of Masai people from East Africa, silhouetted against a sunset over the flat grasslands of Africa.

Tropic of Cancer

Madeira (Portugal)

Canary Islands (Spain)

Algiers   Tunis

Rabat

MOROCCO   TUNISIA   Tripoli

Laayoune

ALGERIA   LIBYA

WESTERN
SAHARA
(Morocco)

MAURITANIA
Nouakchott

MALI   NIGER

Niger

CHAD

CAPE VERDE
Praia

Dakar   Niamey
SENEGAL   Bamako   Ndjamena
THE GAMBIA Banjul
Bissau   Ouagadougou
GUINEA-BISSAU   BURKINA FASO   NIGERIA
Conakry   GUINEA   BENIN   Abuja
Freetown   TOGO
SIERRA LEONE   IVORY
Monrovia   COAST   GHANA   Porto-Novo   CENTRA
LIBERIA   Yamoussoukro   Lome   AFRICA
Accra   CAMEROON   REPUBLI
Malabo   Bangui
EQUATORIAL   Yaounde
GUINEA   Congo

Equator   Libreville   CONGO
SAO TOME
AND PRINCIPE   GABON

Brazzaville
Kinshasa

ATLANTIC

OCEAN   Luanda

ANGOLA

NAMIBIA

Tropic of Capricorn   Windhoek

Orange

Cape Town

Copyright © Usborne Publishing Ltd.

The shading on this map is there to help you see clearly the different countries that make up the continent.

Cairo

EGYPT

Tropic of Cancer

Nile

Khartoum

ERITREA
Asmara

SUDAN

DJIBOUTI **Djibouti**

Addis Ababa

SOMALIA

ETHIOPIA

Mogadishu

UGANDA
Kampala

CONGO

KENYA

Equator

Kigali

Nairobi

(DEM.

RWANDA
BURUNDI
Bujumbura

REP.)

Victoria
SEYCHELLES

Dodoma

TANZANIA
Dar es Salaam

INDIAN

MALAWI

Moroni
COMOROS

OCEAN

ZAMBIA
Lusaka

Lilongwe

Zambezi

Harare
ZIMBABWE

MOZAMBIQUE

Antananarivo

MAURITIUS
Port Louis

OTSWANA

MADAGASCAR

Reunion
(France)

Tropic of Capricorn

aborone

Pretoria
Maputo

Mbabane **SWAZILAND**
Lobamba

loemfontein
Maseru

LESOTHO

SOUTH
AFRICA

Facts

Total land area 30,311,690 sq km (11,703,343 sq miles)

Total population 794 million

Biggest city Lagos, Nigeria

Biggest country Sudan *2,505,810 sq km (967,493 sq miles)*

Smallest country Seychelles *455 sq km (176 sq miles)*

Highest mountain Kilimanjaro, Tanzania *5,895m (19,340ft)*

Longest river Nile, running from to Burundi to Egypt *6,671km (4,145 miles)*

Biggest lake Lake Victoria, between Tanzania, Kenya and Uganda *69,215 sq km (26,724 sq miles)*

Highest waterfall Tugela Falls, on the Tugela River, South Africa *610m (2,000ft)*

Biggest desert Sahara, North Africa *9,100,000 sq km (3,500,000 sq miles)*

Biggest island Madagascar *587,040 sq km (226,656 sq miles)*

Main mineral deposits Gold, copper, diamonds, iron ore, manganese, bauxite

Main fuel deposits Coal, uranium, natural gas

This greater flamingo is from the Transvaal National Park, South Africa.

Africa is home to the world's longest river, the Nile, and its largest desert, the Sahara. In southern Africa there are two more large deserts, the Kalahari and the Namib. Africa also has enormous rainforests in central areas, near the Equator.

A convoy of camels moves across the Sahara Desert in North Africa. The strange swirls of sand are formed by strong winds.

Desert weather

Temperatures in the Sahara Desert can rise as high as 55°C (131°F) during the day, but often fall below freezing point at night. Strong winds blow across the desert and whip up mini whirlwinds called dust devils. These suck up sand and hurl it high into the air.

This satellite image clearly shows the vast Sahara Desert in North Africa. It covers an area about the size of the U.S.A.

Moroccan mountain life

The Atlas Mountains dominate the country of Morocco, north of the Sahara Desert. High in the mountains are villages which are home to groups of African people called Berbers. Berbers have lived in Morocco for thousands of years and today still follow their traditional way of life, herding sheep and goats.

This image shows the curves and folds of the Atlas Mountains in Morocco. They were formed by earthquakes and other movements of the Earth.

Internet links

For a link to a Web site which has all kinds of useful facts about deserts, including the Sahara Desert, go to
www.usborne-quicklinks.com

River in the desert

The River Nile winds its way through eastern Africa, from Burundi all the way to the Mediterranean Sea. It is almost the only water source in this dry, arid part of Africa, so major cities, such as Cairo in Egypt, have grown up near it. The soil near the Nile's banks is fertile enough to farm on, especially near the coast where the river splits into many streams.

Wild forests

The large, dense rainforests of central Africa are home to more than half of Africa's wild animals, including chimpanzees, gorillas and elephants. Many of these animals have never come into contact with humans.

The dark blue water in the lower right of this satellite image is the Red Sea. The triangular piece of land jutting into it is part of Egypt.

This is the River Nile, running through Egypt. As the river reaches the sea, it splits into many streams that create an expanse of fertile, swampy land. This is the large green area at the top of the image.

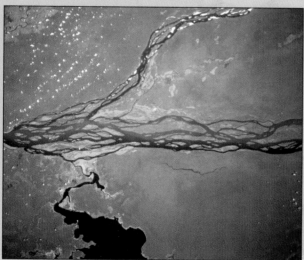

The dense rainforest of central Africa is pink in this satellite image. Running across the middle of the picture is the large Congo River. It splits into many smaller rivers, creating a huge swampy area.

One of Africa's most populous countries is Egypt, which has busy cities such as its capital, Cairo, as well as the remains of ancient civilizations. Africa also has many areas of natural beauty, such as the vast wildlife parks in the south and east of the continent.

Pyramids and the Sphinx

One of the ancient wonders of the world is found at Giza, in Egypt – the group of three Great Pyramids. These stone structures were built by the ancient Egyptians as tombs for their pharaohs, or kings. The biggest pyramid is about 140m (480ft) high, and probably took 20 years to build. You can see a picture of the pyramids on page 1 of this atlas.

In front of the pyramids stands the Great Sphinx, an enormous statue of a lion with a man's head. It was probably carved as a monument to a pharaoh, though no one is sure which one. Some historians believe there are secret rooms and tunnels underneath the Sphinx.

This is the Great Sphinx of Egypt. It was carved out of soft limestone which has crumbled over the years. Part of the Sphinx's nose is now missing.

Cape Town

At Africa's southern tip, in the country of South Africa, is the city of Cape Town. It is famous for its elegant buildings, sandy beaches and busy waterfront. The city is right next to Table Mountain, which gets its name from its distinctive flat top. Thick clouds often cover the mountain and are nicknamed the Table Cloth.

This is Cape Town, with Table Mountain behind.

A panther chameleon clings to a branch. It can wrap its tail around the branch too, for extra grip. Panther chameleons live only in Madagascar.

On safari

Wild animals such as lions, elephants, buffaloes and zebras live on the grasslands of eastern and southern Africa. The land is divided into many specially protected wildlife parks that tourists can visit on safari trips.

These parks are some of the last remaining places where cheetahs live. These big cats were once found all over Africa but are now endangered. Cheetahs are the world's fastest land animals, able to run at a speed of 115kph (70mph).

Wildlife island

Madagascar is a large island in the Indian Ocean, off Africa's southeastern coast. It has thick, steamy rainforests which are home to many animals not found anywhere else in the world. These include rare chameleons and over 50 species of monkey-like animals called lemurs.

Internet links

For a link to a Web site where you can discover more about Madagascar's unusual wildlife, including chameleons, go to **www.usborne-quicklinks.com**

A cheetah in Kenya, eastern Africa, hisses and spits fiercely to scare away enemies.

GREECE Ather

Annaba Bizerte
Menzel Carthage
Bourguiba **Tunis**

Saida

Djelfa Batna Tebessa Kairouan

Biskra Sousse
Monastir
El Jem

Sfax

Atlas Mountains

Ghardaia El Oued Gafsa Kerkenah
Islands

Touggourt Tozeur Gulf of Gabes
Chott Gabes Jerba
el Jerid

Ouargla Tataouine **TUNISIA**

Pantelleria
(Italy)

MALTA
Valletta

Sicily
(Italy) Catania
Syracuse

*Pelagian
Islands*
(Italy)

M e d i t e r r a n e a

Tripoli
Al Khums
Leptis Magna Misratah
Gharyan

Cyrene Darnah
Al Bayda

Benghazi

Tubruq

30°
N

*Tademait
Plateau*

Ghadamis

Surt *Gulf of
Sidra*

Ajdabiya

ALGERIA

*Great
Eastern Erg*

3

Illizi

Sabha

LIBYA

Libyar

25°

Murzuq

Ahaggar

Ghat

Mount Tahat
2,918m
(9,573ft) *Mountains*

Tropic of Cancer

Al Jawf

4

Tamanrasset

*Djado
Plateau*

*Tibesti
Mountains*

20°

Emi Koussi
3,415m
(11,204ft)

MALI

5

S

A

H

A

R

A

Agadez

Faya-Largeau

*Bodele
Depression*

*Ennedi
Plateau*

NIGER

15°

Tahoua

CHAD

Dosso

Mao

Sokoto Maradi Zinder

S

A

H

E

L

Abeche

6

Birnin-Kebbi Katsina

Kano

Lake Chad

Kandi Gusau

Mount Mar
3,088m
(10,131f

Zaria Potiskum Maiduguri **Ndjamena** Mongo Nya

Kaduna **Nigeria**

Minna

Kainji
Reservoir Jos Kumo Maroua
Am Timan

Saki Bida *Niger* **CAMEROON** Bongor Birao

Abuja

B 5°E C 10° D 15° E 20° F

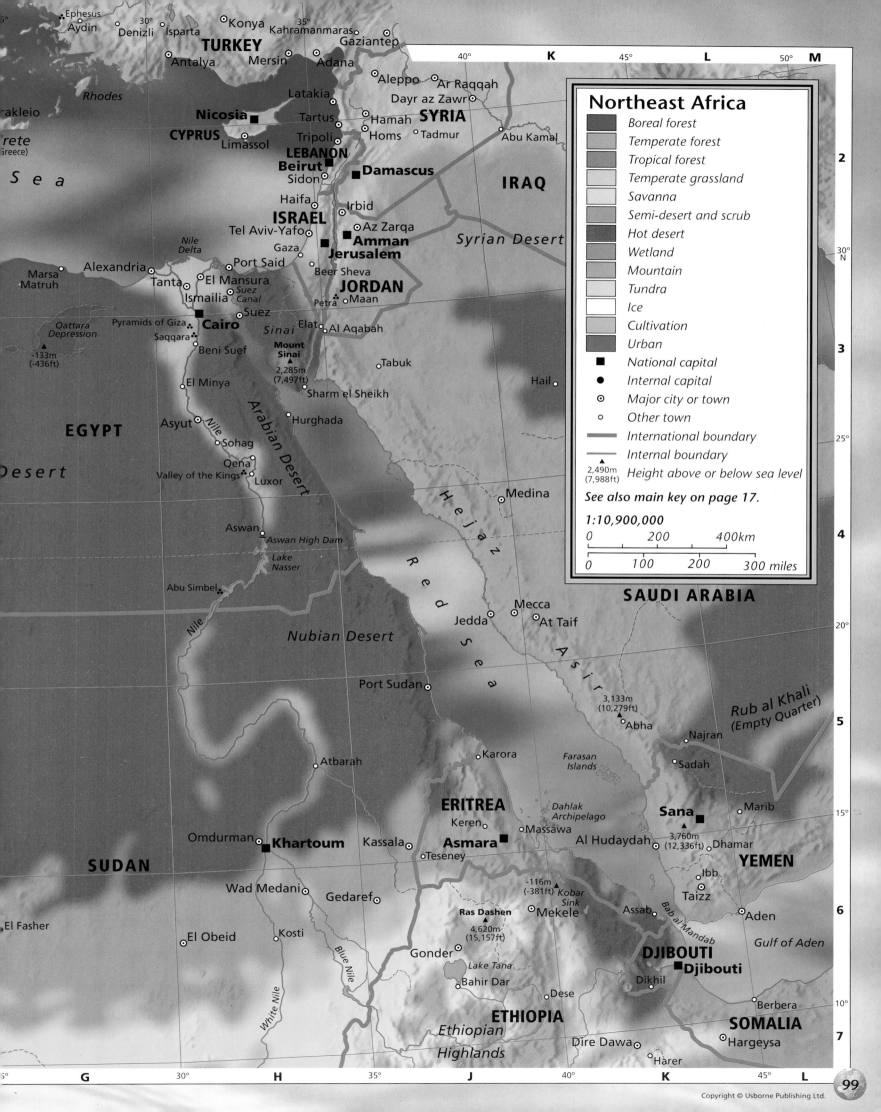

A B C D E F G H

Mediterranean Sea

ATLANTIC OCEAN

SPAIN
Lisbon **PORTUGAL**
Sines
Lagos
Seville
Cadiz
Cordoba
Granada
Malaga
Gibraltar (U.K.)
Ceuta (Spain)
Alicante
Murcia
Almeria
Ibiza
Majorca
Balearic Islands
(Spain)

Azores
(Portugal)
Flores
Terceira
Angra do Heroismo
Pico
Sao Miguel
Ponta Delgada

Same scale as main map

ATLANTIC OCEAN

Madeira *(Portugal)*
Funchal

Canary Islands
(Spain)
Lanzarote
Fuerteventura
La Palma
Tenerife
La Gomera
El Hierro
Gran Canaria

Algiers
Blida
Mostaganem
Oran
Sidi-Bel-Abbes
Tlemcen
Saida
Melilla (Spain)
Oujda
Al Hoceima
Taza
Fes
Meknes
Tetouan
Tangier
Larache
Kenitra
Khouribga
Beni-Mellal
Rabat
Casablanca
El Jadida
Safi
Essaouira
Agadir
Marrakech
Toubkal ▲ 4,165m (13,665ft)
Ouarzazate
Atlas Mountains
MOROCCO

Tunis
Menzel Bourguiba
Bizerte
Carthage
Annaba
Constantine
Skikda
Bejaia
Djemila
Setif
Bordj Bou Arreridj
Batna
Tebessa
Biskra
El Oued
Touggourt
Ouargla
Ghardaia
Djelfa
El Jem
Kairouan
Sousse
Monastir
Sfax
Gafsa
Tozeur
Gabes
Tataouine
Chott el Jerid
Kerkenah Islands
Jerba
Ghadamis

TUNISIA

LIBYA

ALGERIA

Bechar
Er Rachidia
Erfoud
Adrar
Tindouf

Great Western Erg
Tademait Plateau
Great Eastern Erg

Ahaggar Mountains
Mount Tahat 2,918m (9,573ft) ▲
Tamanrasset
Illizi
Tropic of Cancer

Chech Erg

S A H A R A

Es Semara
Tan-Tan
WESTERN SAHARA *(Morocco)*
Laayoune
Boujdour
Ad Dakhla
Nouadhibou
Cape Blanc
Tropic of Cancer

Zouerat
Atar
Akjoujt
Tidjikja
Kidal

MAURITANIA

MALI

Nouakchott

1 2 3 4

NIGER

Agadez
Tahoua
Maradi
Katsina
Gusau
Zaria
Kaduna
Minna
Bida
Abuja
Sokoto
Birnin-Kebbi
Enugu

NIGERIA

Ilorin
Ogbomoso
Owo
Benin City
Onitsha
Warri
Port Harcourt
Niger Delta
Ibadan
Abeokuta
Lagos
Porto-Novo
Saki
Kainji Reservoir
Niger

Tombouctou (Timbuktu)
Goundam
Dosso
Niamey
Tillaberi
Kandio
Parakou
Natitingou
Djougou

BENIN

TOGO

Abomey
Cotonou
Lome
Bight of Benin
Sokode

Ouahigouya
Ouagadougou
Fada-Ngourma
Tenkodogo
Bawku
Dori

BURKINA FASO

White Volta
Wa
Tamale
Damongo
Wenchi

GHANA

Accra
Cape Coast
Sekondi-Takoradi
Cape Three Points
Koforidua
Tarkwa
Kumasi
Lake Volta

Koudougou
Bobo Dioulasso
Banfora
San
Tougan
Segou
Bougouni
Sikasso
Kouttiala
Niono

Bamako
Kita
Kayes

Mopti
Nioro du Sahel

Bouna
Bondoukou
Katiola
Yamoussoukro
Bouake
Korhogo
Odienne
Adzope
Divo
Abidjan
Gagnoa
Daloa
Man
San Pedro
Cape Palmas
Harper

IVORY COAST

Nzerekore
▲ 1,752m (5,748ft)
Gueckedou
Zorzor
Tubmanburg

LIBERIA

Monrovia

GUINEA

Siguiri
Kankan
Labe
Boke
Kindia
Conakry
Freetown

SIERRA LEONE

Makeni
Sefadu
Bo
Kenema

Kedougou
Selibabi
Kaedi
Rosso
Louga
Dara
Thies
Dakar
Kaolack
Kolda

SENEGAL

St. Louis
Kiffa
Nema
Ayoun el Atrous
Senegal

GUINEA-BISSAU

Bissau
Banjul
THE GAMBIA
Ziguinchor
Bignona
Bissagos Archipelago
Tambacounda

Niger
Gao

SAO TOME AND PRINCIPE

Principe
Sao Tome
Equator

Gulf of Guinea

ATLANTIC OCEAN

Inset: CAPE VERDE

L 25°W   ATLANTIC OCEAN   11
M
Santo Antao
Sao Nicolau
Mindelo
Sal
Boa Vista
Sao Tiago
Maio
Praia
Fogo
12
Same scale as main map

Key

Northwest Africa

Boreal forest
Temperate forest
Tropical forest
Temperate grassland
Savanna
Semi-desert and scrub
Hot desert
— International boundary
— Internal boundary
▲ 2,490m (7,988ft) Height above or below sea level

Wetland
Mountain
Tundra
Ice
Cultivation
Urban

■ National capital
● Internal capital
⊙ Major city or town
○ Other town
See also main key on page 17.

1:10,900,000

0   100   200   300 miles
0   200   400km

ATLANTIC OCEAN

Copyright © Usborne Publishing Ltd.

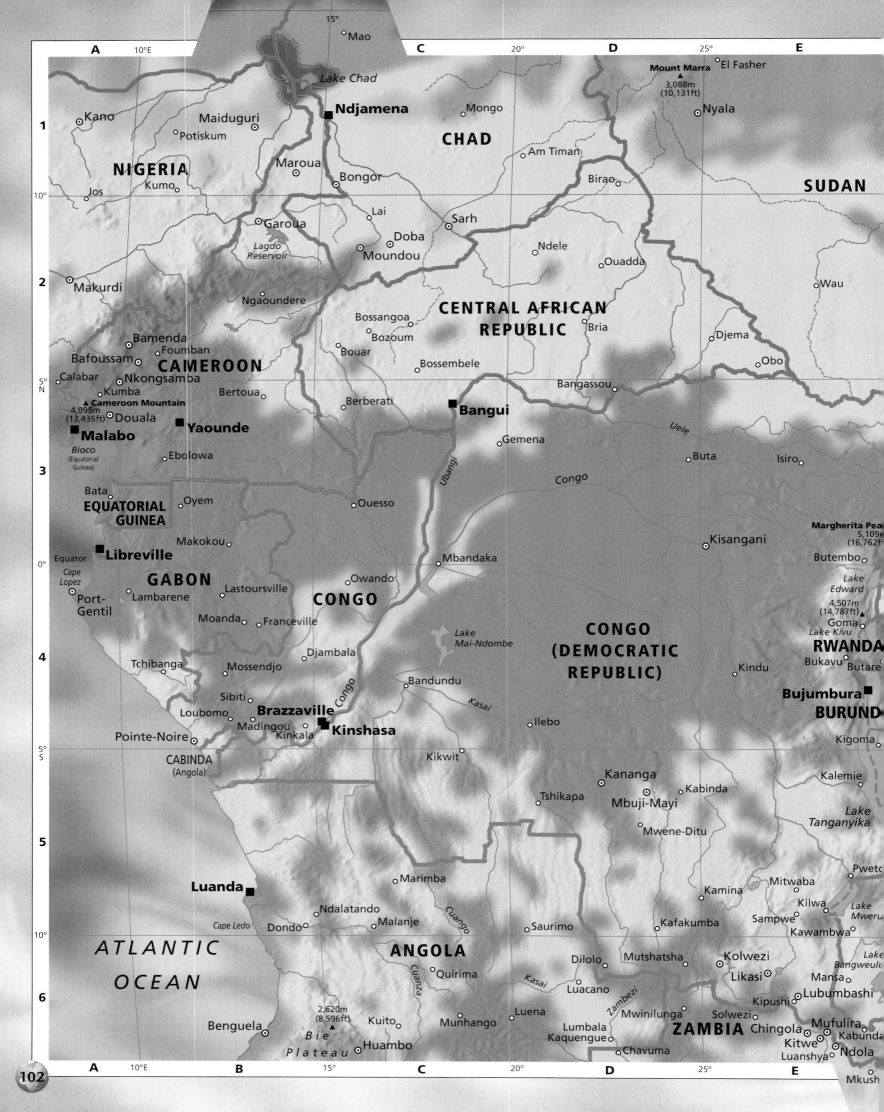

El Obeid
Kosti
Ras Dashen
4,620m
(15,157ft)
Mekele
Assab
Bab al Mandab
Taizz
YEMEN
Aden
Gulf of Aden
Cape
Guardafui

Gonder
White Nile
Blue Nile
Lake Tana
Bahir Dar
DJIBOUTI
Dikhil
Djibouti
Boosaaso

Malakal
Dese
Berbera

Ethiopian
Highlands
Dire Dawa
Hargeysa
SOMALIA

Gambela
Nekemte
Addis Ababa
Harer

White Nile
Debre Zeyit
Nazret
ETHIOPIA
Jima
Eyl

Awasa
Lake
Abaya
Gode

Juba
Beledweyne

Gulu
Moyale
Mandera
Baydhabo

UGANDA
Lake
Turkana
Juba
Baardheere

Soroti
Mount Elgon
4,321m
(14,176ft)
Mogadishu

Lake
Albert
Lake
Kyoga
Mbale
Kitale
KENYA
Marka

Kampala
Jinja
Eldoret
Meru

Entebbe
Kisumu
Kirinyaga
(Mount Kenya)
5,199m
(17,057ft)
Garissa

Masaka
Nakuru
Nyeri

Mbarara
Kisii
Nairobi
Thika

Kigali
Lake Victoria
Machakos
Kismaayo

Mwanza
Kilimanjaro
5,895m
(19,340ft)
Moshi

Great Rift Valley
Arusha
Malindi

Tabora
Mombasa

Tanga
Pemba Island
INDIAN
OCEAN

Great Rift Valley
Dodoma
Zanzibar
Zanzibar Island

TANZANIA
Morogoro
Dar es Salaam

Lake Rukwa
Iringa
Mafia
Island

Mbala
Mbeya
Makumbako
Ilonga
Njinjo

Kasama
Tunduma
Liwale

Isoka
Karonga
Lindi
Mtwara

ZAMBIA
Songea
Masasi
Palma
COMOROS
Grand Comoro
(Njazidja)

Mpika
Mzuzu
Lake Nyasa
(Lake Malawi)
Tunduru
Cape Delgado
Moroni
Anjouan
Island
(Nzwani)

Lundazi
Lupilichi
Mecula
Mueda
Mutsamudu
Mayotte
(France)

Chipata
MALAWI
Lichinga
Nungo
Fomboni
Mamoudzou

Kasungu
MOZAMBIQUE
Mohilla Island
(Mwali)

Petauke
Cuamba
Ruvuma
Pemba

Luangwa

Central Africa

Boreal forest
Temperate forest
Tropical forest
Temperate grassland
Savanna
Semi-desert and scrub
Hot desert
Wetland
Mountain
Tundra
Ice
Cultivation
Urban

■ National capital
● Internal capital
⊙ Major city or town
○ Other town

International boundary
Internal boundary
▲ 2,490m
(7,988ft) Height above or below sea level

See also main key on page 17.

1:10,900,000

0   200   400km

0   100   200   300 miles

Copyright © Usborne Publishing Ltd.

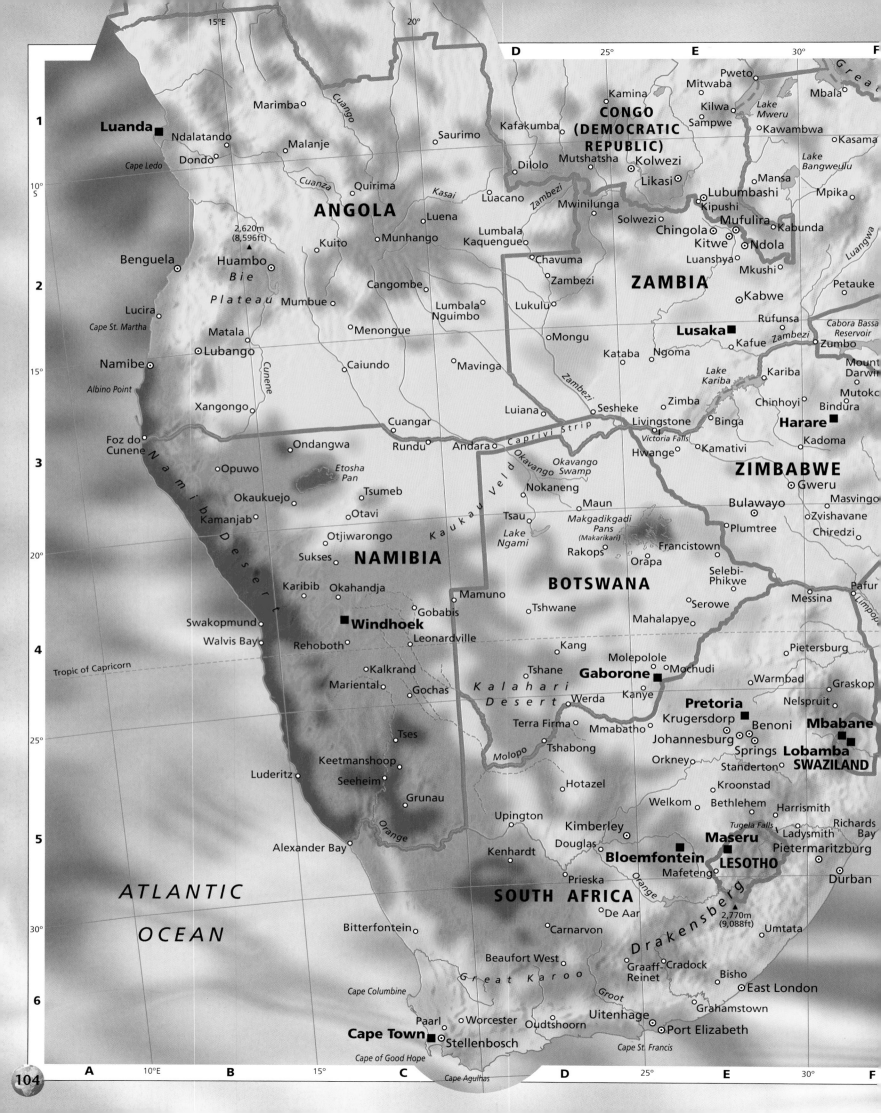

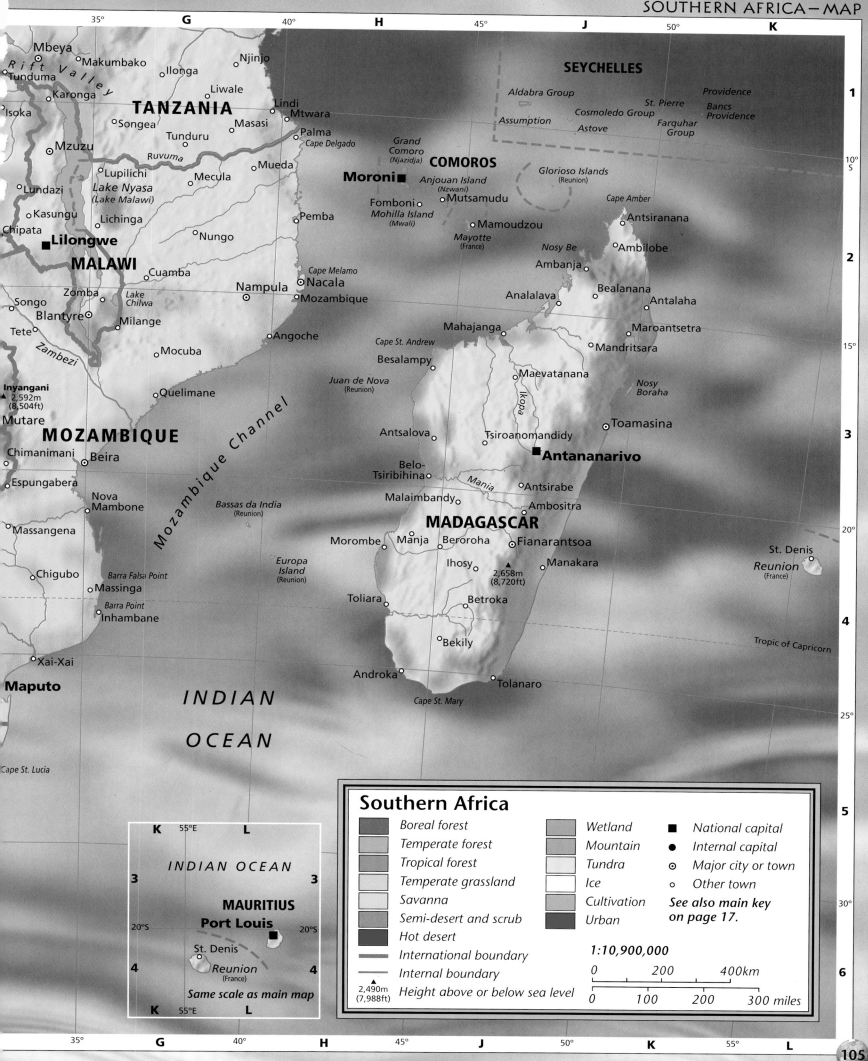

35° **G** 40° **H** 45° **J** 50° **K**

Mbeya
Rift Valley
Makumbako
Tunduma
Isoka
Karonga
Mzuzu
Ilonga
Njinjo
Liwale
Lindi
Mtwara
SEYCHELLES
Aldabra Group
St. Pierre
Providence
Bancs
Providence
Assumption
Cosmoledo Group
Astove
Farquhar
Group

TANZANIA
Songea
Tunduru
Masasi
Palma
Cape Delgado
Ruvuma
Mueda
Mecula

1

Lupilichi
Mecula
Grand
Comoro
(Njazidja)
COMOROS
Glorioso Islands
(Reunion)
10°
S

Lundazi
Chipata
*Lake Nyasa
(Lake Malawi)*
Lichinga
Pemba
Moroni ■
Anjouan Island
(Nzwani)
Mutsamudu
Cape Amber

Kasungu
Nungo
Fomboni
Mohilla Island
(Mwali)
Mamoudzou
Mayotte
(France)
Nosy Be
Ambanja
Antsiranana
Ambilobe

Lilongwe ■
MALAWI
Cuamba
Nampula
Cape Melamo
Nacala
Mozambique
Analalava
Bealanana
Antalaha
2

Zomba
Songo
*Lake
Chilwa*
Milange
Angoche
Mahajanga
Mandritsara
Maroantsetra

Blantyre
Tete
Zambezi
Mocuba
Cape St. Andrew
Besalampy
Ikopa
Maevatanana
*Nosy
Boraha*
15°

Inyangani
▲ 2,592m
(8,504ft)
Mutare
Quelimane
*Juan de Nova
(Reunion)*
Antsalova
Tsiroanomandidy
Toamasina

MOZAMBIQUE
Mozambique Channel
MADAGASCAR
Belo-
Tsiribihina
Antananarivo ■
3

Chimanimani
Beira
Mania
Antsirabe
Espungabera
Nova
Mambone
*Bassas da India
(Reunion)*
Malaimbandy
Ambositra

Massangena
*Europa
Island
(Reunion)*
Morombe
Manja
Beroroha
Fianarantsoa
St. Denis
*Reunion
(France)*
20°

Chigubo
Barra Falsa Point
Ihosy
▲ 2,658m
(8,720ft)
Manakara

Massinga
Barra Point
Inhambane
Toliara
Betroka
Tropic of Capricorn
4

Xai-Xai
Androka
Bekily

Maputo
INDIAN
Tolanaro
25°

Cape St. Mary

OCEAN

Cape St. Lucia

5

K 55°E **L**
Southern Africa

INDIAN OCEAN

3

MAURITIUS
Port Louis ■
30°

20°S
St. Denis
20°S

4
*Reunion
(France)*

Same scale as main map

K 55°E **L**
6

Boreal forest	Wetland	■ National capital
Temperate forest	Mountain	● Internal capital
Tropical forest	Tundra	⊙ Major city or town
Temperate grassland	Ice	○ Other town
Savanna	Cultivation	

Semi-desert and scrub
Urban
***See also main key
on page 17.***

Hot desert
1:10,900,000

International boundary
0   200   400km

Internal boundary
0   100   200   300 miles

▲ 2,490m
(7,988ft)
Height above or below sea level

35° **G** 40° **H** 45° **J** 50° **K** 55° **L**

Copyright © Usborne Publishing Ltd.

THE ARCTIC AND ANTARCTICA

The Arctic and Antarctica are the world's coldest places. The Arctic is the area around the North Pole, including the Arctic Ocean and the most northerly parts of Europe, North America and Asia. Antarctica is a huge continent at the South Pole.

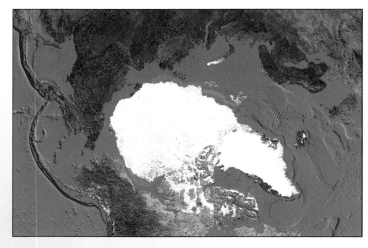

The large white area in this satellite image is ice, covering the Arctic Ocean and Greenland. At the top left of the image is the edge of Russia and at the top right is part of Europe.

Frozen island

Within the Arctic is Greenland, the world's largest island. Most Greenlanders live along the rocky coast, as the main body of land is covered in thick ice for most of the year.

This is the entrance to Sweden's Arctic ice hotel. The hotel is open in winter, then melts in the spring when the weather gets milder. The next winter, it is built all over again.

Internet links

For a link to a Web site where you can discover all kinds of information about animals that live in the Arctic, such as walruses, snowy owls, polar bears and arctic foxes, go to
www.usborne-quicklinks.com

A hotel of ice

Every winter, a hotel made entirely of ice is built in the far north of Sweden. Each piece of furniture is sculpted from ice, and even the beds are made of ice blocks. Guests sleep in special thermal sleeping bags with animal skins piled on top for extra warmth.

Icy continent

A huge, jagged sheet of ice permanently covers almost all of Antarctica, and spreads out over nearby seas as well. Scientists think that the area in the far west of the continent may be made up of many islands, but it is hard to tell because they are so far beneath the ice.

Mountains run down the middle of Antarctica, and in the west there are volcanoes. Amazingly, one volcano heats the sea near it so much that it is warm enough to swim in.

The darkest shading on this satellite image of Antarctica indicates ice that is over 3km (2 miles) deep.

These penguins are on the coast of Antarctica. They live in the ocean but come onto land to breed.

Life in Antarctica

The temperature in Antarctica can fall as low as -80°C (-112°F) in winter. It is too cold for people to live there, though scientists visit to study the area. No plants grow in the ice, and the only land animals are tiny mites. But many animals live in the seas around Antarctica, including penguins, seals, whales and fish.

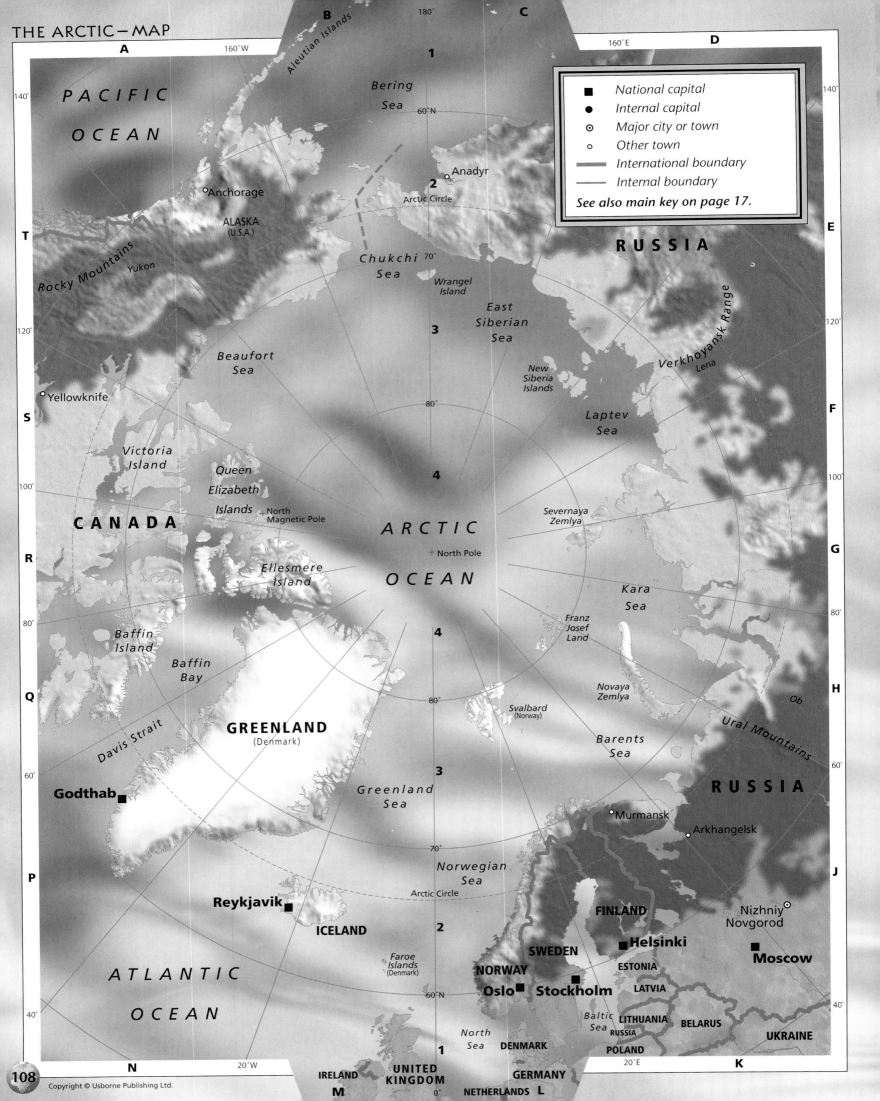

THE ARCTIC—MAP

PACIFIC OCEAN

140°

Aleutian Islands

Bering Sea

1

60°N

T

°Anchorage

Anadyr °

2

Arctic Circle

ALASKA (U.S.A.)

RUSSIA

E

Rocky Mountains

Chukchi Sea

70°

140°

Yukon

Wrangel Island

S

Beaufort Sea

East Siberian Sea

3

120°

Verkhoyansk Range

New Siberia Islands

Lena

° Yellowknife

Victoria Island

80°

Laptev Sea

120°

F

Queen Elizabeth Islands

4

100°

Severnaya Zemlya

CANADA

+ North Magnetic Pole

ARCTIC

+ North Pole

Ellesmere Island

OCEAN

Kara Sea

100°

G

R

80°

Baffin Island

Franz Josef Land

80°

Baffin Bay

4

Novaya Zemlya

Ob

H

Q

Davis Strait

80°

Svalbard (Norway)

Ural Mountains

GREENLAND (Denmark)

Barents Sea

60°

RUSSIA

Murmansk °

Godthab ■

Greenland Sea

3

Arkhangelsk °

J

60°N

70°

P

Norwegian Sea

Arctic Circle

Nizhniy Novgorod °

Reykjavik ■

2

FINLAND

ATLANTIC

ICELAND

Helsinki ■

Moscow ■

SWEDEN

ESTONIA

OCEAN

Faroe Islands (Denmark)

NORWAY

LATVIA

40°

Oslo ■

Stockholm ■

60°N

LITHUANIA

BELARUS

North Sea

DENMARK

Baltic Sea

RUSSIA

UKRAINE

1

POLAND

M

NETHERLANDS

L

Key:

■ National capital
● Internal capital
⊙ Major city or town
○ Other town
▬ International boundary
— Internal boundary

See also main key on page 17.

Copyright © Usborne Publishing Ltd.

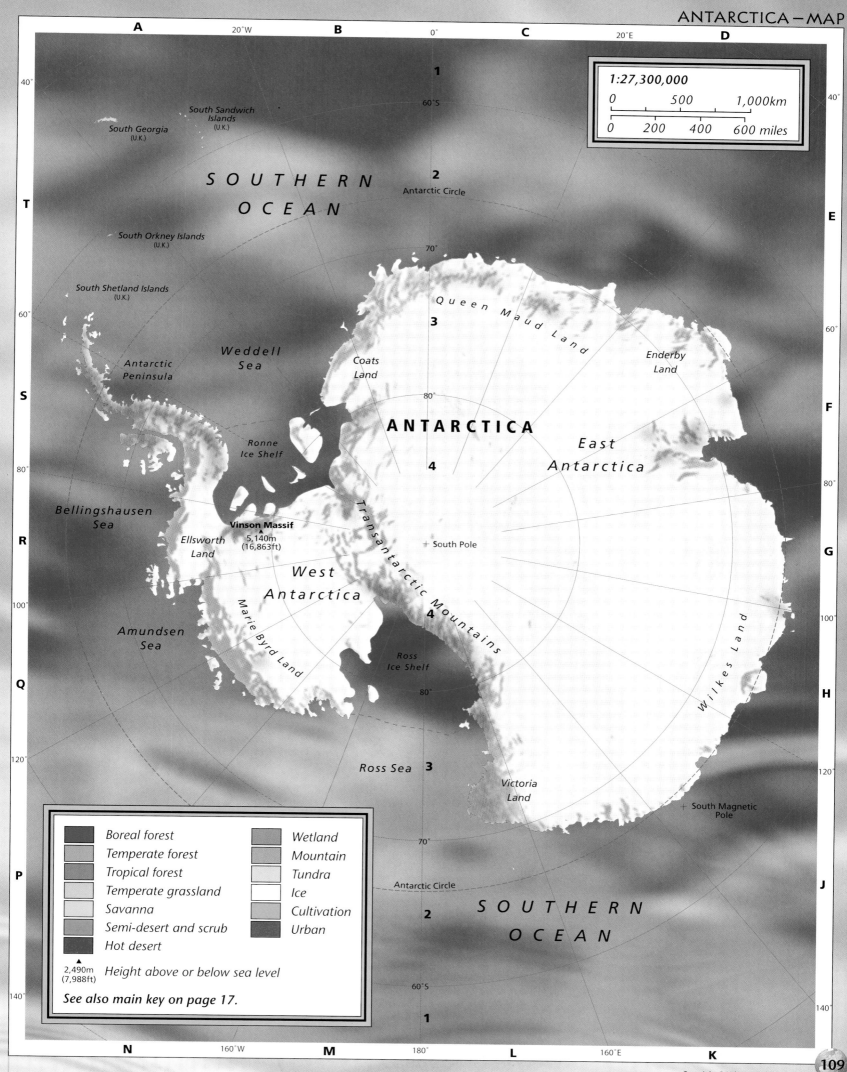

A 20°W B 0° C 20°E D

1

2

Antarctic Circle

1:27,300,000

0   500   1,000km

0   200   400   600 miles

60°S

40°

T

E

70°

S O U T H E R N
O C E A N

South Georgia
(U.K.)

South Sandwich
Islands
(U.K.)

South Orkney Islands
(U.K.)

South Shetland Islands
(U.K.)

Weddell
Sea

Queen Maud Land

Enderby
Land

80°

Coats
Land

ANTARCTICA

East
Antarctica

3

S

60°

F

80°

Antarctic
Peninsula

Ronne
Ice Shelf

4

Bellingshausen
Sea

Vinson Massif
▲
5,140m
(16,863ft)

Ellsworth
Land

+ South Pole

West
Antarctica

Transantarctic Mountains

Wilkes Land

R

G

100°

Amundsen
Sea

Marie Byrd Land

Ross
Ice Shelf

4

Q

H

100°

Ross Sea

3

Victoria
Land

+ South Magnetic
Pole

80°

120°

70°

Antarctic Circle

P

J

120°

Boreal forest   Wetland

Temperate forest   Mountain

Tropical forest   Tundra

Temperate grassland Ice

Savanna   Cultivation

Semi-desert and scrub Urban

Hot desert

▲ 2,490m
(7,988ft)   Height above or below sea level

See also main key on page 17.

S O U T H E R N

O C E A N

60°S

1

N 160°W M 180° L 160°E K

40°

60°

80°

100°

120°

140°

Copyright © Usborne Publishing Ltd.

GEOGRAPHY QUIZ

Test your knowledge of the world's countries, cities, sights and animals with these quiz questions. The answers are on page 129.

The enormous, elaborate church above was designed by a famous Spanish architect named Antonio Gaudí.

Mystery places

Which famous sights are shown in the photographs on this page? Each has clues to help you.

The marble building on the left is one of the Seven Wonders of the World. It was built by an Indian emperor.

This famous steel bridge crosses the bay of a large North American city. It opened in 1937 and for many years was the longest suspension bridge in the world.

This city skyline is dominated by the tallest freestanding structure in the world. Visitors can go up the tower to a glass-bottomed viewing platform and a revolving restaurant. Can you name the tower and the city?

The ruins above are the remains of some of Europe's most important ancient temples and other public buildings.

Quick quiz

1. Which country's flag consists of a red circle on a white background?

2. When it is noon in Britain, what time is it in Mexico?

3. In which country is the Great Victoria Desert?

4. Which continent is the third-largest in the world?

5. In which country is Brno?

6. What is the world's deepest lake?

7. Name the smallest country in Europe.

8. Which country lies between Nicaragua and Panama?

9. In which country would you pay using naira and kobo as currency?

10. What is Turkey's capital city?

Internet links

For a link to a Web site where you can test and improve your knowledge of the countries and cities of the world, go to **www.usborne-quicklinks.com**

Survival challenge

Could you survive in the world's toughest terrains? Take this test to find out.

1. Which of the following would not be very useful on a trip to Antarctica?
a) A warm hat and gloves
b) An umbrella
c) Sunglasses and sunscreen

2. You are in the Sahara Desert and are short of drinking water. What should you do?
a) Stay active, so you produce sweat to cool yourself down.
b) Put on extra clothes and rest as much as possible.
c) Talk and sing songs to keep yourself alert.

3. When on safari in Africa, which of these spiders should you avoid?
a) Six-eyed crab spiders
b) Button spiders
c) Violin spiders

4. You are walking in the Rocky Mountains and meet a grizzly bear. What should you do?
a) Lie on the ground and play dead.
b) Turn and run away as fast as possible.
c) Back away slowly and calmly.

This grizzly bear is in the Rocky Mountains in Utah, U.S.A. Grizzly bears like to keep well away from humans, but will occasionally attack if they feel threatened.

GAZETTEER OF STATES

Afghanistan

Albania

Algeria

Andorra

Angola

Antigua and Barbuda

• **Argentina**

This gazetteer lists the world's 193 independent states, along with key facts about each one. In the lists of languages, the language that is most widely spoken is given first, even if it is not the official language. In the lists of religions, the one followed by the most people is also placed first. Every state has a national flag, which is usually used to represent the country abroad. A few states also have a state flag which they prefer to use instead. The state flags appear here with a dot beside them.

AFGHANISTAN (Asia)
Area: 647,500 sq km (249,935 sq miles)
Population: 25,838,797
Capital city: Kabul
Main languages: Dari, Pashto
Main religion: Muslim
Government: transitional
Currency: 1 afghani = 100 puls

ALBANIA (Europe)
Area: 28,750 sq km (11,100 sq miles)
Population: 3,510,484
Capital city: Tirana
Main language: Albanian
Main religions: Muslim, Albanian Orthodox
Government: emerging democracy
Currency: 1 lek = 100 qintars

ALGERIA (Africa)
Area: 2,381,740 sq km (919,589 sq miles)
Population: 31,193,917
Capital city: Algiers
Main languages: Arabic, French, Berber dialects
Main religion: Sunni Muslim
Government: republic
Currency: 1 Algerian dinar = 100 centimes

ANDORRA (Europe)
Area: 468 sq km (181 sq miles)
Population: 67,627
Capital city: Andorra la Vella
Main languages: Catalan, Spanish
Main religion: Roman Catholic
Government: parliamentary democracy
Currency: 1 euro = 100 cents

ANGOLA (Africa)
Area: 1,246,700 sq km (481,351 sq miles)
Population: 10,366,031
Capital city: Luanda
Main languages: Kilongo, Kimbundu, other Bantu languages, Portuguese
Main religions: indigenous, Roman Catholic, Protestant
Government: transitional
Currency: 1 kwanza = 100 lwei

ANTIGUA AND BARBUDA (North America)
Area: 442 sq km (171 sq miles)
Population: 66,970
Capital city: Saint John's
Main languages: Caribbean Creole, English
Main religion: Protestant
Government: constitutional monarchy
Currency: 1 East Caribbean dollar = 100 cents

ARGENTINA (South America)
Area: 2,780,400 sq km (1,073,512 sq miles)
Population: 36,955,182
Capital city: Buenos Aires
Main language: Spanish
Main religion: Roman Catholic
Government: republic
Currency: 1 peso = 100 centavos

ARMENIA (Asia)
Area: 29,800 sq km (11,506 sq miles)
Population: 3,336,100
Capital city: Yerevan
Main language: Armenian
Main religion: Armenian Orthodox
Government: republic
Currency: 1 dram = 100 luma

AUSTRALIA (Australasia/Oceania)
Area: 7,686,850 sq km (2,967,124 sq miles)
Population: 19,357,594
Capital city: Canberra
Main language: English
Main religion: Christian
Government: federal democratic monarchy
Currency: 1 Australian dollar = 100 cents

AUSTRIA (Europe)
Area: 83,858 sq km (32,378 sq miles)
Population: 8,150,835
Capital city: Vienna
Main language: German
Main religion: Roman Catholic
Government: federal republic
Currency: 1 euro = 100 cents

Armenia

Australia

Austria

Azerbaijan

Bahamas, The

Bahrain

Bangladesh

Barbados

Belarus

Belgium

Belize

Benin

Bhutan

• **Bolivia**

AZERBAIJAN (Asia)
Area: 86,600 sq km (33,436 sq miles)
Population: 7,771,092
Capital city: Baku
Main language: Azeri
Main religion: Muslim
Government: republic
Currency: 1 manat = 100 gopiks

BAHAMAS, THE (North America)
Area: 13,940 sq km (5,382 sq miles)
Population: 297,852
Capital city: Nassau
Main languages: Bahamian Creole, English
Main religion: Christian
Government: parliamentary democracy
Currency: 1 Bahamian dollar = 100 cents

BAHRAIN (Asia)
Area: 678 sq km (261 sq miles)
Population: 645,361
Capital city: Manama
Main languages: Arabic, English
Main religion: Muslim
Government: traditional monarchy
Currency: 1 Bahraini dinar = 1,000 fils

BANGLADESH (Asia)
Area: 144,000 sq km (55,598 sq miles)
Population: 131,269,860
Capital city: Dhaka
Main languages: Bengali, English
Main religions: Muslim, Hindu
Government: republic
Currency: 1 taka = 100 poisha

BARBADOS (North America)
Area: 430 sq km (166 sq miles)
Population: 275,330
Capital city: Bridgetown
Main languages: Bajan, English
Main religion: Christian
Government: parliamentary democracy
Currency: 1 Barbadian dollar = 100 cents

BELARUS (Europe)
Area: 207,600 sq km (80,154 sq miles)
Population: 10,350,194
Capital city: Minsk
Main language: Belarusian
Main religion: Eastern Orthodox
Government: republic
Currency: 1 Belarusian ruble = 100 kopecks

BELGIUM (Europe)
Area: 30,510 sq km (11,780 sq miles)
Population: 10,258,762
Capital city: Brussels
Main languages: Dutch, French
Main religions: Roman Catholic, Protestant
Government: constitutional monarchy
Currency: 1 euro = 100 cents

BELIZE (North America)
Area: 22,960 sq km (8,865 sq miles)
Population: 256,062
Capital city: Belmopan
Main languages: Spanish, Belize Creole, English, Garifuna, Maya

Main religions: Roman Catholic, Protestant
Government: parliamentary democracy
Currency: 1 Belizean dollar = 100 cents

BENIN (Africa)
Area: 112,620 sq km (43,483 sq miles)
Population: 6,590,782
Capital city: Porto-Novo
Main languages: Fon, French, Yoruba
Main religions: indigenous, Christian, Muslim
Government: republic
Currency: 1 CFA* franc = 100 centimes

BHUTAN (Asia)
Area: 47,000 sq km (18,146 sq miles)
Population: 2,049,412
Capital city: Thimphu
Main languages: Dzongkha, Nepali
Main religions: Muslim, Hindu
Government: monarchy
Currency: 1 ngultrum = 100 chetrum

BOLIVIA (South America)
Area: 1,098,580 sq km (424,162 sq miles)
Population: 8,300,463
Capital cities: La Paz, Sucre
Main languages: Spanish, Quechua, Aymara
Main religion: Roman Catholic
Government: republic
Currency: 1 boliviano = 100 centavos

BOSNIA AND HERZEGOVINA (Europe)
Area: 51,129 sq km (19,741 sq miles)
Population: 3,922,205
Capital city: Sarajevo
Main languages: Bosnian, Serbian, Croatian
Main religions: Muslim, Orthodox, Roman Catholic
Government: emerging federal democracy
Currency: 1 marka = 100 pfenninga

BOTSWANA (Africa)
Area: 600,372 sq km (231,743 sq miles)
Population: 1,586,119
Capital city: Gaborone
Main languages: Setswana, Kalanga, English
Main religions: indigenous, Christian
Government: parliamentary republic
Currency: 1 pula = 100 thebe

BRAZIL (South America)
Area: 8,547,400 sq km (3,300,151 sq miles)
Population: 174,468,575
Capital city: Brasilia
Main language: Portuguese
Main religion: Roman Catholic
Government: federal republic
Currency: 1 real = 100 centavos

BRUNEI (Asia)
Area: 5,770 sq km (2,228 sq miles)
Population: 343,653
Capital city: Bandar Seri Begawan
Main languages: Malay, English, Chinese
Main religions: Muslim, Buddhist
Government: constitutional sultanate (a type of monarchy)
Currency: 1 Bruneian dollar = 100 cents

Bosnia and Herzegovina

Botswana

Brazil

Brunei

Bulgaria

Burkina Faso

Burma (Myanmar)

*CFA = Communaute Financiere Africaine

GAZETTEER OF STATES CONTINUED:

Burundi

Cambodia

Cameroon

Canada

Cape Verde

Central African Republic

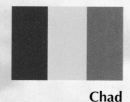

Chad

BULGARIA (Europe)
Area: 110,910 sq km (42,822 sq miles)
Population: 7,707,495
Capital city: Sofia
Main language: Bulgarian
Main religions: Bulgarian Orthodox, Muslim
Government: republic
Currency: 1 lev = 100 stotinki

BURKINA FASO (Africa)
Area: 274,200 sq km (105,869 sq miles)
Population: 12,272,289
Capital city: Ouagadougou
Main languages: Moore, Jula, French
Main religions: Muslim, indigenous
Government: republic
Currency: 1 CFA* franc = 100 centimes

BURMA (MYANMAR) (Asia)
Area: 678,500 sq km (261,969 sq miles)
Population: 50,438,300
Capital city: Rangoon
Main language: Burmese
Main religion: Buddhist
Government: military dictatorship
Currency: 1 kyat = 100 pyas

BURUNDI (Africa)
Area: 27,830 sq km (10,745 sq miles)
Population: 6,223,897
Capital city: Bujumbura
Main languages: Kirundi, French, Swahili
Main religions: Christian, indigenous
Government: republic
Currency: 1 Burundi franc = 100 centimes

CAMBODIA (Asia)
Area: 181,040 sq km (69,900 sq miles)
Population: 12,491,501
Capital city: Phnom Penh
Main language: Khmer
Main religion: Buddhist
Government: constitutional monarchy
Currency: 1 new riel = 100 sen

CAMEROON (Africa)
Area: 475,440 sq km (183,567 sq miles)
Population: 15,803,220
Capital city: Yaounde
Main languages: Cameroon Pidgin English, Ewondo, Fula, French, English
Main religions: indigenous, Christian, Muslim
Government: republic
Currency: 1 CFA* franc = 100 centimes

CANADA (North America)
Area: 9,970,610 sq km (3,849,653 sq miles)
Population: 31,592,805
Capital city: Ottawa
Main languages: English, French
Main religions: Roman Catholic, Protestant
Government: federal democracy
Currency: 1 Canadian dollar = 100 cents

CAPE VERDE (Africa)
Area: 4,033 sq km (1,557 sq miles)
Population: 405,163
Capital city: Praia
Main languages: Crioulo*, Portuguese

Main religions: Roman Catholic, Protestant
Government: republic
Currency: 1 Cape Verdean escudo = 100 centavos

CENTRAL AFRICAN REPUBLIC (Africa)
Area: 622,436 sq km (240,322 sq miles)
Population: 3,576,884
Capital city: Bangui
Main languages: Sangho, French
Main religions: indigenous, Christian, Muslim
Government: republic
Currency: 1 CFA* franc = 100 centimes

CHAD (Africa)
Area: 1,284,000 sq km (495,752 sq miles)
Population: 8,707,078
Capital city: Ndjamena
Main languages: Arabic, Sara, French
Main religions: Muslim, Christian, indigenous
Government: republic
Currency: 1 CFA* franc = 100 centimes

CHILE (South America)
Area: 756,626 sq km (292,133 sq miles)
Population: 15,328,467
Capital city: Santiago
Main language: Spanish
Main religions: Roman Catholic, Protestant
Government: republic
Currency: 1 Chilean peso = 100 centavos

CHINA (Asia)
Area: 9,596,960 sq km (3,705,386 sq miles)
Population: 1,273,111,290
Capital city: Beijing
Main languages: Mandarin Chinese, Yue, Wu
Main religions: Taoist, Buddhist
Government: Communist state
Currency: 1 yuan = 10 jiao

COLOMBIA (South America)
Area: 1,138,910 sq km (439,733 sq miles)
Population: 40,349,388
Capital city: Bogota
Main language: Spanish
Main religion: Roman Catholic
Government: republic
Currency: 1 Colombian peso = 100 centavos

COMOROS (Africa)
Area: 1,862 sq km (719 sq miles)
Population: 596,202
Capital city: Moroni
Main languages: Comorian*, French, Arabic
Main religion: Sunni Muslim
Government: republic
Currency: 1 Comoran franc = 100 centimes

CONGO (Africa)
Area: 342,000 sq km (132,046 sq miles)
Population: 2,894,336
Capital city: Brazzaville
Main languages: Munukutuba, Lingala, French
Main religions: Christian, animist
Government: republic
Currency: 1 CFA* franc = 100 centimes

Chile

China

Colombia

Comoros

Congo

Congo (Democratic Republic)

Costa Rica

*CFA = Communaute Financiere Africaine; Comorian = a blend of Swahili and Arabic; Crioulo = a blend of Portuguese and West African

Croatia

Cuba

Cyprus

Czech Republic

Denmark

Djibouti

Dominica

CONGO (DEMOCRATIC REPUBLIC) (Africa)
Area: 2,345,410 sq km (905,563 sq miles)
Population: 53,624,718
Capital city: Kinshasa
Main languages: Lingala, Swahili, Kikongo, Tshiluba, French
Main religions: Roman Catholic, Protestant, Kimbanguist, Muslim
Government: transitional
Currency: 1 Congolese franc = 100 centimes

COSTA RICA (North America)
Area: 51,100 sq km (19,730 sq miles)
Population: 3,773,057
Capital city: San Jose
Main language: Spanish
Main religions: Roman Catholic, Evangelical
Government: democratic republic
Currency: 1 Costa Rican colon = 100 centimos

CROATIA (Europe)
Area: 56,538 sq km (21,829 sq miles)
Population: 4,334,142
Capital city: Zagreb
Main language: Croatian
Main religions: Roman Catholic, Orthodox
Government: parliamentary democracy
Currency: 1 kuna = 100 lipas

CUBA (North America)
Area: 110,860 sq km (42,803 sq miles)
Population: 11,184,023
Capital city: Havana
Main language: Spanish
Main religion: Roman Catholic
Government: Communist state
Currency: 1 Cuban peso = 100 centavos

CYPRUS (Europe)
Area: 9,250 sq km (3,571 sq miles)
Population: 762,887
Capital city: Nicosia
Main languages: Greek, Turkish
Main religions: Greek Orthodox, Muslim
Government: republic with a self-proclaimed independent Turkish area
Currency: Greek Cypriot area: 1 Cypriot pound = 100 cents; Turkish Cypriot area: 1 Turkish lira = 100 kurus

CZECH REPUBLIC (Europe)
Area: 78,866 sq km (30,450 sq miles)
Population: 10,264,212
Capital city: Prague
Main language: Czech
Main religion: Roman Catholic
Government: parliamentary democracy
Currency: 1 koruna = 100 haleru

DENMARK (Europe)
Area: 43,094 sq km (16,639 sq miles)
Population: 5,352,815
Capital city: Copenhagen
Main language: Danish
Main religion: Evangelical Lutheran
Government: constitutional monarchy
Currency: 1 Danish krone = 100 oere

DJIBOUTI (Africa)
Area: 23,200 sq km (8,957 sq miles)
Population: 460,700
Capital city: Djibouti
Main languages: Afar, Somali, Arabic, French
Main religion: Muslim
Government: republic
Currency: 1 Djiboutian franc = 100 centimes

DOMINICA (North America)
Area: 751 sq km (290 sq miles)
Population: 70,786
Capital city: Roseau
Main languages: English, French patois
Main religions: Roman Catholic, Protestant
Government: democratic republic
Currency: 1 East Caribbean dollar = 100 cents

DOMINICAN REPUBLIC (North America)
Area: 48,511 sq km (18,731 sq miles)
Population: 8,581,477
Capital city: Santo Domingo
Main language: Spanish
Main religion: Roman Catholic
Government: democratic republic
Currency: 1 Dominican peso = 100 centavos

EAST TIMOR (Asia)
Area: 24,000 sq km (9,266 sq miles)
Population: 737,811
Capital city: Dili
Main languages: Tetun (Tetum), Bahasa Indonesia, Portuguese
Main religions: Roman Catholic, animist
Government: republic
Currency: 1 U.S. dollar = 100 cents

ECUADOR (South America)
Area: 283,560 sq km (109,483 sq miles)
Population: 13,183,978
Capital city: Quito
Main languages: Spanish, Quechua
Main religion: Roman Catholic
Government: republic
Currency: 1 sucre = 100 centavos

EGYPT (Africa)
Area: 1,001,450 sq km (386,660 sq miles)
Population: 69,536,644
Capital city: Cairo
Main language: Arabic
Main religion: Sunni Muslim
Government: republic
Currency: 1 Egyptian pound = 100 piasters

EL SALVADOR (North America)
Area: 21,040 sq km (8,124 sq miles)
Population: 6,237,662
Capital city: San Salvador
Main language: Spanish
Main religion: Roman Catholic
Government: republic
Currency: 1 Salvadoran colon = 100 centavos

EQUATORIAL GUINEA (Africa)
Area: 28,050 sq km (10,830 sq miles)
Population: 486,060
Capital city: Malabo
Main languages: Fang, Bubi, other Bantu

• Dominican Republic

East Timor

• Ecuador

Egypt

• El Salvador

Equatorial Guinea

Eritrea

GAZETTEER OF STATES CONTINUED:

Estonia

Ethiopia

Federated States of Micronesia

Fiji

Finland

France

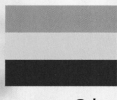

Gabon

languages, Spanish, French, Pidgin English
Main religion: Christian
Government: republic
Currency: 1 CFA* franc = 100 centimes

ERITREA (Africa)
Area: 117,600 sq km (45,405 sq miles)
Population: 4,298,269
Capital city: Asmara
Main languages: Tigrinya, Afar, Arabic
Main religions: Muslim, Coptic Christian, Roman Catholic, Protestant
Government: transitional
Currency: 1 nafka = 100 cents

ESTONIA (Europe)
Area: 45,226 sq km (17,462 sq miles)
Population: 1,423,316
Capital city: Tallinn
Main languages: Estonian, Russian
Main religions: Evangelical Lutheran, Russian and Estonian Orthodox, other Christian
Government: parliamentary democracy
Currency: 1 Estonian kroon = 100 senti

ETHIOPIA (Africa)
Area: 1,127,127 sq km (435,184 sq miles)
Population: 65,891,874
Capital city: Addis Ababa
Main languages: Amharic, Tigrinya, Arabic
Main religions: Muslim, Ethiopian Orthodox, animist
Government: federal republic
Currency: 1 birr = 100 cents

FEDERATED STATES OF MICRONESIA (Australasia/Oceania)
Area: 702 sq km (271 sq miles)
Population: 134,597
Capital city: Palikir
Main languages: Chuuk, Ponapean, English
Main religions: Roman Catholic, Protestant
Government: democracy
Currency: 1 U.S. dollar = 100 cents

FIJI (Australasia/Oceania)
Area: 18,270 sq km (7,054 sq miles)
Population: 844,330
Capital city: Suva
Main languages: Fijian, Hindustani, English
Main religions: Christian, Hindu
Government: republic
Currency: 1 Fijian dollar = 100 cents

FINLAND (Europe)
Area: 337,030 sq km (130,127 sq miles)
Population: 5,175,783
Capital city: Helsinki
Main language: Finnish
Main religion: Evangelical Lutheran
Government: republic
Currency: 1 euro = 100 cents

FRANCE (Europe)
Area: 547,030 sq km (211,208 sq miles)
Population: 59,551,227
Capital city: Paris
Main language: French

Main religion: Roman Catholic
Government: republic
Currency: 1 euro = 100 cents

GABON (Africa)
Area: 267,670 sq km (103,347 sq miles)
Population: 1,221,175
Capital city: Libreville
Main languages: Fang, Myene, French
Main religions: Christian, animist
Government: republic
Currency: 1 CFA* franc = 100 centimes

GAMBIA, THE (Africa)
Area: 11,300 sq km (4,363 sq miles)
Population: 1,411,205
Capital city: Banjul
Main languages: Mandinka, Fula, Wolof, English
Main religion: Muslim
Government: democratic republic
Currency: 1 dalasi = 100 butut

GEORGIA (Asia)
Area: 69,700 sq km (26,911 sq miles)
Population: 4,989,285
Capital city: Tbilisi
Main languages: Georgian, Russian
Main religions: Georgian Orthodox, Muslim, Russian Orthodox
Government: republic
Currency: 1 lari = 100 tetri

GERMANY (Europe)
Area: 357,021 sq km (137,846 sq miles)
Population: 83,029,536
Capital city: Berlin
Main language: German
Main religions: Protestant, Roman Catholic
Government: federal republic
Currency: 1 euro = 100 cents

GHANA (Africa)
Area: 238,540 sq km (92,100 sq miles)
Population: 19,894,014
Capital city: Accra
Main languages: Twi, Fante, Ga, Hausa, Dagbani, Ewe, Nzemi, English
Main religions: indigenous, Muslim, Christian
Government: democratic republic
Currency: 1 new cedi = 100 pesewas

GREECE (Europe)
Area: 131,940 sq km (50,942 sq miles)
Population: 10,623,835
Capital city: Athens
Main language: Greek
Main religion: Greek Orthodox
Government: parliamentary republic
Currency: 1 euro = 100 cents

GRENADA (North America)
Area: 340 sq km (131 sq miles)
Population: 89,227
Capital city: Saint George's
Main languages: English, French patois
Main religions: Roman Catholic, Protestant
Government: constitutional monarchy
Currency: 1 East Caribbean dollar = 100 cents

Gambia, The

Georgia

Germany

Ghana

Greece

Grenada

Guatemala

*CFA = Communaute Financiere Africaine

Guinea

Guinea-Bissau

Guyana

• **Haiti**

Honduras

Hungary

Iceland

GUATEMALA (North America)
Area: 108,890 sq km (42,042 sq miles)
Population: 12,974,361
Capital city: Guatemala City
Main languages: Spanish, Amerindian languages including Quiche, Kekchi, Cakchiquel, Mam
Main religions: Roman Catholic, Protestant, indigenous Mayan beliefs
Government: democratic republic
Currency: 1 quetzal = 100 centavos

GUINEA (Africa)
Area: 245,860 sq km (94,927 sq miles)
Population: 7,613,870
Capital city: Conakry
Main languages: Fuuta Jalon, Mallinke, Susu, French
Main religion: Muslim
Government: republic
Currency: 1 Guinean franc = 100 centimes

GUINEA-BISSAU (Africa)
Area: 36,120 sq km (13,946 sq miles)
Population: 1,315,822
Capital city: Bissau
Main languages: Crioulo*, Balante, Pulaar, Mandjak, Mandinka, Portuguese
Main religions: indigenous, Muslim
Government: republic
Currency: 1 CFA* franc = 100 centimes

GUYANA (South America)
Area: 214,970 sq km (83,000 sq miles)
Population: 697,181
Capital city: Georgetown
Main languages: Guyanese Creole, English, Amerindian languages, Caribbean Hindi
Main religions: Christian, Hindu
Government: republic
Currency: 1 Guyanese dollar = 100 cents

HAITI (North America)
Area: 27,750 sq km (10,714 sq miles)
Population: 6,964,549
Capital city: Port-au-Prince
Main languages: Haitian Creole, French
Main religions: Roman Catholic, Protestant, Voodoo
Government: republic
Currency: 1 gourde = 100 centimes

HONDURAS (North America)
Area: 112,090 sq km (43,278 sq miles)
Population: 6,406,052
Capital city: Tegucigalpa
Main languauge: Spanish
Main religion: Roman Catholic
Government: republic
Currency: 1 lempira = 100 centavos

HUNGARY (Europe)
Area: 93,030 sq km (35,919 sq miles)
Population: 10,106,017
Capital city: Budapest
Main language: Hungarian
Main religions: Roman Catholic, Calvinist
Government: parliamentary democracy
Currency: 1 forint = 100 filler

ICELAND (Europe)
Area: 103,000 sq km (39,768 sq miles)
Population: 277,906
Capital city: Reykjavik
Main language: Icelandic
Main religion: Evangelical Lutheran
Government: republic
Currency: 1 Icelandic krona = 100 aurar

INDIA (Asia)
Area: 3,287,590 sq km (1,269,339 sq miles)
Population: 1,029,991,145
Capital city: New Delhi
Main languages: Hindi, English, Bengali, Urdu, over 1,600 other languages and dialects
Main religions: Hindu, Muslim
Government: federal republic
Currency: 1 Indian rupee = 100 paise

INDONESIA (Asia)
Area: 1,919,440 sq km (741,096 sq miles)
Population: 228,437,870
Capital city: Jakarta
Main languages: Bahasa Indonesia, English, Dutch, Javanese
Main religion: Muslim
Government: republic
Currency: 1 Indonesian rupiah = 100 sen

IRAN (Asia)
Area: 1,648,000 sq km (636,293 sq miles)
Population: 66,128,965
Capital city: Tehran
Main languages: Farsi and other Persian dialects, Azeri
Main religions: Shi'a Muslim, Sunni Muslim
Government: Islamic republic
Currency: 10 Iranian rials = 1 toman

IRAQ (Asia)
Area: 437,072 sq km (168,754 sq miles)
Population: 23,331,985
Capital city: Baghdad
Main languages: Arabic, Kurdish
Main religion: Muslim
Government: republic under a military regime
Currency: 1 Iraqi dinar = 1,000 fils

IRELAND (Europe)
Area: 70,280 sq km (27,135 sq miles)
Population: 3,840,838
Capital city: Dublin
Main languages: English, Irish (Gaelic)
Main religion: Roman Catholic
Government: republic
Currency: 1 euro = 100 cents

ISRAEL (Asia)
Area: 20,770 sq km (8,019 sq miles)
Population: 5,938,093
Capital city: Jerusalem
Main languages: Hebrew, Arabic
Main religions: Jewish, Muslim
Government: parliamentary democracy
Currency: 1 Israeli shekel = 100 agorot

ITALY (Europe)
Area: 301,230 sq km (116,305 sq miles)

India

Indonesia

Iran

Iraq

Ireland

Israel

Italy

*CFA = Communaute Financiere Africaine;
Crioulo = a blend of Portuguese and West African

GAZETTEER OF STATES CONTINUED:

Ivory Coast

Population: 57,679,825
Capital city: Rome
Main language: Italian
Main religion: Roman Catholic
Government: republic
Currency: 1 euro = 100 cents

IVORY COAST (Africa)
Area: 322,460 sq km (124,502 sq miles)
Population: 16,393,221
Capital city: Yamoussoukro
Main languages: Baoule, Dioula, French
Main religions: Christian, Muslim, animist
Government: republic
Currency: 1 CFA* = 100 centimes

Jamaica

JAMAICA (North America)
Area: 10,990 sq km (4,243 sq miles)
Population: 2,665,636
Capital city: Kingston
Main languages: Southwestern Caribbean Creole, English
Main religion: Protestant
Government: parliamentary democracy
Currency: 1 Jamaican dollar = 100 cents

Japan

JAPAN (Asia)
Area: 377,835 sq km (145,882 sq miles)
Population: 126,771,662
Capital city: Tokyo
Main language: Japanese
Main religions: Shinto, Buddhist
Government: constitutional monarchy
Currency: 1 yen = 100 sen

Jordan

JORDAN (Asia)
Area: 92,190 sq km (35,585 sq miles)
Population: 5,153,378
Capital city: Amman
Main languages: Arabic, English
Main religion: Sunni Muslim
Government: constitutional monarchy
Currency: 1 Jordanian dinar = 1,000 fils

Kazakhstan

KAZAKHSTAN (Asia)
Area: 2,717,300 sq km (1,049,150 sq miles)
Population: 16,731,303
Capital city: Astana
Main languages: Kazakh, Russian
Main religions: Muslim, Russian Orthodox
Government: republic
Currency: 1 Kazakhstani tenge = 100 tiyn

Kenya

KENYA (Africa)
Area: 582,650 sq km (224,961 sq miles)
Population: 30,765,916
Capital city: Nairobi
Main languages: Swahili, English, Bantu languages
Main religions: Christian, indigenous
Government: republic
Currency: 1 Kenyan shilling = 100 cents

Kiribati

KIRIBATI (Australasia/Oceania)
Area: 717 sq km (277 sq miles)
Population: 94,149
Capital city: Bairiki (on Tarawa island)
Main languages: Gilbertese, English
Main religions: Roman Catholic, Protestant

Government: republic
Currency: 1 Australian dollar = 100 cents

KUWAIT (Asia)
Area: 17,820 sq km (6,880 sq miles)
Population: 2,041,961
Capital city: Kuwait City
Main languages: Arabic, English
Main religion: Muslim
Government: monarchy
Currency: 1 Kuwaiti dinar = 1,000 fils

Kuwait

KYRGYZSTAN (Asia)
Area: 198,500 sq km (76,641 sq miles)
Population: 4,753,003
Capital city: Bishkek
Main languages: Kyrgyz, Russian
Main religions: Muslim, Russian Orthodox
Government: republic
Currency: 1 Kyrgyzstani som = 100 tyiyn

Kyrgyzstan

LAOS (Asia)
Area: 236,800 sq km (91,428 sq miles)
Population: 5,638,967
Capital city: Vientiane
Main languages: Lao, French, English
Main religions: Buddhist, animist
Government: Communist state
Currency: 1 new kip = 100 at

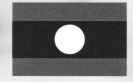

Laos

LATVIA (Europe)
Area: 64,589 sq km (24,938 sq miles)
Population: 2,385,231
Capital city: Riga
Main languages: Latvian, Russian
Main religions: Lutheran, Roman Catholic, Russian Orthodox
Government: parliamentary democracy
Currency: 1 Latvian lat = 100 santims

Latvia

LEBANON (Asia)
Area: 10,400 sq km (4,015 sq miles)
Population: 3,627,774
Capital city: Beirut
Main languages: Arabic, French, English
Main religions: Muslim, Christian
Government: republic
Currency: 1 Lebanese pound = 100 piasters

Lebanon

LESOTHO (Africa)
Area: 30,350 sq km (11,718 sq miles)
Population: 2,177,062
Capital cities: Maseru, Lobamba
Main languages: Sesotho, English, Zulu, Xhosa
Main religions: Christian, indigenous
Government: constitutional monarchy
Currency: 1 loti = 100 lisente

Lesotho

LIBERIA (Africa)
Area: 111,370 sq km (43,000 sq miles)
Population: 3,225,837
Capital city: Monrovia
Main languages: Kpelle, English, Bassa
Main religions: indigenous, Christian, Muslim
Government: republic
Currency: 1 Liberian dollar = 100 cents

LIBYA (Africa)
Area: 1,759,540 sq km (679,358 sq miles)

Liberia

Libya

Population: 5,240,599
Capital city: Tripoli
Main languages: Arabic, Italian, English
Main religion: Sunni Muslim
Government: military rule
Currency: 1 Libyan dinar = 1,000 dirhams

LIECHTENSTEIN (Europe)
Area: 160 sq km (62 sq miles)
Population: 32,528
Capital city: Vaduz
Main languages: German, Alemannic
Main religion: Roman Catholic
Government: constitutional monarchy
Currency: 1 Swiss franc = 100 centimes

Liechtenstein

LITHUANIA (Europe)
Area: 65,200 sq km (25,174 sq miles)
Population: 3,610,535
Capital city: Vilnius
Main languages: Lithuanian, Polish, Russian
Main religions: Roman Catholic, Lutheran, Russian Orthodox
Government: democracy
Currency: 1 Lithuanian litas = 100 centas

Lithuania

LUXEMBOURG (Europe)
Area: 2,586 sq km (998 sq miles)
Population: 442,972
Capital city: Luxembourg
Main languages: Luxemburgish, German, French
Main religion: Roman Catholic
Government: constitutional monarchy
Currency: 1 euro = 100 cents

Luxembourg

MACEDONIA (Europe)
Area: 25,333 sq km (9,781 sq miles)
Population: 2,046,209
Capital city: Skopje
Main languages: Macedonian, Albanian
Main religions: Macedonian Orthodox, Muslim
Government: emerging democracy
Currency: 1 Macedonian denar = 100 deni

Macedonia

MADAGASCAR (Africa)
Area: 587,040 sq km (226,656 sq miles)
Population: 15,982,563
Capital city: Antananarivo
Main languages: Malagasy, French
Main religions: indigenous beliefs, Christian
Government: republic
Currency: 1 Malagasy franc = 100 centimes

Madagascar

MALAWI (Africa)
Area: 118,480 sq km (45,745 sq miles)
Population: 10,548,250
Capital city: Lilongwe
Main languages: Chichewa, English
Main religions: Protestant, Roman Catholic, Muslim
Government: parliamentary democracy
Currency: 1 Malawian kwacha = 100 tambala

Malawi

MALAYSIA (Asia)
Area: 329,750 sq km (127,316 sq miles)
Population: 22,229,040
Capital city: Kuala Lumpur

Main languages: Bahasa Melayu, English, Chinese dialects, Tamil
Main religions: Muslim, Buddhist, Daoist
Government: constitutional monarchy
Currency: 1 ringgit = 100 sen

Malaysia

MALDIVES (Asia)
Area: 300 sq km (116 sq miles)
Population: 310,764
Capital city: Male
Main languages: Maldivian, English
Main religion: Sunni Muslim
Government: republic
Currency: 1 rufiyaa = 100 laari

Maldives

MALI (Africa)
Area: 1,240,000 sq km (478,764 sq miles)
Population: 11,008,518
Capital city: Bamako
Main languages: Bambara, Fulani, Songhai, French
Main religion: Muslim
Government: republic
Currency: 1 CFA* franc = 100 centimes

Mali

MALTA (Europe)
Area: 316 sq km (122 sq miles)
Population: 394,583
Capital city: Valletta
Main languages: Maltese, English
Main religion: Roman Catholic
Government: democratic republic
Currency: 1 Maltese lira = 100 cents

Malta

MARSHALL ISLANDS (Australasia/Oceania)
Area: 181 sq km (70 sq miles)
Population: 70,822
Capital city: Majuro
Main languages: Marshallese, English
Main religion: Protestant
Government: republic
Currency: 1 U.S. dollar = 100 cents

Marshall Islands

MAURITANIA (Africa)
Area: 1,030,700 sq km (397,953 sq miles)
Population: 2,747,312
Capital city: Nouakchott
Main languages: Arabic, Wolof, French
Main religion: Muslim
Government: republic
Currency: 1 ouguiya = 5 khoums

Mauritania

MAURITIUS (Africa)
Area: 1,860 sq km (718 sq miles)
Population: 1,189,825
Capital city: Port Louis
Main languages: Mauritius Creole French, French, Hindi, Bhojpuri, Urdu, Tamil, English
Main religions: Hindu, Christian, English
Government: parliamentary democracy
Currency: 1 Mauritian rupee = 100 cents

MEXICO (North America)
Area: 1,972,550 sq km (761,602 sq miles)
Population: 101,879,171
Capital city: Mexico City
Main languages: Spanish, Mayan, Nahuatl

Mauritius

CFA = Communaute Financiere Africaine

GAZETTEER OF STATES CONTINUED:

Mexico

Main religion: Roman Catholic
Government: federal republic
Currency: 1 New Mexican peso = 100 centavos

MOLDOVA (Europe)
Area: 33,843 sq km (13,067 sq miles)
Population: 4,431,570
Capital city: Chisinau
Main languages: Moldovan, Russian, Gagauz
Main religion: Eastern Orthodox
Government: republic
Currency: 1 Moldovan leu = 100 bani

Moldova

MONACO (Europe)
Area: 1.95 sq km (0.75 sq miles)
Population: 31,842
Capital city: Monaco
Main languages: French, Monegasque, Italian
Main religion: Roman Catholic
Government: constitutional monarchy
Currency: 1 euro = 100 cents

Monaco

MONGOLIA (Asia)
Area: 1,565,000 sq km (604,247 sq miles)
Population: 2,654,999
Capital city: Ulan Bator
Main language: Khalkha Mongol
Main religion: Tibetan Buddist Lamaist
Government: republic
Currency: 1 tugrik = 100 mongos

Mongolia

MOROCCO (Africa)
Area: 446,550 sq km (172,413 sq miles)
Population: 30,645,305
Capital city: Rabat
Main languages: Arabic, Berber, French
Main religion: Muslim
Government: constitutional monarchy
Currency: 1 Moroccan dirham = 100 centimes

Morocco

MOZAMBIQUE (Africa)
Area: 801,590 sq km (309,494 sq miles)
Population: 19,371,057
Capital city: Maputo
Main languages: Makua, Tsonga, Portuguese
Main religions: indigenous, Christian, Muslim
Government: republic
Currency: 1 metical = 100 centavos

Mozambique

NAMIBIA (Africa)
Area: 825,418 sq km (318,694 sq miles)
Population: 1,797,677
Capital city: Windhoek
Main languages: Afrikaans, German, English
Main religions: Christian, indigenous
Government: republic
Currency: 1 Namibian dollar = 100 cents

NAURU (Australasia/Oceania)
Area: 21 sq km (8 sq miles)
Population: 12,088
Capital: Yaren
Main languages: Nauruan, English
Main religion: Christian
Government: republic
Currency: 1 Australian dollar = 100 cents

Namibia

NEPAL (Asia)
Area: 147,181 sq km (56,827 sq miles)
Population: 25,284,463
Capital city: Kathmandu
Main languages: Nepali, Maithili
Main religions: Hindu, Buddhist
Government: constitutional monarchy
Currency: 1 Nepalese rupee = 100 paisa

NETHERLANDS (Europe)
Area: 41,532 sq km (16,036 sq miles)
Population: 15,981,472
Capital cities: Amsterdam, The Hague
Main language: Dutch
Main religion: Christian
Government: constitutional monarchy
Currency: 1 euro = 100 cents

NEW ZEALAND (Australasia/Oceania)
Area: 268,680 sq km (103,737 sq miles)
Population: 3,864,129
Capital city: Wellington
Main languages: English, Maori
Main religion: Christian
Government: parliamentary democracy
Currency: 1 New Zealand dollar = 100 cents

NICARAGUA (North America)
Area: 129,494 sq km (49,998 sq miles)
Population: 4,918,393
Capital city: Managua
Main language: Spanish
Main religion: Roman Catholic
Government: republic
Currency: 1 gold cordoba = 100 centavos

NIGER (Africa)
Area: 1,267,000 sq km (489,189 sq miles)
Population: 10,355,156
Capital city: Niamey
Main languages: Hausa, Djerma, French
Main religion: Muslim
Government: republic
Currency: 1 CFA* franc = 100 centimes

NIGERIA (Africa)
Area: 923,768 sq km (356,667 sq miles)
Population: 126,635,626
Capital city: Abuja
Main languages: Hausa, Yoruba, Igbo, English
Main religions: Muslim, Christian, indigenous
Government: republic
Currency: 1 naira = 100 kobo

NORTH KOREA (Asia)
Area: 120,540 sq km (46,540 sq miles)
Population: 21,968,228
Capital city: Pyongyang
Main language: Korean
Main religions: Buddhist, Confucianist
Government: authoritarian socialist
Currency: 1 North Korean won = 100 chon

NORWAY (Europe)
Area: 324,220 sq km (125,181 sq miles)
Population: 4,503,440
Capital city: Oslo
Main language: Norwegian

Nauru

Nepal

Netherlands

New Zealand

Nicaragua

Niger

Nigeria

*CFA = Communaute Financiere Africaine

North Korea

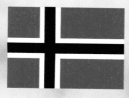

Norway

Oman

Pakistan

Palau

Panama

Papua New Guinea

Main religion: Evangelical Lutheran
Government: constitutional monarchy
Currency: 1 Norwegian krone = 100 oere

OMAN (Asia)
Area: 212,460 sq km (82,031 sq miles)
Population: 2,622,198
Capital city: Muscat
Main languages: Arabic, English, Baluchi
Main religion: Muslim
Government: monarchy
Currency: 1 Omani rial = 1,000 baiza

PAKISTAN (Asia)
Area: 803,940 sq km (310,401 sq miles)
Population: 144,616,639
Capital city: Islamabad
Main languages: Punjabi, Sindhi, Urdu, English
Main religion: Muslim
Government: federal republic
Currency: 1 Pakistani rupee = 100 paisa

PALAU (Australasia/Oceania)
Area: 459 sq km (177 sq miles)
Population: 19,092
Capital city: Koror
Main languages: Palauan, English
Main religions: Christian, Modekngei
Government: democratic republic
Currency: 1 U.S. dollar = 100 cents

PANAMA (North America)
Area: 78,200 sq km (30,193 sq miles)
Population: 2,845,647
Capital city: Panama City
Main languages: Spanish, English
Main religions: Roman Catholic, Protestant
Government: democracy
Currency: 1 balboa = 100 centesimos

PAPUA NEW GUINEA (Australasia/Oceania)
Area: 462,840 sq km (178,703 sq miles)
Population: 5,049,055
Capital city: Port Moresby
Main languages: Tok Pisin, Hiri Motu, English
Main religions: Christian, indigenous
Government: parliamentary democracy
Currency: 1 kina = 100 toea

PARAGUAY (South America)
Area: 406,750 sq km (157,046 sq miles)
Population: 5,734,139
Capital city: Asuncion
Main languages: Guarani, Spanish
Main religion: Roman Catholic
Government: republic
Currency: 1 guarani = 100 centimos

PERU (South America)
Area: 1,285,220 sq km (496,223 sq miles)
Population: 27,483,864
Capital city: Lima
Main languages: Spanish, Quechua, Aymara
Main religion: Roman Catholic
Government: republic
Currency: 1 nuevo sol = 100 centimos

PHILIPPINES (Asia)
Area: 300,000 sq km (115,830 sq miles)
Population: 82,841,518
Capital city: Manila
Main languages: Tagalog, English, Ilocano
Main religion: Roman Catholic
Government: republic
Currency: 1 Philippine peso = 100 centavos

POLAND (Europe)
Area: 312,685 sq km (120,727 sq miles)
Population: 38,633,912
Capital city: Warsaw
Main language: Polish
Main religion: Roman Catholic
Government: democratic republic
Currency: 1 zloty = 100 groszy

PORTUGAL (Europe)
Area: 92,391 sq km (35,672 sq miles)
Population: 10,066,253
Capital city: Lisbon
Main language: Portuguese
Main religion: Roman Catholic
Government: democratic republic
Currency: 1 euro = 100 cents

QATAR (Asia)
Area: 11,437 sq km (4,416 sq miles)
Population: 769,152
Capital city: Doha
Main languages: Arabic, English
Main religion: Muslim
Government: monarchy
Currency: 1 Qatari riyal = 100 dirhams

ROMANIA (Europe)
Area: 237,500 sq km (91,699 sq miles)
Population: 22,364,022
Capital city: Bucharest
Main languages: Romanian, Hungarian, German
Main religion: Romanian Orthodox
Government: republic
Currency: 1 leu = 100 bani

RUSSIA (Europe and Asia)
Area: 17,075,200 sq km (6,592,735 sq miles)
Population: 145,470,197
Capital city: Moscow
Main language: Russian
Main religions: Russian Orthodox, Muslim
Government: federal government
Currency: 1 ruble = 100 kopeks

RWANDA (Africa)
Area: 26,338 sq km (10,169 sq miles)
Population: 7,312,756
Capital city: Kigali
Main languages: Kinyarwanda, French, English, Swahili
Main religions: Roman Catholic, Protestant, Adventist
Government: transitional
Currency: 1 Rwandan franc = 100 centimes

SAINT KITTS AND NEVIS (North America)
Area: 269 sq km (104 sq miles)
Population: 38,756

Paraguay

• **Peru**

Philippines

Poland

Portugal

Qatar

Romania

GAZETTEER OF STATES CONTINUED:

Russia

Capital city: Basseterre
Main language: English
Main religions: Protestant, Roman Catholic
Government: constitutional monarchy
Currency: 1 East Caribbean dollar = 100 cents

SAINT LUCIA (North America)
Area: 620 sq km (239 sq miles)
Population: 158,178
Capital city: Castries
Main languages: French patois, English
Main religion: Roman Catholic
Government: parliamentary democracy
Currency: 1 East Caribbean dollar = 100 cents

Rwanda

SAINT VINCENT AND THE GRENADINES (North America)
Area: 389 sq km (150 sq miles)
Population: 115,942
Capital city: Kingstown
Main languages: English, French patois
Main religions: Protestant, Roman Catholic
Government: parliamentary democracy
Currency: 1 East Caribbean dollar = 100 cents

Saint Kitts and Nevis

SAMOA (Australasia/Oceania)
Area: 2,860 sq km (1,104 sq miles)
Population: 179,058
Capital city: Apia
Main languages: Samoan, English
Main religion: Christian
Government: constitutional monarchy
Currency: 1 tala = 100 sene

Saint Lucia

SAN MARINO (Europe)
Area: 61 sq km (24 sq miles)
Population: 27,336
Capital city: San Marino
Main language: Italian
Main religion: Roman Catholic
Government: republic
Currency: 1 euro = 100 cents

Saint Vincent and the Grenadines

SAO TOME AND PRINCIPE (Africa)
Area: 1,001 sq km (386 sq miles)
Population: 165,034
Capital city: Saó Tome
Main languages: Crioulo* dialects, Portuguese
Main religion: Christian
Government: republic
Currency: 1 dobra = 100 centimos

Samoa

SAUDI ARABIA (Asia)
Area: 2,149,690 sq km (829,995 sq miles)
Population: 22,757,092
Capital city: Riyadh
Main language: Arabic
Main religion: Muslim
Government: monarchy
Currency: 1 Saudi riyal = 100 halalah

• San Marino

SENEGAL (Africa)
Area: 196,190 sq km (75,749 sq miles)
Population: 10,284,929
Capital city: Dakar
Main languages: Wolof, French, Pulaar
Main religion: Muslim
Government: democratic republic
Currency: 1 CFA* franc = 100 centimes

SEYCHELLES (Africa)
Area: 455 sq km (176 sq miles)
Population: 79,715
Capital city: Victoria
Main language: Seselwa
Main religion: Roman Catholic
Government: republic
Currency: 1 Seychelles rupee = 100 cents

SIERRA LEONE (Africa)
Area: 71,740 sq km (27,699 sq miles)
Population: 5,426,618
Capital city: Freetown
Main languages: Mende, Temne, Krio, English
Main religions: Muslim, indigenous, Christian
Government: republic
Currency: 1 leone = 100 cents

SINGAPORE (Asia)
Area: 648 sq km (250 sq miles)
Population: 4,300,419
Capital city: Singapore
Main languages: Chinese, Malay, English, Tamil
Main religions: Buddhist, Muslim
Government: parliamentary republic
Currency: 1 Singapore dollar = 100 cents

SLOVAKIA (Europe)
Area: 48,845 sq km (18,859 sq miles)
Population: 5,414,937
Capital city: Bratislava
Main languages: Slovak, Hungarian
Main religion: Roman Catholic
Government: parliamentary democracy
Currency: 1 koruna = 100 halierov

SLOVENIA (Europe)
Area: 20,253 sq km (7,820 sq miles)
Population: 1,930,132
Capital city: Ljubljana
Main language: Slovenian
Main religion: Roman Catholic
Government: democratic republic
Currency: 1 tolar = 100 stotins

SOLOMON ISLANDS (Australasia/Oceania)
Area: 28,450 sq km (10,985 sq miles)
Population: 480,442
Capital city: Honiara
Main languages: Solomon pidgin, Kwara'ae, To'abaita, English
Main religion: Christian
Government: parliamentary democracy
Currency: 1 Solomon Islands dollar = 100 cents

SOMALIA (Africa)
Area: 637,657 sq km (246,199 sq miles)
Population: 7,488,773
Capital city: Mogadishu
Main languages: Somali, Arabic, Oromo
Main religion: Sunni Muslim
Government: transitional
Currency: 1 Somali shilling = 100 cents

SOUTH AFRICA (Africa)
Area: 1,219,912 sq km (471,008 sq miles)
Population: 43,586,097
Capital cities: Pretoria, Cape Town, Bloemfontein
Main languages: Zulu, Xhosa, Afrikaans, Pedi,

Sao Tome and Principe

Saudi Arabia

Senegal

Seychelles

Sierra Leone

Singapore

Slovakia

*CFA = Communaute Financiere Africaine; Crioulo = a blend of Portuguese and West African

• Slovenia

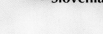

Solomon Islands

Somalia

South Africa

South Korea

• Spain

Sri Lanka

English, Tswana, Sotho, Tsonga, Swati, Venda, Ndebele
Main religions: Christian, indigenous
Government: republic
Currency: 1 rand = 100 cents

SOUTH KOREA (Asia)
Area: 98,480 sq km (38,023 sq miles)
Population: 47,904,370
Capital city: Seoul
Main language: Korean
Main religions: Christian, Buddhist
Government: republic
Currency: 1 South Korean won = 100 chun

SPAIN (Europe)
Area: 504,750 sq km (194,884 sq miles)
Population: 40,037,995
Capital city: Madrid
Main languages: Castilian Spanish, Catalan
Main religion: Roman Catholic
Government: constitutional monarchy
Currency: 1 euro = 100 cents

SRI LANKA (Asia)
Area: 65,610 sq km (25,332 sq miles)
Population: 19,408,635
Capital cities: Colombo, Sri Jayewardenepura Kotte
Main languages: Sinhala, Tamil, English
Main religions: Buddhist, Hindu
Government: republic
Currency: 1 Sri Lankan rupee = 100 cents

SUDAN (Africa)
Area: 2,505,810 sq km (967,493 sq miles)
Population: 36,080,373
Capital city: Khartoum
Main languages: Arabic, English
Main religions: Sunni Muslim, indigenous
Government: Islamic republic
Currency: 1 Sudanese dinar = 100 piastres

SURINAM (South America)
Area: 163,270 sq km (63,039 sq miles)
Population: 433,998
Capital city: Paramaribo
Main languages: Sranang Tongo, Dutch, English
Main religions: Christian, Hindu, Muslim
Government: republic
Currency: 1 Surinamese guilder, gulden or florin = 100 cents

SWAZILAND (Africa)
Area: 17,363 sq km (6,704 sq miles)
Population: 1,104,343
Capital cities: Mbabane, Lobamba
Main languages: Swati, English
Main religions: Protestant, indigenous, Muslim
Government: monarchy
Currency: 1 lilangeni = 100 cents

SWEDEN (Europe)
Area: 449,964 sq km (173,731 sq miles)
Population: 8,875,053
Capital city: Stockholm
Main language: Swedish

Main religion: Lutheran
Government: constitutional monarchy
Currency: 1 Swedish krona = 100 oere

SWITZERLAND (Europe)
Area: 41,290 sq km (15,942 sq miles)
Population: 7,283,274
Capital city: Bern
Main languages: German, French, Italian
Main religions: Roman Catholic, Protestant
Government: federal republic
Currency: 1 Swiss franc, franken or frano = 100 centimes, rappen or centesimi

SYRIA (Asia)
Area: 185,180 sq km (71,498 sq miles)
Population: 16,728,808
Capital city: Damascus
Main languages: Arabic, Kurdish
Main religions: Muslim, Christian
Government: republic under military regime
Currency: 1 Syrian pound = 100 piastres

TAIWAN (Asia)
Area: 35,980 sq km (13,892 sq miles)
Population: 22,370,461
Capital city: Taipei
Main languages: Taiwanese, Mandarin Chinese, Hakka Chinese
Main religions: Buddhist, Confucian, Daoist
Government: democracy
Currency: 1 New Taiwan dollar = 100 cents

TAJIKISTAN (Asia)
Area: 143,100 sq km (55,251 sq miles)
Population: 6,578,681
Capital city: Dushanbe
Main languages: Tajik, Russian
Main religion: Sunni Muslim
Government: republic
Currency: 1 somoni = 100 dirams

TANZANIA (Africa)
Area: 945,087 sq km (364,898 sq miles)
Population: 36,232,074
Capital cities: Dar es Salaam, Dodoma
Main languages: Swahili, English, Sukuma
Main religions: Christian, Muslim, indigenous
Government: republic
Currency: 1 Tanzanian shilling = 100 cents

THAILAND (Asia)
Area: 514,000 sq km (198,455 sq miles)
Population: 61,797,751
Capital city: Bangkok
Main languages: Thai, English, Chaochow
Main religion: Buddhist
Government: constitutional monarchy
Currency: 1 baht = 100 satang

TOGO (Africa)
Area: 56,785 sq km (21,925 sq miles)
Population: 5,153,088
Capital city: Lome
Main languages: Mina, Ewe, Kabye, French
Main religions: indigenous, Christian, Muslim
Government: republic
Currency: 1 CFA* franc = 100 centimes

Sudan

Surinam

Swaziland

Sweden

Switzerland

Syria

Taiwan

*CFA = Communaute Financiere Africaine

GAZETTEER OF STATES CONTINUED:

Tajikistan

Trinidad and Tobago

(left column, flags labeled top to bottom): Tanzania, Thailand, Togo, Tonga

TONGA (Australasia/Oceania)
Area: 748 sq km (289 sq miles)
Population: 104,227
Capital city: Nukualofa
Main languages: Tongan, English
Main religion: Christian
Government: constitutional monarchy
Currency: 1 pa'anga = 100 seniti

TRINIDAD AND TOBAGO (North America)
Area: 5,128 sq km (1,980 sq miles)
Population: 1,169,682
Capital city: Port-of-Spain
Main languages: English, French, Spanish, Hindi
Main religions: Christian, Hindu
Government: republic
Currency: 1 Trinidad and Tobago dollar = 100 cents

TUNISIA (Africa)
Area: 163,610 sq km (63,170 sq miles)
Population: 9,705,102
Capital city: Tunis
Main languages: Arabic, French
Main religion: Muslim
Government: republic
Currency: 1 Tunisian dinar = 1,000 millimes

TURKEY (Europe and Asia)
Area: 780,580 sq km (301,382 sq miles)
Population: 66,493,970
Capital city: Ankara
Main language: Turkish
Main religion: Muslim
Government: democratic republic
Currency: 1 Turkish lira = 100 kurus

TURKMENISTAN (Asia)
Area: 488,100 sq km (188,455 sq miles)
Population: 4,603,244
Capital city: Ashgabat (Ashkhabad)
Main languages: Turkmen, Russian
Main religion: Muslim
Government: republic
Currency: 1 Turkmen manat = 100 tenesi

TUVALU (Australasia/Oceania)
Area: 26 sq km (10 sq miles)
Population: 10,991
Capital city: Funafuti
Main languages: Tuvaluan, English
Main religion: Congregationalist
Government: constitutional monarchy
Currency: 1 Tuvaluan dollar or 1 Australian dollar = 100 cents

UGANDA (Africa)
Area: 236,040 sq km (91,135 sq miles)
Population: 23,985,712
Capital city: Kampala
Main languages: Luganda, English, Swahili
Main religions: Christian, Muslim, indigenous
Government: republic
Currency: 1 Ugandan shilling = 100 cents

UKRAINE (Europe)
Area: 603,700 sq km (233,089 sq miles)
Population: 49,153,027
Capital city: Kiev

Main languages: Ukrainian, Russian
Main religion: Ukrainain Orthodox
Government: republic
Currency: 1 hryvnia = 100 kopiykas

UNITED ARAB EMIRATES (Asia)
Area: 82,880 sq km (32,000 sq miles)
Population: 2,407,460
Capital city: Abu Dhabi
Main languages: Arabic, English
Main religion: Muslim
Government: federation
Currency: 1 Emirati dirham = 100 fils

UNITED KINGDOM (Europe)
Area: 244,820 sq km (94,525 sq miles)
Population: 59,647,790
Capital city: London
Main language: English
Main religions: Anglican, Roman Catholic
Government: constitutional monarchy
Currency: 1 British pound = 100 pence

UNITED STATES OF AMERICA (North America)
Area: 9,629,091 sq km (3,717,792 sq miles)
Population: 278,058,881
Capital city: Washington D.C.
Main language: English
Main religions: Protestant, Roman Catholic
Government: federal republic
Currency: 1 U.S. dollar = 100 cents

URUGUAY (South America)
Area: 176,220 sq km (68,039 sq miles)
Population: 3,360,105
Capital city: Montevideo
Main language: Spanish
Main religion: Roman Catholic
Government: republic
Currency: 1 Uruguayan peso = 100 centesimos

UZBEKISTAN (Asia)
Area: 447,400 sq km (172,741 sq miles)
Population: 25,155,064
Capital city: Tashkent
Main languages: Uzbek, Russian
Main religions: Muslim, Eastern Orthodox
Government: republic
Currency: 1 Uzbekistani sum = 100 tyyn

VANUATU (Australasia/Oceania)
Area: 12,189 sq km (4,706 sq miles)
Population: 192,910
Capital city: Port-Vila
Main languages: Bislama, French, English
Main religion: Christian
Government: republic
Currency: 1 vatu = 100 centimes

VATICAN CITY (Europe)
Area: 0.44 sq km (0.17 sq miles)
Population: 880
Capital city: Vatican City
Main languages: Italian, Latin
Main religion: Roman Catholic
Government: led by the Pope
Currency: 1 euro = 100 cents

Tunisia

Turkey

Turkmenistan

Tuvalu

Uganda

Ukraine

United Arab Emirates

VENEZUELA (South America)
Area: 912,050 sq km (352,143 sq miles)
Population: 23,916,810
Capital city: Caracas
Main language: Spanish
Main religion: Roman Catholic
Government: federal republic
Currency: 1 bolivar = 100 centimos

VIETNAM (Asia)
Area: 329,560 sq km (127,243 sq miles)
Population: 79,939,014
Capital city: Hanoi
Main languages: Vietnamese, French, English, Khmer, Chinese
Main religion: Buddhist
Government: Communist state
Currency: 1 new dong = 100 xu

YEMEN (Asia)
Area: 527,970 sq km (203,849 sq miles)
Population: 18,078,035
Capital city: Sana
Main language: Arabic
Main religion: Muslim
Government: republic
Currency: 1 Yemeni rial = 100 fils

YUGOSLAVIA (Europe)
Area: 102,350 sq km (39,517 sq miles)
Population: 10,677,290
Capital city: Belgrade
Main language: Serbian
Main religions: Orthodox, Muslim
Government: republic
Currency: 1 Yugoslavian new dinar = 100 paras

ZAMBIA (Africa)
Area: 752,614 sq km (290,584 sq miles)
Population: 9,770,199
Capital city: Lusaka
Main languages: Bemba, Tonga, Nyanja, English
Main religions: Christian, Muslim, Hindu
Government: republic
Currency: 1 Zambian kwacha = 100 ngwee

ZIMBABWE (Africa)
Area: 390,580 sq km (150,803 sq miles)
Population: 11,365,366
Capital city: Harare
Main languages: Shona, Ndebele, English
Main religions: Christian, indigenous
Government: republic
Currency: 1 Zimbabwean dollar = 100 cents

United Kingdom

United States of America

Uruguay

Uzbekistan

Vanuatu

Vatican City

Venezuela

Vietnam

Yemen

Yugoslavia

Zambia

Zimbabwe

The United Nations

The United Nations (U.N.) is an organization which aims to bring countries together to work for peace and development. Of the world's 193 states, 189 belong to the U.N. Those that don't belong are Taiwan, Switzerland, East Timor and the Vatican City.

Kofi Annan, the Secretary-General of the U.N., with U.N. ambassador Pele

Internet links

For a link to a Web site where you can test your flag knowledge by playing a game where you have to match countries and their flags, go to **www.usborne-quicklinks.com**

TIME ZONES

When it's midday in Rio de Janeiro, it's midnight in Tokyo. This is because the Earth is divided into different time zones. Within each zone, people usually set their clocks to the same time. If you fly between two zones, you change your watch to the time in the new zone.

Dividing up time

There are 25 main time zones. They are separated by one-hour intervals and there is a new time zone every 15 degrees of longitude. There are 12 one-hour zones both ahead of and behind Greenwich Mean Time, or GMT, which is the time at the Prime Meridian Line.

Governments can change their countries' time zones. So, for convenience, whole countries usually keep the same local time instead of sticking to the zones exactly. For example, China could be divided into several time zones, but instead the whole country keeps the same time. A few areas, such as India, use non-standard half hour deviations.

Summer time

Some countries adjust their clocks in summer. For example, in the U.K. all clocks go forward one hour. This is known as Daylight Saving Time or Summer Time. It is a way of getting more out of the days by having an extra hour of daylight in the evening. It reduces energy use as people don't use as much electricity for lights.

Changing dates

On the opposite side of the world from the Prime Meridian Line is the International Date Line, which runs mostly through the Pacific Ocean and bends to avoid the land. Places to the west of it are 24 hours ahead of places to the east. This means that if you travel east across it you lose a day and if you travel west across it you gain a day.

This map shows the time zones. The times at the top of the map tell you the time in the different zones when it is noon at the Prime Meridian Line. There are two midnight zones, one for each day on either side of the International Date Line. The numbers in circles tell you how many hours ahead of or behind Greenwich Mean Time an area is.

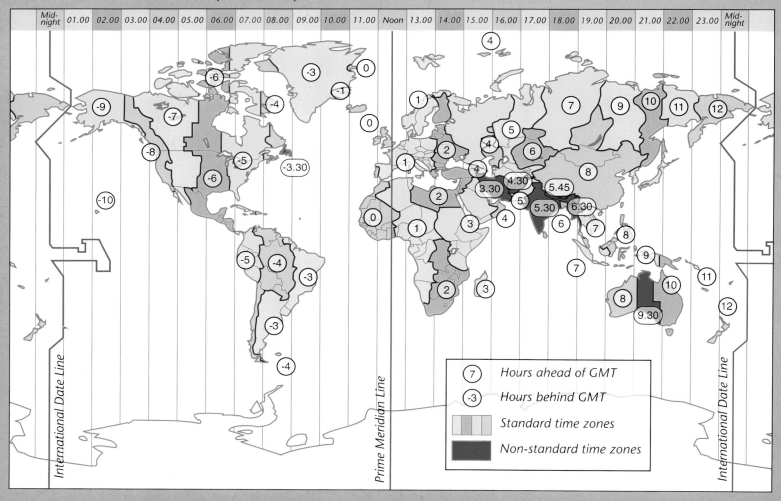

126

GENERAL INDEX

Places featured in the maps in this atlas are listed in a separate index on pages 130–143.

Answers to geography quiz (pages 110–111)

Mystery places

Top left: La Sagrada Familia church in Barcelona, Spain
Top right: The Taj Mahal near Agra, India
Middle left: The Golden Gate Bridge in San Francisco, U.S.A.
Middle right: The Acropolis in Athens, Greece
Bottom: The CN Tower in Toronto, Canada

Quick quiz

1. Japan
2. 6 a.m.
3. Australia
4. North America
5. Czech Republic
6. Lake Baikal, Russia
7. Vatican City
8. Costa Rica
9. Nigeria
10. Ankara

Survival challenge

1. b. An umbrella would not be useful as it doesn't rain in Antarctica. It's also the world's windiest continent, so an umbrella wouldn't last long! You would need sunglasses and sunscreen, however, as the reflection of the sun off snow is dazzling and can cause sunburn.

2. b. Extra clothes would help to conserve your sweat, which cools down your skin, and resting in the shade (if there is any) would help your body stay as cool as possible. Being active, talking or singing would cause your body to lose moisture and your mouth to dry out – which would make you even thirstier.

3. All of them. Six-eyed crab spiders are one of the most venomous types of spiders in the world. Their bites are so severe that they can cause death. Button spiders have a bite which is very painful, though not lethal, while a bite from a violin spider causes painful swelling.

4. c. A bear will only attack if it thinks you are a threat to it. If you moved away slowly, not making any sudden movements, it would probably leave you alone. You should only lie down (preferably curled into a ball) and play dead if the bear actually takes a swipe at you.

MAP INDEX

This is an index of the places and features named on the maps. Each entry consists of the following parts: the name (given in bold type), the country or region within which it is located (given in italics), the page on which the name can be found (given in bold type), and the grid reference (also given in bold type). For some names, there is also a description explaining what kind of place it is – for example a country, internal administrative area (state or province), national capital or internal capital. To find a place on a map, first find the map indicated by the page reference. Then use the grid reference to find the square containing the name or town symbol. See page 11 for help with using the grid.

a

Abaco, *The Bahamas,* **33 L5**
Abadan, *Iran,* **73 E5**
Abakan, *Russia,* **74 E3**
Abaya, Lake, *Ethiopia,* **103 G2**
Abeche, *Chad,* **98 F6**
Abeokuta, *Nigeria,* **101 F7**
Aberdeen, *United Kingdom,* **88 D2**
Aberystwyth, *United Kingdom,* **88 C3**
Abha, *Saudi Arabia,* **73 D8**
Abidjan, *Ivory Coast,* **32 G4**
Abomey, *Benin,* **101 F7**
Abu Dhabi, *United Arab Emirates, national capital,* **73 F7**
Abuja, *Nigeria, national capital,* **101 G7**
Abu Kamal, *Syria,* **72 D5**
Abu Simbel, *Egypt,* **99 H4**
Acapulco, *Mexico,* **34 E4**
Accra, *Ghana, national capital,* **101 E7**
Acklins Island, *The Bahamas,* **33 L6**
Aconcagua, *Argentina,* **44 E6**
Adana, *Turkey,* **72 C4**
Adapazari, *Turkey,* **91 J3**
Ad Dakhla, *Western Sahara,* **100 B4**
Ad Dammam, *Saudi Arabia,* **73 F6**
Addis Ababa, *Ethiopia, national capital,* **103 G2**
Adelaide, *Australia, internal capital,* **54 G6**
Aden, *Yemen,* **73 E9**
Aden, Gulf of, *Africa/Asia,* **73 E9**
Admiralty Islands, *Papua New Guinea,* **65 L4**
Adrar, *Algeria,* **100 E3**
Adriatic Sea, *Europe,* **90 E3**
Adzope, *Ivory Coast,* **101 E7**
Aegean Sea, *Europe,* **91 H4**
Afghanistan, *Asia, country,* **70 A4**
Africa, **20–21**
Agadez, *Niger,* **98 C5**
Agadir, *Morocco,* **100 D2**
Agra, *India,* **70 D5**
Agrigento, *Italy,* **90 E4**
Agua Prieta, *Mexico,* **34 C1**
Aguascalientes, *Mexico,* **34 D3**
Agulhas, Cape, *South Africa,* **104 C6**
Agulhas Negras, Mount, *Brazil,* **44 K4**
Ahaggar Mountains, *Algeria,* **100 G4**
Ahmadabad, *India,* **71 C6**
Ahvaz, *Iran,* **73 E5**
Aix-en-Provence, *France,* **89 F6**
Aizawl, *India,* **71 G6**
Ajaccio, *France,* **89 G6**
Ajdabiya, *Libya,* **98 F2**
Ajmer, *India,* **70 C5**
Akhisar, *Turkey,* **91 H4**
Akita, *Japan,* **69 P3**
Akjoujt, *Mauritania,* **100 C5**
Akola, *India,* **71 D6**
Aksaray, *Turkey,* **91 K4**
Aksu, *China,* **70 E2**
Alabama, *U.S.A., internal admin. area,* **33 J4**
Al Amarah, *Iraq,* **73 E5**
Aland Islands, *Finland,* **86 F3**
Alanya, *Turkey,* **91 J4**
Al Aqabah, *Jordan,* **73 C6**
Alaska, *U.S.A., internal admin. area,* **30 D2**

Alaska, Gulf of, *North America,* **30 E3**
Alaska Peninsula, *U.S.A.,* **30 D3**
Alaska Range, *U.S.A.,* **30 D2**
Alavus, *Finland,* **86 G3**
Al Ayn, *United Arab Emirates,* **73 G7**
Albacete, *Spain,* **89 D7**
Albania, *Europe, country,* **91 F3**
Albany, *Australia,* **54 C7**
Albany, *Georgia, U.S.A.,* **33 K4**
Albany, *New York, U.S.A., internal capital,* **33 M2**
Al Bayda, *Libya,* **98 F2**
Alberta, *Canada, internal admin. area,* **30 H3**
Albert, Lake, *Africa,* **103 F3**
Albino Point, *Angola,* **104 B3**
Alboran Island, *Spain,* **89 D7**
Alborg, *Denmark,* **87 D4**
Albuquerque, *U.S.A.,* **32 E3**
Aldabra Group, *Seychelles,* **105 J1**
Aleppo, *Syria,* **72 C4**
Alesund, *Norway,* **86 C3**
Aleutian Islands, *U.S.A.,* **31 A3**
Alexander Archipelago, *Canada,* **30 F3**
Alexander Bay, *South Africa,* **104 C5**
Alexandria, *Egypt,* **99 G2**
Algeciras, *Spain,* **89 C7**
Algeria, *Africa, country,* **100 F3**
Algiers, *Algeria, national capital,* **100 F1**
Al Hillah, *Iraq,* **72 D5**
Al Hoceima, *Morocco,* **100 E1**
Al Hudaydah, *Yemen,* **73 D9**
Ali Bayramli, *Azerbaijan,* **72 E4**
Alicante, *Spain,* **89 D7**
Alice Springs, *Australia,* **54 F4**
Aligarh, *India,* **70 D5**
Al Jawf, *Libya,* **98 F4**
Al Khums, *Libya,* **98 D2**
Al Kut, *Iraq,* **73 E5**
Allahabad, *India,* **70 E5**
Almaty, *Kazakhstan,* **70 D2**
Almeria, *Spain,* **89 D7**
Almetyevsk, *Russia,* **85 G3**
Almirante, *Panama,* **35 H6**
Al Mubarrez, *Saudi Arabia,* **73 E6**
Al Mukalla, *Yemen,* **73 E9**
Alor Setar, *Malaysia,* **64 B2**
Alps, *Europe,* **90 D2**
Al Qamishli, *Syria,* **72 D4**
Alta, *Norway,* **86 G1**
Altai Mountains, *Asia,* **68 D1**
Altamira, *Brazil,* **43 H4**
Altay, *China,* **70 F1**
Altay, *Mongolia,* **68 E1**
Altun Mountains, *China,* **70 G3**
Aluksne, *Latvia,* **87 H4**
Alytus, *Lithuania,* **87 H5**
Amadjuak Lake, *Canada,* **31 M2**
Amami, *Japan,* **69 L5**
Amarillo, *U.S.A.,* **32 F3**
Amazon, *South America,* **43 H4**
Amazon Delta, *Brazil,* **43 J3**
Ambanja, *Madagascar,* **105 J2**
Ambato, *Ecuador,* **42 C4**
Amber, Cape, *Madagascar,* **105 J2**
Ambilobe, *Madagascar,* **105 J2**
Ambon, *Indonesia,* **65 G4**
Ambositra, *Madagascar,* **105 J4**

American Samoa, *Oceania, dependency,* **52 F6**
America, United States of, *North America, country,* **32 F3**
Amiens, *France,* **88 E4**
Amman, *Jordan, national capital,* **73 C5**
Amravati, *India,* **71 D6**
Amritsar, *India,* **70 C4**
Amsterdam, *Netherlands, national capital,* **88 F3**
Am Timan, *Chad,* **98 F6**
Amu Darya, *Asia,* **72 H4**
Amundsen Gulf, *Canada,* **30 G1**
Amundsen Sea, *Antarctica,* **109 Q3**
Amur, *Asia,* **75 G3**
Anadyr, *Russia,* **75 J2**
Anadyr, Gulf of, *Asia,* **75 K2**
Analalava, *Madagascar,* **105 J2**
Anambas Islands, *Indonesia,* **64 C3**
Anchorage, *U.S.A.,* **30 E2**
Ancona, *Italy,* **90 E3**
Andaman Islands, *India,* **71 G8**
Andaman Sea, *Asia,* **66 C5**
Andara, *Namibia,* **104 D3**
Andes, *South America,* **44 E5**
Andorra, *Europe, country,* **89 E6**
Andorra la Vella, *Andorra, national capital,* **89 E6**
Andreanof Islands, *U.S.A.,* **31 B3**
Androka, *Madagascar,* **105 H5**
Andros, *The Bahamas,* **33 L6**
Aneto, Pico de, *Spain,* **89 E6**
Angel Falls, *Venezuela,* **42 F2**
Angers, *France,* **88 D5**
Angkor, *Cambodia,* **66 D5**
Angoche, *Mozambique,* **105 G3**
Angola, *Africa, country,* **104 C2**
Angra do Heroismo, *Azores,* **100 K10**
Angren, *Uzbekistan,* **70 C2**
Anguilla, *North America,* **34 M4**
Anjouan Island, *Comoros,* **105 H2**
Ankara, *Turkey, national capital,* **91 K3**
Annaba, *Algeria,* **100 G1**
An Najaf, *Iraq,* **73 D5**
Annapolis, *U.S.A., internal capital,* **33 L3**
An Nasiriyah, *Iraq,* **73 E5**
Anqing, *China,* **69 J4**
Anshan, *China,* **69 K2**
Antalaha, *Madagascar,* **105 K2**
Antalya, *Turkey,* **91 J4**
Antalya, Gulf of, *Turkey,* **91 J4**
Antananarivo, *Madagascar, national capital,* **105 J3**
Antarctica, **109 B4**
Antarctic Peninsula, *Antarctica,* **109 T2**
Anticosti Island, *Canada,* **31 N4**
Antigua and Barbuda, *North America, country,* **34 M4**
Antofagasta, *Chile,* **44 D4**
Antsalova, *Madagascar,* **105 H3**
Antsirabe, *Madagascar,* **105 J3**
Antsiranana, *Madagascar,* **105 J2**
Antwerp, *Belgium,* **88 F4**
Aomori, *Japan,* **69 P2**
Aoraki, *New Zealand,* **55 P8**
Apalachee Bay, *U.S.A.,* **33 K5**
Aparri, *Philippines,* **67 H4**
Apatity, *Russia,* **86 K2**

Apennines, *Italy,* **90 E3**
Apia, *Samoa, national capital,* **52 F6**
Appalachian Mountains, *U.S.A.,* **33 K3**
Aqsay, *Kazakhstan,* **85 G3**
Aqtau, *Kazakhstan,* **72 F3**
Aqtobe, *Kazakhstan,* **85 H3**
Arabian Desert, *Africa,* **99 H3**
Arabian Peninsula, *Asia,* **73 E7**
Arabian Sea, *Asia,* **73 G8**
Aracaju, *Brazil,* **43 L6**
Arad, *Romania,* **91 G2**
Arafura Sea, *Asia/Australasia,* **65 H5**
Araguaia, *Brazil,* **43 H6**
Araguaina, *Brazil,* **43 J5**
Arak, *Iran,* **72 E5**
Aral, *Kazakhstan,* **72 H2**
Aral Sea, *Asia,* **72 G2**
Arapiraca, *Brazil,* **43 L5**
Araraquara, *Brazil,* **44 J4**
Araure, *Venezuela,* **42 E2**
Arbil, *Iraq,* **72 D4**
Arctic Ocean, **108 A4**
Ardabil, *Iran,* **72 E4**
Arendal, *Norway,* **86 D4**
Arequipa, *Peru,* **42 D7**
Argentina, *South America, country,* **45 E7**
Argentino, Lake, *Argentina,* **45 D10**
Arhus, *Denmark,* **87 D4**
Arica, *Chile,* **44 D3**
Arica, Gulf of, *South America,* **42 D7**
Arizona, *U.S.A., internal admin. area,* **32 D4**
Arkansas, *U.S.A.,* **33 G3**
Arkansas, *U.S.A., internal admin. area,* **33 H4**
Arkhangelsk, *Russia,* **74 C2**
Armenia, *Asia, country,* **72 D3**
Armidale, *Australia,* **55 K6**
Arnhem, *Netherlands,* **88 F4**
Arnhem Land, *Australia,* **54 F2**
Arqalyq, *Kazakhstan,* **72 J1**
Ar Ramadi, *Iraq,* **72 D5**
Ar Raqqah, *Syria,* **72 C4**
Aruba, *North America,* **35 K5**
Aru Islands, *Indonesia,* **65 J5**
Arusha, *Tanzania,* **103 G4**
Arzamas, *Russia,* **84 E2**
Asahikawa, *Japan,* **69 P2**
Asansol, *India,* **71 F6**
Ashgabat (Ashkhabad), *Turkmenistan, national capital,* **72 G4**
Asia, **21**
Asir, *Saudi Arabia,* **73 D7**
Asmara, *Eritrea, national capital,* **99 J5**
Assab, *Eritrea,* **99 K6**
As Sulaymaniyah, *Iraq,* **72 E4**
Assumption, *Seychelles,* **105 J1**
Astana, *Kazakhstan, national capital,* **74 D3**
Astove, *Seychelles,* **105 J2**
Astrakhan, *Russia,* **85 F4**
Asuncion, *Paraguay, national capital,* **44 G5**
Aswan, *Egypt,* **99 H4**
Aswan High Dam, *Egypt,* **99 H4**
Asyut, *Egypt,* **99 H3**
Atacama Desert, *Chile,* **44 E3**
Atalaia do Norte, *Brazil,* **42 D4**

Atar, *Mauritania*, 100 C4
Atbarah, *Sudan*, 99 H5
Atbasar, *Kazakhstan*, 72 J1
Athabasca, *Canada*, 30 H3
Athabasca, Lake, *Canada*, 30 J3
Athens, *Greece, national capital*, 91 G4
Atka Island, *U.S.A.*, 31 B3
Atlanta, *U.S.A., internal capital*, 33 K4
Atlantic City, *U.S.A.*, 33 M3
Atlantic Ocean, 20
Atlas Mountains, *Africa*, 100 D2
At Taif, *Saudi Arabia*, 73 D7
Attapu, *Laos*, 66 E5
Attu Island, *U.S.A.*, 31 A3
Atyrau, *Kazakhstan*, 85 G4
Auckland, *New Zealand*, 55 P7
Augsburg, *Germany*, 88 G4
Augusta, *U.S.A., internal capital*, 33 N2
Aurangabad, *India*, 71 D7
Austin, *U.S.A., internal capital*, 32 G4
Australasia and Oceania, 21
Australia, *Australasia, country*, 54 E4
Australian Capital Territory, *Australia, internal admin. area*, 55 J6
Austria, *Europe, country*, 90 E2
Awasa, *Ethiopia*, 103 G2
Ayacucho, *Peru*, 42 D6
Aydin, *Turkey*, 91 H4
Ayers Rock, *Australia*, 54 F5
Ayoun el Atrous, *Mauritania*, 101 D5
Azerbaijan, *Asia, country*, 72 E3
Azores, *Atlantic Ocean*, 100 K10
Azov, Sea of, *Europe*, 91 K2
Az Zarqa, *Jordan*, 73 C5

b

Baardheere, *Somalia*, 103 H3
Babahoyo, *Ecuador*, 42 C4
Bab al Mandab, *Africa/Asia*, 99 K6
Babruysk, *Belarus*, 87 J5
Babuyan Islands, *Philippines*, 67 H4
Babylon, *Iraq*, 72 D5
Bacabal, *Brazil*, 43 K4
Bacau, *Romania*, 91 H2
Bac Lieu, *Vietnam*, 66 E6
Bacolod, *Philippines*, 67 H5
Badajoz, *Spain*, 89 C7
Baffin Bay, *Canada*, 31 N1
Baffin Island, *Canada*, 31 M2
Bafoussam, *Cameroon*, 102 B2
Bage, *Brazil*, 44 H6
Baghdad, *Iraq, national capital*, 72 D5
Bahamas, The, *North America, country*, 33 L5
Bahawalpur, *Pakistan*, 70 C5
Bahia, *Brazil*, 43 L6
Bahia Blanca, *Argentina*, 45 F7
Bahir Dar, *Ethiopia*, 103 G1
Bahrain, *Asia, country*, 73 F6
Baia Mare, *Romania*, 91 G2
Baie-Comeau, *Canada*, 31 N4
Baikal, Lake, *Russia*, 75 F3
Bairiki, *Kiribati, national capital*, 52 E4
Bakersfield, *U.S.A.*, 32 C3
Baku, *Azerbaijan, national capital*, 72 E3
Balakovo, *Russia*, 85 F3
Balaton, Lake, *Hungary*, 87 F7
Balbina Reservoir, *Brazil*, 43 G4
Baldy Peak, *U.S.A.*, 32 E4
Balearic Islands, *Spain*, 89 E7
Bali, *Indonesia*, 64 E5
Balikesir, *Turkey*, 91 H4
Balikpapan, *Indonesia*, 64 E4
Balkanabat, *Turkmenistan*, 72 F4
Balkan Mountains, *Europe*, 91 G3
Balkhash, Lake, *Kazakhstan*, 70 D1
Balkuduk, *Kazakhstan*, 85 F4
Balqash, *Kazakhstan*, 70 D1
Balti, *Moldova*, 91 H2
Baltic Sea, *Europe*, 87 F4
Baltimore, *U.S.A.*, 33 L3
Bamako, *Mali, national capital*, 101 D6
Bamenda, *Cameroon*, 102 B2
Bancs Providence, *Seychelles*, 105 K1
Banda Aceh, *Indonesia*, 64 A2
Bandar-e Abbas, *Iran*, 73 G6

Bandar Seri Begawan, *Brunei, national capital*, 64 D2
Banda Sea, *Indonesia*, 65 G5
Bandundu, *Democratic Republic of Congo*, 102 C4
Bandung, *Indonesia*, 64 C5
Banfora, *Burkina Faso*, 101 E6
Bangalore, *India*, 71 D8
Bangassou, *Central African Republic*, 102 D3
Bangka, *Indonesia*, 64 C4
Bangkok, *Thailand, national capital*, 66 D5
Bangladesh, *Asia, country*, 71 F6
Bangor, *U.S.A.*, 33 N2
Bangui, *Central African Republic, national capital*, 102 C3
Bangweulu, Lake, *Zambia*, 104 E2
Banja Luka, *Bosnia and Herzegovina*, 90 F2
Banjarmasin, *Indonesia*, 64 D4
Banjul, *The Gambia, national capital*, 101 B6
Banks Island, *Canada*, 30 G1
Banks Islands, *Vanuatu*, 55 N2
Banska Bystrica, *Slovakia*, 87 F6
Baoding, *China*, 69 J3
Baoji, *China*, 68 G4
Baotou, *China*, 68 G2
Baqubah, *Iraq*, 72 D5
Baranavichy, *Belarus*, 87 H5
Barbacena, *Brazil*, 44 K4
Barbados, *North America, country*, 34 N5
Barcelona, *Spain*, 89 E6
Barcelona, *Venezuela*, 42 F1
Bareilly, *India*, 70 D5
Barents Sea, *Europe*, 74 B2
Bari, *Italy*, 90 F3
Barinas, *Venezuela*, 42 D2
Barkly Tableland, *Australia*, 54 G3
Barnaul, *Russia*, 74 E3
Barquisimeto, *Venezuela*, 42 E1
Barra Falsa Point, *Mozambique*, 105 G4
Barranquilla, *Colombia*, 42 D1
Barra Point, *Mozambique*, 105 G4
Barreiras, *Brazil*, 44 J2
Barrow, Point, *U.S.A.*, 30 D1
Barysaw, *Belarus*, 87 J5
Basel, *Switzerland*, 90 C2
Basra, *Iraq*, 73 E5
Bassas da India, *Africa*, 105 G4
Basse-Terre, *Guadeloupe*, 34 M4
Basseterre, *St. Kitts and Nevis, national capital*, 34 M4
Bass Strait, *Australia*, 54 J7
Bastia, *France*, 89 G6
Batan Islands, *Philippines*, 67 H3
Batdambang, *Cambodia*, 66 D5
Bathurst, *Canada*, 31 N4
Bathurst, *U.S.A.*, 33 N1
Bathurst Island, *Canada*, 31 K1
Batna, *Algeria*, 100 G1
Baton Rouge, *U.S.A., internal capital*, 33 H4
Batumi, *Georgia*, 72 D3
Baturaja, *Indonesia*, 64 B4
Bawku, *Ghana*, 101 E6
Bayamo, *Cuba*, 35 J3
Baydhabo, *Somalia*, 103 H3
Bealanana, *Madagascar*, 105 J2
Beaufort Sea, *North America*, 30 F1
Beaufort West, *South Africa*, 104 D6
Beaumont, *U.S.A.*, 33 H4
Bechar, *Algeria*, 100 E2
Beer Sheva, *Israel*, 73 B5
Beijing, *China, national capital*, 69 J3
Beira, *Mozambique*, 105 G3
Beirut, *Lebanon, national capital*, 72 C5
Bejaia, *Algeria*, 100 F1
Bekescsaba, *Hungary*, 87 G7
Bekily, *Madagascar*, 105 J4
Belarus, *Europe, country*, 87 J5
Belaya, *Russia*, 85 G2
Belcher Islands, *Canada*, 31 L3
Beledweyne, *Somalia*, 103 J3
Belem, *Brazil*, 43 J4

Belfast, *United Kingdom, internal capital*, 88 C3
Belgaum, *India*, 71 C7
Belgium, *Europe, country*, 88 E4
Belgrade, *Yugoslavia, national capital*, 91 G2
Belitung, *Indonesia*, 64 C4
Belize, *North America, country*, 34 G4
Bellingham, *U.S.A.*, 32 B1
Bellingshausen Sea, *Antarctica*, 109 R2
Belmopan, *Belize, national capital*, 34 G4
Belo Horizonte, *Brazil*, 44 K3
Belomorsk, *Russia*, 86 K2
Beloretsk, *Russia*, 85 H3
Belo-Tsiribihina, *Madagascar*, 105 H3
Bendigo, *Australia*, 54 H7
Bengal, Bay of, *Asia*, 71 F7
Benghazi, *Libya*, 98 F2
Bengkulu, *Indonesia*, 64 B4
Benguela, *Angola*, 104 B2
Beni Mellal, *Morocco*, 100 D2
Benin, *Africa, country*, 101 F6
Benin, Bight of, *Africa*, 101 F7
Benin City, *Nigeria*, 101 G7
Beni Suef, *Egypt*, 99 H3
Ben Nevis, *United Kingdom*, 88 C2
Benoni, *South Africa*, 104 E5
Berbera, *Somalia*, 103 J1
Berberati, *Central African Republic*, 102 C3
Berdyansk, *Ukraine*, 84 D4
Berezniki, *Russia*, 85 H2
Bergamo, *Italy*, 90 D2
Bergen, *Norway*, 86 C3
Bering Sea, *North America*, 30 C2
Bering Strait, *U.S.A.*, 30 B2
Berlin, *Germany, national capital*, 88 H3
Bern, *Switzerland, national capital*, 90 C2
Beroroha, *Madagascar*, 105 J4
Bertoua, *Cameroon*, 102 B3
Besalampy, *Madagascar*, 105 H3
Besancon, *France*, 89 F5
Bethel, *U.S.A.*, 30 C2
Bethlehem, *South Africa*, 104 E5
Betroka, *Madagascar*, 105 J4
Beyneu, *Kazakhstan*, 72 G2
Beysehir Lake, *Turkey*, 91 J4
Beziers, *France*, 89 E6
Bhagalpur, *India*, 70 F5
Bhavnagar *India*, 71 C6
Bhopal, *India*, 71 D6
Bhutan, *Asia, country*, 70 G5
Biak, *Indonesia*, 65 J4
Bialystok, *Poland*, 87 G5
Bida, *Nigeria*, 101 G7
Biel, *Switzerland*, 90 C2
Bielefeld, *Germany*, 88 G3
Bien Hoa, *Vietnam*, 66 E5
Bie Plateau, *Angola*, 104 B2
Bignona, *Senegal*, 101 B6
Bikaner, *India*, 70 C5
Bila Tserkva, *Ukraine*, 87 J6
Bilbao, *Spain*, 89 D6
Bilhorod Dnistrovskyy, *Ukraine*, 84 C4
Billings, *U.S.A.*, 32 E1
Bindura, *Zimbabwe*, 104 F3
Binga, *Zimbabwe*, 104 E3
Binga, Mont, *Mozambique*, 104 E3
Bintulu, *Malaysia*, 64 D3
Bioco, *Equatorial Guinea*, 102 A3
Birao, *Central African Republic*, 102 D1
Biratnagar, *Nepal*, 70 F5
Birjand, *Iran*, 72 G5
Birmingham, *United Kingdom*, 88 D3
Birmingham, *U.S.A.*, 33 J4
Birnin-Kebbi, *Nigeria*, 101 F6
Biscay, Bay of, *Europe*, 89 C5
Bishkek, *Kyrgyzstan, national capital*, 70 C2
Bisho, *South Africa*, 104 E6
Biskra, *Algeria*, 100 G2
Bismarck, *U.S.A., internal capital*, 32 F1
Bismarck Sea, *Papua New Guinea*, 65 L4
Bissagos Archipelago, *Guinea-Bissau*, 101 B6
Bissau, *Guinea-Bissau, national capital*, 101 B6
Bitola, *Macedonia*, 91 G3

Bitterfontein, *South Africa*, 104 C6
Bizerte, *Tunisia*, 98 C1
Blackpool, *United Kingdom*, 88 D3
Black Sea, *Asia/Europe*, 74 B3
Black Volta, *Africa*, 101 E6
Blagoevgrad, *Bulgaria*, 91 G3
Blagoveshchensk, *Russia*, 75 G3
Blanca Bay, *Argentina*, 45 F7
Blanc, Cape, *Africa*, 100 B4
Blanc, Mont, *Europe*, 89 F5
Blantyre, *Malawi*, 105 F3
Blida, *Algeria*, 100 F1
Bloemfontein, *South Africa, national capital*, 104 E5
Blue Nile, *Africa*, 99 H6
Bo, *Sierra Leone*, 101 C7
Boa Vista, *Brazil*, 42 F3
Boa Vista, *Cape Verde*, 101 M11
Bobo Dioulasso, *Burkina Faso*, 101 E6
Bodele Depression, *Africa*, 98 E5
Boden, *Sweden*, 86 G2
Bodo, *Norway*, 86 E2
Bogor, *Indonesia*, 64 C5
Bogota, *Colombia, national capital*, 42 D3
Bohol, *Philippines*, 67 H6
Boise, *U.S.A., internal capital*, 32 C2
Bojnurd, *Iran*, 72 G4
Boke, *Guinea*, 101 C6
Bolivar Peak, *Venezuela*, 42 D2
Bolivia, *South America, country*, 44 E3
Bologna, *Italy*, 90 D2
Bolzano, *Italy*, 90 D2
Bombay, *India*, 71 C7
Bondoukou, *Ivory Coast*, 101 E7
Bongor, *Chad*, 102 C1
Bonin Islands, *Japan*, 52 B2
Bonn, *Germany*, 88 F4
Boosaaso, *Somalia*, 103 J1
Boothia, Gulf of, *Canada*, 31 K1
Boothia Peninsula, *Canada*, 31 K1
Bordeaux, *France*, 89 D5
Bordj Bou Arreridj, *Algeria*, 100 F1
Borlange, *Sweden*, 86 E3
Borneo, *Asia*, 64 D4
Bornholm, *Denmark*, 87 E5
Borovichi, *Russia*, 86 K4
Bosnia and Herzegovina, *Europe, country*, 90 F2
Bosporus, *Turkey*, 91 J3
Bossangoa, *Central African Republic*, 102 C2
Bossembele, *Central African Republic*, 102 C2
Bosten Lake, *China*, 70 F2
Boston, *U.S.A., internal capital*, 33 M2
Bothnia, Gulf of, *Europe*, 86 F3
Botosani, *Romania*, 91 H2
Botswana, *Africa, country*, 104 D4
Bouake, *Ivory Coast*, 101 E7
Bouar, *Central African Republic*, 102 C2
Bougouni, *Mali*, 101 D6
Boujdour, *Western Sahara*, 100 C3
Bouna, *Ivory Coast*, 101 E7
Bozoum, *Central African Republic*, 102 C2
Braga, *Portugal*, 89 B6
Braganca, *Brazil*, 43 J4
Brahmapur, *India*, 71 E7
Brahmaputra, *Asia*, 70 G5
Braila, *Romania*, 91 H2
Brandon, *Canada*, 31 K4
Brandon, *U.S.A.*, 32 G1
Brasilia, *Brazil, national capital*, 44 J3
Brasov, *Romania*, 91 H2
Bratislava, *Slovakia, national capital*, 87 F6
Brazil, *South America, country*, 43 H5
Brazilian Highlands, *Brazil*, 44 K2
Brazzaville, *Congo, national capital*, 102 C4
Bremen, *Germany*, 88 G3
Bremerhaven, *Germany*, 88 G3
Brescia, *Italy*, 90 D2
Brest, *Belarus*, 87 G5
Brest, *France*, 88 C4
Bria, *Central African Republic*, 102 D2
Bridgetown, *Barbados, national capital*, 34 N5
Brisbane, *Australia, internal capital*, 55 K5

Florencia, *Colombia*, 42 C3
Flores, *Azores*, 100 J10
Flores, *Indonesia*, 65 F5
Flores Sea, *Indonesia*, 65 F5
Floresta, *Brazil*, 43 L5
Floriano, *Brazil*, 43 K5
Florianopolis, *Brazil*, 44 J5
Florida, *U.S.A., internal admin. area*, 33 K5
Florida Keys, *U.S.A.*, 33 K6
Florida, Straits of, *North America*, 33 K6
Focsani, *Romania*, 91 H2
Foggia, *Italy*, 90 E3
Fogo, *Cape Verde*, 101 M12
Fomboni, *Comoros*, 105 H2
Formosa, *Argentina*, 44 G5
Fort Albany, *Canada*, 31 L3
Fortaleza, *Brazil*, 43 L4
Fort Chipewyan, *Canada*, 30 H3
Fort-de-France, *Martinique*, 34 M5
Fort Lauderdale, *U.S.A.*, 33 K5
Fort McMurray, *Canada*, 30 H3
Fort Nelson, *Canada*, 30 G3
Fort Peck Lake, *U.S.A.*, 32 E1
Fort Providence, *Canada*, 30 H2
Fort St. John, *Canada*, 30 G3
Fort Severn, *Canada*, 31 L3
Fort Vermilion, *Canada*, 30 H3
Fort Wayne, *U.S.A.*, 33 J2
Fort Worth, *U.S.A.*, 32 G4
Foumban, *Cameroon*, 102 B2
Foxe Basin, *Canada*, 31 M2
Foxe Peninsula, *Canada*, 31 M2
Fox Islands, *U.S.A.*, 31 C3
Foz do Cunene, *Angola*, 104 B3
Foz do Iguacu, *Brazil*, 44 H5
France, *Europe, country*, 89 E5
Franceville, *Gabon*, 102 B4
Francistown, *Botswana*, 104 E4
Frankfort, *U.S.A., internal capital*, 33 K3
Frankfurt, *Germany*, 88 G4
Franz Josef Land, *Russia*, 74 C1
Fraser Island, *Australia*, 55 K5
Fredericton, *Canada, internal capital*, 31 N4
Fredrikstad, *Norway*, 86 D4
Freeport City, *The Bahamas*, 33 L5
Freetown, *Sierra Leone, national capital*, 101 C7
Freiburg, *Germany*, 88 F4
French Guiana, *South America, dependency*, 43 H3
French Polynesia, *Oceania, dependency*, 53 J6
Fresno, *U.S.A.*, 32 C3
Frisian Islands, *Europe*, 88 F3
Froya, *Norway*, 86 D3
Fuerteventura, *Canary Islands*, 100 B3
Fuji, Mount, *Japan*, 69 N3
Fukui, *Japan*, 69 N3
Fukuoka, *Japan*, 69 M4
Fukushima, *Japan*, 69 P3
Funafuti, *Tuvalu, national capital*, 52 E5
Funchal, *Madeira*, 100 B2
Furnas Reservoir, *Brazil*, 44 J4
Fushun, *China*, 69 K2
Fuxin, *China*, 69 K2
Fyn, *Denmark*, 87 D5

g

Gabes, *Tunisia*, 98 D2
Gabes, Gulf of, *Africa*, 98 D2
Gabon, *Africa, country*, 102 B4
Gaborone, *Botswana, national capital*, 104 E4
Gafsa, *Tunisia*, 98 C2
Gagnoa, *Ivory Coast*, 101 D7
Gairdner, Lake, *Australia*, 54 F6
Galapagos Islands, *Ecuador*, 42 N9
Galati, *Romania*, 91 J2
Galdhopiggen, *Norway*, 86 D3
Galle, *Sri Lanka*, 71 E9
Gallinas, Cape, *Colombia*, 42 D1
Galveston, *U.S.A.*, 33 H5
Galway, *Ireland*, 88 B3
Gambela, *Ethiopia*, 103 F2

Gambia, The, *Africa, country*, 101 B6
Ganca, *Azerbaijan*, 72 E3
Gander, *Canada*, 31 P4
Ganges, *Asia*, 70 E5
Ganges, Mouths of the, *Asia*, 71 F6
Ganzhou, *China*, 69 H5
Gao, *Mali*, 101 F5
Garda, Lake, *Italy*, 90 D2
Garissa, *Kenya*, 103 G4
Garonne, *France*, 89 E5
Garoua, *Cameroon*, 102 B2
Gaspe, *Canada*, 31 N4
Gatchina, *Russia*, 86 J4
Gavle, *Sweden*, 86 F3
Gaza, *Israel*, 73 B5
Gaziantep, *Turkey*, 72 C4
Gdansk, *Poland*, 87 F5
Gdansk, Gulf of, *Poland*, 87 F5
Gdynia, *Poland*, 87 F5
Gedaref, *Sudan*, 99 J6
Geelong, *Australia*, 54 H7
Gejiu, *China*, 68 F6
Gemena, *Democratic Republic of Congo*, 102 C3
General Roca, *Argentina*, 45 E7
General Santos, *Philippines*, 67 J6
General Villegas, *Argentina*, 44 F7
Geneva, *Switzerland*, 90 C2
Geneva, Lake, *Europe*, 90 C2
Genoa, *Italy*, 90 D2
Genoa, Gulf of, *Italy*, 90 D2
Gent, *Belgium*, 88 E4
Georgetown, *Guyana, national capital*, 43 G2
George Town, *Malaysia*, 64 B2
Georgia, *Asia, country*, 72 D3
Georgia, *U.S.A., internal admin. area*, 33 K4
Gera, *Germany*, 88 H4
Geraldton, *Australia*, 54 B5
Gerlachovsky stit, *Slovakia*, 87 G6
Germany, *Europe, country*, 88 G4
Gerona, *Spain*, 89 E6
Ghadamis, *Libya*, 98 C2
Ghana, *Africa, country*, 101 E7
Ghardaia, *Algeria*, 100 F2
Gharyan, *Libya*, 98 D2
Ghat, *Libya*, 98 D3
Gibraltar, *Europe*, 89 C7
Gibson Desert, *Australia*, 54 E4
Gijon, *Spain*, 89 C6
Gilbert Islands, *Kiribati*, 52 E5
Gilgit, *Pakistan*, 70 C3
Girardeau, Cape, *U.S.A.*, 33 J3
Giza, Pyramids of, *Egypt*, 99 H3
Gladstone, *Australia*, 55 K4
Glama, *Norway*, 86 D3
Glasgow, *United Kingdom*, 88 C3
Glazov, *Russia*, 85 G2
Glorioso Islands, *Africa*, 105 J2
Gloucester, *United Kingdom*, 88 D4
Gobabis, *Namibia*, 104 C4
Gobi Desert, *Asia*, 68 F2
Gochas, *Namibia*, 104 C4
Godavari, *India*, 71 D7
Gode, *Ethiopia*, 103 H2
Goiania, *Brazil*, 44 J3
Gold Coast, *Australia*, 55 K5
Golmud, *China*, 70 G3
Goma, *Democratic Republic of Congo*, 102 E4
Gonaives, *Haiti*, 35 K4
Gonder, *Ethiopia*, 103 G1
Gongga Shan, *China*, 68 F5
Good Hope, Cape of, *South Africa*, 104 C6
Goose Lake, *U.S.A.*, 32 B2
Gorakhpur, *India*, 71 E5
Gorgan, *Iran*, 72 F4
Gori, *Georgia*, 72 D3
Gorki Reservoir, *Russia*, 84 E2
Gorontalo, *Indonesia*, 65 F3
Gorzow Wielkopolski, *Poland*, 87 E5
Gothenburg, *Sweden*, 87 E4
Gotland, *Sweden*, 87 F4
Gottingen, *Germany*, 88 G4

Gouin Reservoir, *Canada*, 33 L1
Goundam, *Mali*, 101 E5
Governador Valadares, *Brazil*, 44 K3
Graaff-Reinet, *South Africa*, 104 D6
Grafton, *Australia*, 55 K5
Grahamstown, *South Africa*, 104 E6
Granada, *Spain*, 89 D7
Gran Canaria, *Canary Islands*, 100 B3
Gran Chaco, *South America*, 44 F4
Grand Bahama, *The Bahamas*, 33 L5
Grand Canal, *China*, 69 J4
Grand Canyon, *U.S.A.*, 32 D3
Grand Comoro, *Comoros*, 105 H2
Grande Bay, *Argentina*, 45 E10
Grande Prairie, *Canada*, 30 H3
Grand Forks, *U.S.A.*, 33 G1
Grand Island, *U.S.A.*, 32 G2
Grand Junction, *U.S.A.*, 32 E3
Grand Rapids, *Canada*, 31 K3
Grand Rapids, *U.S.A.*, 33 J2
Grand Teton, *U.S.A.*, 32 D2
Graskop, *South Africa*, 104 F5
Graz, *Austria*, 90 E2
Great Australian Bight, *Australia*, 54 F6
Great Barrier Reef, *Australia*, 54 J3
Great Basin, *U.S.A.*, 32 C2
Great Bear Lake, *Canada*, 30 G2
Great Dividing Range, *Australia*, 55 J6
Great Eastern Erg, *Algeria*, 100 G3
Greater Antilles, *North America*, 35 J4
Greater Khingan Range, *China*, 69 J1
Greater Sunda Islands, *Asia*, 64 C4
Great Falls, *U.S.A.*, 32 D1
Great Inagua, *The Bahamas*, 35 K3
Great Karoo, *South Africa*, 104 D6
Great Plains, *U.S.A.*, 32 F2
Great Rift Valley, *Africa*, 103 F5
Great Salt Desert, *Iran*, 72 F5
Great Salt Lake, *U.S.A.*, 32 D2
Great Salt Lake Desert, *U.S.A.*, 32 D2
Great Sandy Desert, *Australia*, 54 D4
Great Slave Lake, *Canada*, 30 H2
Great Victoria Desert, *Australia*, 54 D5
Great Wall of China, *China*, 68 F3
Great Western Erg, *Algeria*, 100 E2
Greece, *Europe, country*, 91 G4
Green Bay, *U.S.A.*, 33 J2
Greenland, *North America, dependency*, 108 P3
Greenland Sea, *Atlantic Ocean*, 108 M3
Greensboro, *U.S.A.*, 33 L3
Greenville, *U.S.A.*, 33 H4
Grenada, *North America, country*, 34 M5
Grenoble, *France*, 89 F5
Griffith, *Australia*, 54 J6
Groningen, *Netherlands*, 88 F3
Groot, *South Africa*, 104 D6
Groote Eylandt, *Australia*, 54 G2
Grossglockner, *Austria*, 90 E2
Groznyy, *Russia*, 72 E3
Grudziadz, *Poland*, 87 F5
Grunau, *Namibia*, 104 C5
Grytviken, *South Georgia*, 45 L10
Guadalajara, *Mexico*, 34 D3
Guadalquivir, *Spain*, 89 C7
Guadalupe Island, *Mexico*, 34 A2
Guadeloupe, *North America*, 34 M4
Guadiana, *Europe*, 89 C7
Gualeguaychu, *Argentina*, 44 G6
Guam, *Oceania*, 52 B3
Guangzhou, *China*, 69 H6
Guantanamo, *Cuba*, 35 J3
Guarapuava, *Brazil*, 44 H5
Guardafui, Cape, *Somalia*, 103 K1
Guatemala, *North America, country*, 34 F4
Guatemala City, *Guatemala, national capital*, 34 F5
Guaviare, *Colombia*, 42 E3
Guayaquil, *Ecuador*, 42 C4
Guayaquil, Gulf of, *Ecuador*, 42 B4
Gueckedou, *Guinea*, 101 C7
Guelma, *Algeria*, 90 C4
Guiana Highlands, *Venezuela*, 42 E2
Guilin, *China*, 68 H5
Guinea, *Africa, country*, 101 C6

Guinea-Bissau, *Africa, country*, 101 B6
Guinea, Gulf of, *Africa*, 101 F8
Guiria, *Venezuela*, 42 F1
Guiyang, *China*, 68 G5
Gujranwala, *Pakistan*, 70 C4
Gujrat, *Pakistan*, 70 C4
Gulbarga, *India*, 71 D7
Gulf, The, *Asia*, 73 F6
Gulu, *Uganda*, 103 F3
Gunung Kerinci, *Indonesia*, 64 B4
Gunung Tahan, *Malaysia*, 64 B3
Gurupi, *Brazil*, 44 J2
Gusau, *Nigeria*, 101 G6
Guwahati, *India*, 70 G5
Guyana, *South America, country*, 43 G2
Gwalior, *India*, 70 D5
Gweru, *Zimbabwe*, 104 E3
Gympie, *Australia*, 55 K5
Gyor, *Hungary*, 87 F7

h

Haapsalu, *Estonia*, 86 G4
Haarlem, *Netherlands*, 88 F3
Hadhramaut, *Yemen*, 73 E9
Ha Giang, *Vietnam*, 66 E3
Hague, The, *Netherlands, national capital*, 88 F3
Haifa, *Israel*, 72 B5
Haikou, *China*, 68 H6
Hail, *Saudi Arabia*, 73 D6
Hailar, *China*, 69 J1
Hainan, *China*, 68 H7
Hai Phong, *Vietnam*, 66 E3
Haiti, *North America, country*, 35 K4
Hakodate, *Japan*, 69 P2
Halifax, *Canada, internal capital*, 31 N4
Halmahera, *Indonesia*, 65 G3
Halmstad, *Sweden*, 87 E4
Hamadan, *Iran*, 72 E5
Hamah, *Syria*, 72 C4
Hamamatsu, *Japan*, 69 N4
Hamburg, *Germany*, 88 G3
Hameenlinna, *Finland*, 86 H3
Hamhung, *North Korea*, 69 L3
Hami, *China*, 70 G2
Hamilton, *Canada*, 31 M4
Hamilton, *New Zealand*, 55 Q7
Hammerfest, *Norway*, 86 G1
Handan, *China*, 69 H3
Hangzhou, *China*, 69 K4
Hannover, *Germany*, 88 G3
Hanoi, *Vietnam, national capital*, 66 E3
Happy Valley-Goose Bay, *Canada*, 31 N3
Haradh, *Saudi Arabia*, 73 E7
Harare, *Zimbabwe, national capital*, 104 F3
Harbin, *China*, 69 L1
Harer, *Ethiopia*, 103 H2
Hargeysa, *Somalia*, 103 H2
Harney Basin, *U.S.A.*, 32 C2
Harper, *Liberia*, 101 D8
Harrisburg, *U.S.A., internal capital*, 33 L2
Harrismith, *South Africa*, 104 E5
Hartford, *U.S.A., internal capital*, 33 M2
Hatteras, Cape, *U.S.A.*, 33 L3
Hattiesburg, *U.S.A.*, 33 J4
Hat Yai, *Thailand*, 66 D6
Hauki Lake, *Finland*, 86 J3
Havana, *Cuba, national capital*, 35 H3
Hawaii, *Pacific Ocean, internal admin. area*, 33 P7
Hawaiian Islands, *Pacific Ocean*, 33 P7
Hebrides, *United Kingdom*, 88 C2
Hefei, *China*, 69 J4
Hegang, *China*, 69 M1
Hejaz, *Saudi Arabia*, 73 C6
Helena, *U.S.A., internal capital*, 32 D1
Helmand, *Asia*, 70 B4
Helsingborg, *Sweden*, 87 E4
Helsinki, *Finland, national capital*, 86 H3
Hengyang, *China*, 68 H5
Henzada, *Burma*, 66 C4
Herat, *Afghanistan*, 70 A4
Hermosillo, *Mexico*, 34 B2
Hiiumaa, *Estonia*, 86 G4
Hilo, *U.S.A.*, 33 P8

Himalayas, *Asia*, 70 E4
Hindu Kush, *Asia*, 70 B3
Hinton, *Canada*, 30 H3
Hiroshima, *Japan*, 69 M4
Hispaniola, *North America*, 35 K4
Hitra, *Norway*, 86 D3
Hobart, *Australia, internal capital*, 54 J8
Ho Chi Minh City, *Vietnam*, 66 E5
Hohhot, *China*, 68 H2
Hokkaido, *Japan*, 69 P2
Holguin, *Cuba*, 35 J3
Homs, *Syria*, 72 C5
Homyel, *Belarus*, 87 J5
Honduras, *North America, country*, 35 G4
Honduras, Gulf of, *North America*, 35 G4
Honefoss, *Norway*, 86 D3
Hong Kong, *China*, 69 H6
Honiara, *Solomon Islands, national capital*, 52 D5
Honolulu, *U.S.A., internal capital*, 33 P7
Honshu, *Japan*, 69 N3
Horlivka, *Ukraine*, 84 D4
Hormuz, Strait of, *Asia*, 73 G6
Horn, Cape, *Chile*, 45 D11
Horn Lake, *Sweden*, 86 F2
Hotan, *China*, 70 D3
Hotazel, *South Africa*, 104 D5
Houston, *U.S.A.*, 33 G5
Hradec Kralove, *Czech Republic*, 90 E1
Hrodna, *Belarus*, 87 G5
Huacrachuco, *Peru*, 42 C5
Huaihua, *China*, 68 H5
Huambo, *Angola*, 104 C2
Huancayo, *Peru*, 42 C6
Huang He, *China*, 69 H3
Huanuco, *Peru*, 42 C5
Huascaran, Mount, *Peru*, 42 C5
Hubli, *India*, 71 D7
Hudiksvall, *Sweden*, 86 F3
Hudson Bay, *Canada*, 31 L3
Hudson Strait, *Canada*, 31 M2
Hue, *Vietnam*, 66 E4
Huelva, *Spain*, 89 C7
Hull, *United Kingdom*, 88 D3
Hulun Lake, *China*, 69 J1
Hungary, *Europe, country*, 87 F7
Huntsville, *Canada*, 31 M4
Huntsville, *U.S.A.*, 33 J4
Hurghada, *Egypt*, 99 H3
Huron, Lake, *U.S.A.*, 33 K2
Hvannadalshnukur, *Iceland*, 86 P2
Hwange, *Zimbabwe*, 104 E3
Hyderabad, *India*, 71 D7
Hyderabad, *Pakistan*, 70 B5
Hyesan, *North Korea*, 69 L2

i

Iasi, *Romania*, 91 H2
Ibadan, *Nigeria*, 101 F7
Ibague, *Colombia*, 42 C3
Ibarra, *Ecuador*, 42 C3
Ibb, *Yemen*, 73 D9
Iberian Mountains, *Spain*, 89 D6
Ibiza, *Spain*, 89 E7
Ica, *Peru*, 42 C6
Iceland, *Europe, country*, 86 P2
Idaho, *U.S.A., internal admin. area*, 32 C2
Idaho Falls, *U.S.A.*, 32 D2
Ierapetra, *Greece*, 91 H5
Iguacu Falls, *South America*, 44 H5
Ihosy, *Madagascar*, 105 J4
Ikopa, *Madagascar*, 105 J3
Ilagan, *Philippines*, 67 H4
Ilebo, *Democratic Republic of Congo*, 102 D4
Ilheus, *Brazil*, 44 L2
Iliamna Lake, *U.S.A.*, 30 D2
Iligan, *Philippines*, 67 H6
Illapel, *Chile*, 44 D6
Illimani, Mount, *Bolivia*, 44 E3
Illinois, *U.S.A., internal admin. area*, 33 J2
Illizi, *Algeria*, 100 G3
Ilmen, Lake, *Russia*, 86 J4
Iloilo, *Philippines*, 67 H5
Ilonga, *Tanzania*, 103 G5
Ilorin, *Nigeria*, 101 F7

Imperatriz, *Brazil*, 43 J5
Imphal, *India*, 71 G6
Inari, Lake, *Finland*, 86 H1
Inchon, *South Korea*, 69 L3
Indals, *Sweden*, 86 E3
Inderbor, *Kazakhstan*, 85 G4
India, *Asia, country*, 71 D6
Indiana, *U.S.A., internal admin. area*, 33 J2
Indianapolis, *U.S.A., internal capital*, 33 J3
Indian Ocean, 21
Indonesia, *Asia, country*, 64 C5
Indore, *India*, 71 D6
Indus, *Asia*, 70 B5
Ingolstadt, *Germany*, 88 G4
Inhambane, *Mozambique*, 105 G4
Inner Mongolia, *China*, 69 H2
Innsbruck, *Austria*, 90 D2
Inukjuak, *Canada*, 31 M3
Inuvik, *Canada*, 30 F2
Invercargill, *New Zealand*, 55 N9
Inyangani, *Zimbabwe*, 105 F3
Ioannina, *Greece*, 91 G4
Ionian Sea, *Europe*, 91 F4
Iowa, *U.S.A., internal admin. area*, 33 H2
Ipiales, *Colombia*, 42 C3
Ipoh, *Malaysia*, 64 B3
Ipswich, *United Kingdom*, 88 E3
Iqaluit, *Canada, internal capital*, 31 N2
Iquique, *Chile*, 44 D4
Iquitos, *Peru*, 42 D4
Irakleio, *Greece*, 91 H5
Iran, *Asia, country*, 72 F5
Iranshahr, *Iran*, 73 H6
Iraq, *Asia, country*, 72 D5
Irbid, *Jordan*, 72 C5
Ireland, *Europe, country*, 88 B3
Iringa, *Tanzania*, 103 G5
Irish Sea, *Europe*, 88 C3
Irkutsk, *Russia*, 75 F3
Irrawaddy, *Burma*, 66 C4
Irrawaddy, Mouths of the, *Burma*, 66 B4
Irtysh, *Asia*, 74 D3
Isabela, *Ecuador*, 42 N10
Isafjordhur, *Iceland*, 86 N2
Isiro, *Democratic Republic of Congo*, 102 E3
Islamabad, *Pakistan, national capital*, 70 C4
Isle of Man, *Europe*, 88 C3
Isle of Wight, *United Kingdom*, 88 D4
Ismailia, *Egypt*, 99 H2
Isoka, *Zambia*, 105 F2
Isparta, *Turkey*, 91 J4
Israel, *Asia, country*, 73 B5
Issyk, Lake, *Kyrgyzstan*, 70 D2
Istanbul, *Turkey*, 91 J3
Itaituba, *Brazil*, 43 G4
Itajai, *Brazil*, 44 J5
Italy, *Europe, country*, 90 D2
Itapetininga, *Brazil*, 44 J4
Ivano-Frankivsk, *Ukraine*, 87 H6
Ivanovo, *Russia*, 84 E2
Ivdel, *Russia*, 85 J1
Ivory Coast, *Africa, country*, 101 D7
Ivujivik, *Canada*, 31 M2
Izhevsk, *Russia*, 85 G2
Izmir, *Turkey*, 91 H4

j

Jabalpur, *India*, 71 D6
Jackson, *Mississippi, U.S.A., internal capital*, 33 H4
Jackson, *Tennessee, U.S.A.*, 33 J3
Jacksonville, *U.S.A.*, 33 K4
Jaen, *Spain*, 89 D7
Jaffna, *Sri Lanka*, 71 E9
Jaipur, *India*, 70 D5
Jakarta, *Indonesia, national capital*, 64 C5
Jalalabad, *Afghanistan*, 70 C4
Jalal-Abad, *Kyrgyzstan*, 70 C2
Jamaica, *North America, country*, 35 J4
Jambi, *Indonesia*, 64 B4
James Bay, *Canada*, 31 L3
Jamestown, *U.S.A.*, 33 L2

Jammu, *India*, 70 C4
Jammu and Kashmir, *Asia*, 70 D4
Jamnagar, *India*, 71 C6
Jamshedpur, *India*, 71 F6
Japan, *Asia, country*, 69 N3
Japan, Sea of, *Asia*, 69 M2
Japura, *Brazil*, 42 E4
Jatai, *Brazil*, 44 H3
Java, *Indonesia*, 64 C5
Java Sea, *Indonesia*, 64 C5
Jayapura, *Indonesia*, 65 K4
Jedda, *Saudi Arabia*, 73 C7
Jefferson City, *U.S.A., internal capital*, 33 H3
Jekabpils, *Latvia*, 87 H4
Jelgava, *Latvia*, 87 G4
Jember, *Indonesia*, 64 D5
Jerba, *Tunisia*, 98 D2
Jerez de la Frontera, *Spain*, 89 C7
Jerusalem, *Israel, national capital*, 73 C5
Jhansi, *India*, 70 D5
Jiamusi, *China*, 69 M1
Jilin, *China*, 69 L2
Jima, *Ethiopia*, 103 G2
Jinhua, *China*, 69 J5
Jining, *China*, 69 J3
Jinja, *Uganda*, 103 F3
Jinzhou, *China*, 69 K2
Jixi, *China*, 69 M1
Jizzax, *Uzbekistan*, 70 B2
Joao Pessoa, *Brazil*, 43 M5
Jodhpur, *India*, 70 C5
Johannesburg, *South Africa*, 104 E5
Johnston Atoll, *Oceania*, 52 G3
Johor Bahru, *Malaysia*, 64 B3
Jolo, *Philippines*, 67 H6
Jonesboro, *U.S.A.*, 33 H3
Jonkoping, *Sweden*, 87 E4
Jordan, *Asia, country*, 73 C5
Jorhat, *India*, 70 G5
Jos, *Nigeria*, 102 A2
Juan de Nova, *Africa*, 105 H3
Juazeiro, *Brazil*, 43 K5
Juazeiro do Norte, *Brazil*, 43 L5
Juba, *Africa*, 103 H3
Juba, *Sudan*, 103 F3
Juchitan, *Mexico*, 34 E4
Juiz de Fora, *Brazil*, 44 K4
Juliaca, *Peru*, 42 D7
Juneau, *U.S.A., internal capital*, 30 F3
Jurmala, *Latvia*, 87 G4
Jurua, *Brazil*, 42 E5
Jutland, *Europe*, 87 D4
Jyvaskyla, *Finland*, 86 H3

k

K2, *Asia*, 70 D3
Kaamanen, *Finland*, 86 H1
Kabinda, *Democratic Republic of Congo*, 102 D5
Kabul, *Afghanistan, national capital*, 70 B4
Kabunda, *Democratic Republic of Congo*, 102 E6
Kabwe, *Zambia*, 104 E2
Kadoma, *Zimbabwe*, 104 E3
Kaduna, *Nigeria*, 101 G6
Kaedi, *Mauritania*, 101 C5
Kafakumba, *Democratic Republic of Congo*, 102 D5
Kafue, *Zambia*, 104 E3
Kagoshima, *Japan*, 69 M4
Kahramanmaras, *Turkey*, 72 C4
Kahului, *U.S.A.*, 33 P7
Kainji Reservoir, *Nigeria*, 101 F6
Kairouan, *Tunisia*, 98 D1
Kajaani, *Finland*, 86 H2
Kakhovske Reservoir, *Ukraine*, 84 C4
Kalahari Desert, *Africa*, 104 D4
Kalamata, *Greece*, 91 G4
Kalemie, *Democratic Republic of Congo*, 102 E5
Kalgoorlie, *Australia*, 54 D6
Kaliningrad, *Russia*, 87 G5
Kalisz, *Poland*, 87 F6
Kalkrand, *Namibia*, 104 C4

Kalmar, *Sweden*, 87 F4
Kaluga, *Russia*, 84 D3
Kamanjab, *Namibia*, 104 B3
Kama Reservoir, *Russia*, 85 H2
Kamativi, *Zimbabwe*, 104 E3
Kamchatka Peninsula, *Russia*, 75 H3
Kamenka, *Russia*, 84 E3
Kamina, *Democratic Republic of Congo*, 102 E5
Kamloops, *Canada*, 30 G3
Kampala, *Uganda, national capital*, 103 F3
Kampong Cham, *Cambodia*, 66 E5
Kampong Chhnang, *Cambodia*, 66 D5
Kampong Saom, *Cambodia*, 66 D5
Kamyanets-Podilskyy, *Ukraine*, 87 H6
Kamyshin, *Russia*, 84 F3
Kananga, *Democratic Republic of Congo*, 102 D5
Kanazawa, *Japan*, 69 N3
Kandahar, *Afghanistan*, 70 B4
Kandalaksha, *Russia*, 86 K2
Kandi, *Benin*, 101 F6
Kandy, *Sri Lanka*, 71 E9
Kang, *Botswana*, 104 D4
Kangaroo Island, *Australia*, 54 G7
Kanggye, *North Korea*, 69 L2
Kankan, *Guinea*, 101 D6
Kano, *Nigeria*, 98 C6
Kanpur, *India*, 70 E5
Kansas, *U.S.A., internal admin. area*, 32 G3
Kansas City, *U.S.A.*, 33 H3
Kanye, *Botswana*, 104 E4
Kaohsiung, *Taiwan*, 69 K6
Kaolack, *Senegal*, 101 B6
Kara-Balta, *Kyrgyzstan*, 70 C2
Karabuk, *Turkey*, 91 K3
Karachi, *Pakistan*, 71 B6
Karaj, *Iran*, 72 F4
Karakol, *Kyrgyzstan*, 70 D2
Karakorum Range, *Asia*, 70 D3
Kara Kum Desert, *Turkmenistan*, 72 G3
Karaman, *Turkey*, 91 K4
Karamay, *China*, 70 E1
Kara Sea, *Russia*, 74 D2
Kariba, *Zimbabwe*, 104 E3
Kariba, Lake, *Africa*, 104 E3
Karibib, *Namibia*, 104 C4
Karimata Strait, *Indonesia*, 64 C4
Karlovac, *Croatia*, 90 E2
Karlovy Vary, *Czech Republic*, 90 E1
Karlshamn, *Sweden*, 87 E4
Karlsruhe, *Germany*, 88 G4
Karlstad, *Sweden*, 86 E4
Karmoy, *Norway*, 86 C4
Karonga, *Malawi*, 105 F1
Karora, *Eritrea*, 99 J5
Karpathos, *Greece*, 91 H5
Karratha, *Australia*, 54 C4
Kasai, *Africa*, 102 C4
Kasama, *Zambia*, 104 F2
Kashi, *China*, 70 D3
Kassala, *Sudan*, 99 J5
Kassel, *Germany*, 88 G4
Kasungu, *Malawi*, 105 F2
Kataba, *Zambia*, 104 E3
Kathmandu, *Nepal, national capital*, 70 F5
Katiola, *Ivory Coast*, 101 D7
Katowice, *Poland*, 87 F6
Katsina, *Nigeria*, 101 G6
Kattegat, *Europe*, 87 D4
Kauai, *U.S.A.*, 33 P7
Kaukau Veld, *Africa*, 104 C4
Kaunas, *Lithuania*, 87 G5
Kavala, *Greece*, 91 H3
Kawambwa, *Zambia*, 104 E1
Kayes, *Mali*, 101 C6
Kayseri, *Turkey*, 72 C4
Kazakhstan, *Asia, country*, 74 C3
Kazan, *Russia*, 85 F2
Kaztalovka, *Kazakhstan*, 85 F4
Kebnekaise, *Sweden*, 86 F2
Kecskemet, *Hungary*, 87 F7
Kedougou, *Senegal*, 101 C6
Keetmanshoop, *Namibia*, 104 C5

Prince of Wales Island, *Canada*, 31 K1
Prince Rupert, *Canada*, 30 F3
Principe, *Sao Tome and Principe*, 101 G8
Pripet, *Europe*, 87 J6
Pripet Marshes, *Europe*, 87 H5
Pristina, *Yugoslavia*, 91 G3
Providence, *Seychelles*, 105 K1
Providence, *U.S.A., internal capital*, 33 M2
Providence, Cape, *New Zealand*, 55 N9
Provo, *U.S.A.*, 32 D2
Prudhoe Bay, *U.S.A.*, 30 E1
Pskov, *Russia*, 87 J4
Pskov, Lake, *Europe*, 86 J4
Pucallpa, *Peru*, 42 D5
Puebla, *Mexico*, 34 E4
Pueblo, *U.S.A.*, 32 F3
Puerto Ayora, *Ecuador*, 42 N10
Puerto Cabezas, *Nicaragua*, 35 H5
Puerto Deseado, *Argentina*, 45 E9
Puerto Inirida, *Colombia*, 42 E3
Puerto Leguizamo, *Colombia*, 42 D4
Puerto Maldonado, *Peru*, 42 E6
Puerto Montt, *Chile*, 45 D8
Puerto Natales, *Chile*, 45 D10
Puerto Paez, *Venezuela*, 42 E2
Puerto Princesa, *Philippines*, 67 G6
Puerto Rico, *North America*, 34 L4
Puerto Suarez, *Bolivia*, 44 G3
Puerto Vallarta, *Mexico*, 34 C3
Pula, *Croatia*, 90 E2
Pulog, Mount, *Philippines*, 67 H4
Puncak Jaya, *Indonesia*, 65 J4
Pune, *India*, 71 C7
Puno, *Peru*, 42 D7
Punta Arenas, *Chile*, 45 D10
Puntarenas, *Costa Rica*, 35 H5
Purus, *Brazil*, 42 E5
Pusan, *South Korea*, 69 L3
Pushkin, *Russia*, 86 J4
Puula Lake, *Finland*, 86 H3
Pweto, *Democratic Republic of Congo*, 102 E5
Pya, Lake, *Russia*, 86 J2
Pye, *Burma*, 66 C4
Pyinmana, *Burma*, 66 C4
Pyongyang, *North Korea, national capital*, 69 L3
Pyramids of Giza, *Egypt*, 99 H3
Pyrenees, *Europe*, 89 D6
Pyrgos, *Greece*, 91 G4

q

Qaidam Basin, *China*, 70 G3
Qaraghandy, *Kazakhstan*, 74 D3
Qatar, *Asia, country*, 73 F6
Qattara Depression, *Egypt*, 99 G3
Qazvin, *Iran*, 72 E4
Qena, *Egypt*, 99 H3
Qingdao, *China*, 69 K3
Qinghai Lake, *China*, 68 F3
Qinhuangdao, *China*, 69 J3
Qiqihar, *China*, 69 K1
Qom, *Iran*, 72 F5
Qostanay, *Kazakhstan*, 85 J3
Quanzhou, *China*, 69 J6
Quebec, *Canada, internal admin. area*, 31 M3
Quebec, *Canada, internal capital*, 31 M4
Queen Charlotte Islands, *Canada*, 30 F3
Queen Elizabeth Islands, *Canada*, 30 H1
Queen Maud Land, *Antarctica*, 109 C3
Queensland, *Australia, internal admin. area*, 54 H4
Quelimane, *Mozambique*, 105 G3
Quellon, *Chile*, 45 D8
Quetta, *Pakistan*, 70 B4
Quevedo, *Ecuador*, 42 C4
Quezaltenango, *Guatemala*, 34 F4
Quezon City, *Philippines*, 67 H5
Quibdo, *Colombia*, 42 C2
Quillabamba, *Peru*, 42 D6
Quimper, *France*, 88 C5
Quincy, *U.S.A.*, 33 H3
Qui Nhon, *Vietnam*, 66 E5
Quirima, *Angola*, 104 C2

Quito, *Ecuador, national capital*, 42 C4
Qurghonteppa, *Tajikistan*, 70 B3
Qyzylorda, *Kazakhstan*, 72 J3

r

Raahe, *Finland*, 86 H2
Rabat, *Morocco, national capital*, 100 D2
Rabaul, *Papua New Guinea*, 65 M4
Rabnita, *Moldova*, 91 J2
Radisson, *Canada*, 31 M3
Radom, *Poland*, 87 G6
Ragusa, *Italy*, 90 E4
Rahimyar Khan, *Pakistan*, 70 C5
Rainier, Mount, *U.S.A.*, 32 B1
Raipur, *India*, 71 E6
Rajahmundry, *India*, 71 E7
Rajkot, *India*, 71 C6
Rajshahi, *Bangladesh*, 71 F6
Rakops, *Botswana*, 104 D4
Raleigh, *U.S.A., internal capital*, 33 L3
Ralik Islands, *Marshall Islands*, 52 D3
Ramnicu Valcea, *Romania*, 91 H2
Rancagua, *Chile*, 44 D6
Ranchi, *India*, 71 F6
Randers, *Denmark*, 87 D4
Rangoon, *Burma, national capital*, 66 C4
Rangpur, *Bangladesh*, 70 F5
Rapid City, *U.S.A.*, 32 F2
Ras Dashen, *Ethiopia*, 103 G1
Rasht, *Iran*, 72 E4
Ratak Islands, *Marshall Islands*, 52 E3
Rat Islands, *U.S.A.*, 31 A3
Rauma, *Finland*, 86 G3
Ravenna, *Italy*, 90 E2
Rawson, *Argentina*, 45 E8
Rechytsa, *Belarus*, 87 J5
Recife, *Brazil*, 43 M5
Reconquista, *Argentina*, 44 G5
Red, *Asia*, 68 F6
Red, *U.S.A.*, 33 G4
Red Deer, *Canada*, 30 H3
Redding, *U.S.A.*, 32 B2
Red Sea, *Africa/Asia*, 99 J4
Regensburg, *Germany*, 88 H4
Regina, *Canada, internal capital*, 30 J3
Regina, *French Guiana*, 43 H3
Rehoboth, *Namibia*, 104 C4
Reims, *France*, 88 F4
Reindeer Lake, *Canada*, 30 J3
Rennell Island, *Solomon Islands*, 55 M2
Rennes, *France*, 88 D4
Reno, *U.S.A.*, 32 C3
Reunion, *Indian Ocean*, 105 L4
Revelstoke, *Canada*, 30 H3
Revillagigedo Islands, *Mexico*, 34 B4
Reykjavik, *Iceland, national capital*, 86 N2
Rhine, *Europe*, 88 F4
Rhode Island, *U.S.A., internal admin. area*, 33 M2
Rhodes, *Greece*, 91 J4
Rhone, *Europe*, 89 F5
Riau Islands, *Indonesia*, 64 B3
Ribeirao Preto, *Brazil*, 44 J4
Riberalta, *Bolivia*, 44 E2
Richards Bay, *South Africa*, 104 F5
Richmond, *U.S.A., internal capital*, 33 L3
Riga, *Latvia, national capital*, 87 H4
Riga, Gulf of, *Europe*, 87 G4
Rijeka, *Croatia*, 90 E2
Rimini, *Italy*, 90 E2
Rio Branco, *Brazil*, 42 E5
Rio Cuarto, *Argentina*, 44 F6
Rio de Janeiro, *Brazil*, 44 K4
Rio Gallegos, *Argentina*, 45 E10
Rio Grande, *Argentina*, 45 E10
Rio Grande, *Brazil*, 44 H6
Rio Grande, *U.S.A.*, 32 F5
Riohacha, *Colombia*, 42 D1
Rivas, *Nicaragua*, 35 G5
Rivera, *Uruguay*, 44 G6
Riverside, *U.S.A.*, 32 C4
Rivne, *Ukraine*, 87 H6
Riyadh, *Saudi Arabia, national capital*, 73 E7
Roanoke, *U.S.A.*, 33 L3
Robson, Mount, *Canada*, 30 H3

Rochester, *U.S.A.*, 33 L2
Rockford, *U.S.A.*, 33 J2
Rockhampton, *Australia*, 55 K4
Rocky Mountains, *U.S.A.*, 32 D1
Romania, *Europe, country*, 91 G2
Rome, *Italy, national capital*, 90 E3
Rondonopolis, *Brazil*, 44 H3
Ronne, *Denmark*, 87 E5
Ronne Ice Shelf, *Antarctica*, 109 S3
Roraima, Mount, *South America*, 42 F2
Rosario, *Argentina*, 44 F6
Roseau, *Dominica, national capital*, 34 M4
Roslavl, *Russia*, 87 K5
Ross Ice Shelf, *Antarctica*, 109 M4
Rosso, *Mauritania*, 101 B5
Ross Sea, *Antarctica*, 109 M3
Rostock, *Germany*, 88 H3
Rostov, *Russia*, 84 D4
Roti, *Indonesia*, 65 Q7
Rotorua, *Australia*, 55 Q7
Rotterdam, *Netherlands*, 88 F4
Rouen, *France*, 88 E4
Rovaniemi, *Finland*, 86 H2
Roxas, *Philippines*, 67 H5
Rub al Khali, *Asia*, 73 E8
Rudnyy, *Kazakhstan*, 85 J3
Rufino, *Argentina*, 44 F6
Rufunsa, *Zambia*, 104 E3
Rukwa, Lake, *Tanzania*, 103 F5
Rundu, *Namibia*, 104 C3
Rurrenabaque, *Bolivia*, 44 E2
Ruse, *Bulgaria*, 91 H3
Russia, *Asia/Europe, country*, 74 E3
Ruvuma, *Africa*, 103 G6
Rwanda, *Africa, country*, 102 E4
Ryazan, *Russia*, 84 D3
Rybinsk, *Russia*, 84 D2
Rybinsk Reservoir, *Russia*, 84 D2
Rybnik, *Poland*, 87 F6
Ryukyu Islands, *Japan*, 69 L5
Rzeszow, *Poland*, 87 G6
Rzhev, *Russia*, 84 C2

s

Saarbrucken, *Germany*, 88 F4
Saarijarvi, *Finland*, 86 H3
Sabha, *Libya*, 98 D3
Sabzevar, *Iran*, 72 G4
Sacramento, *U.S.A., internal capital*, 32 B3
Sadah, *Yemen*, 73 E8
Safi, *Morocco*, 100 D2
Sahara, *Africa*, 98 C5
Saharanpur, *India*, 70 D5
Sahel, *Africa*, 98 C6
Sahiwal, *Pakistan*, 70 C4
Saida, *Algeria*, 100 F2
Saigon, *Vietnam*, 66 E5
Saimaa Lake, *Finland*, 86 H3
St. Andrew, Cape, *Madagascar*, 105 H3
St. Denis, *Reunion*, 105 L4
St. Etienne, *France*, 89 F5
St. Francis, Cape, *South Africa*, 104 D6
St. George, *U.S.A.*, 32 D3
St. George's, *Grenada, national capital*, 34 M5
St. Helier, *Channel Islands*, 88 D4
Saint John, *Canada*, 31 N4
St. John's, *Antigua and Barbuda, national capital*, 34 M4
St. John's, *Canada, internal capital*, 31 P4
St. Kitts and Nevis, *North America, country*, 34 M4
St. Lawrence, *Canada*, 31 M4
St. Lawrence, Gulf of, *Canada*, 31 N4
St. Lawrence Island, *U.S.A.*, 30 B2
St. Louis, *Senegal*, 101 B5
St. Louis, *U.S.A.*, 33 H3
St. Lucia, *North America, country*, 34 M5
St. Lucia, Cape, *South Africa*, 105 F5
St. Malo, *France*, 88 D4
St. Martha, Cape, *Angola*, 104 B2
St. Martin, *North America*, 34 M4
St. Mary, Cape, *Madagascar*, 105 J5
St. Paul, *U.S.A., internal capital*, 33 H1

St. Petersburg, *Russia*, 86 J4
St. Petersburg, *U.S.A.*, 33 K5
St. Pierre, *Seychelles*, 105 J1
St. Pierre and Miquelon, *North America*, 31 P4
St. Polten, *Austria*, 90 E1
St. Vincent and the Grenadines, *North America, country*, 34 M5
St. Vincent, Cape, *Portugal*, 89 B7
Sakhalin, *Russia*, 75 H3
Saki, *Azerbaijan*, 72 E3
Saki, *Nigeria*, 101 F7
Sakishima Islands, *Japan*, 69 K6
Sal, *Cape Verde*, 101 M11
Salado, *Argentina*, 44 F5
Salalah, *Oman*, 73 F8
Salamanca, *Spain*, 89 C6
Salem, *India*, 71 D8
Salem, *U.S.A., internal capital*, 32 B1
Salerno, *Italy*, 90 E3
Salihorsk, *Belarus*, 87 H5
Salinas, *U.S.A.*, 32 B3
Salta, *Argentina*, 44 E4
Saltillo, *Mexico*, 34 D2
Salt Lake City, *U.S.A., internal capital*, 32 D2
Salto, *Uruguay*, 44 G6
Salton Sea, *U.S.A.*, 32 C4
Salvador, *Brazil*, 43 L6
Salween, *Asia*, 66 C4
Salzburg, *Austria*, 90 E2
Samar, *Philippines*, 67 J5
Samara, *Russia*, 85 G3
Samarinda, *Indonesia*, 64 E4
Samarqand, *Uzbekistan*, 70 B3
Sambalpur, *India*, 71 E6
Samoa, *Oceania, country*, 52 F6
Sampwe, *Democratic Republic of Congo*, 102 E5
Sam Rayburn Reservoir, *U.S.A.*, 33 H4
Samsun, *Turkey*, 72 C3
San, *Mali*, 101 E6
Sana, *Yemen, national capital*, 73 D8
Sanandaj, *Iran*, 72 E4
San Andres Island, *Colombia*, 35 H5
San Antonio, *U.S.A.*, 32 G5
San Antonio, Cape, *Argentina*, 45 G7
San Antonio Oeste, *Argentina*, 45 F8
San Cristobal, *Ecuador*, 42 P10
San Cristobal, *Venezuela*, 42 D2
Sandakan, *Malaysia*, 65 E2
San Diego, *U.S.A.*, 32 C4
Sandoway, *Burma*, 66 B4
San Fernando, *Chile*, 44 D6
San Fernando de Apure, *Venezuela*, 42 E2
San Francisco, *Argentina*, 44 F6
San Francisco, *U.S.A.*, 32 B3
San Francisco, Cape, *Ecuador*, 42 B3
Sangihe Islands, *Indonesia*, 65 G3
San Jorge, Gulf of, *Argentina*, 45 E9
San Jose, *Costa Rica, national capital*, 35 H6
San Jose, *U.S.A.*, 32 B3
San Jose de Chiquitos, *Bolivia*, 44 F3
San Jose del Guaviare, *Colombia*, 42 D3
San Juan, *Argentina*, 44 E6
San Juan, *Puerto Rico*, 34 L4
San Julian, *Argentina*, 45 E9
Sanliurfa, *Turkey*, 72 C4
San Lucas, Cape, *Mexico*, 34 B3
San Luis, *Argentina*, 44 E6
San Luis Obispo, *U.S.A.*, 32 B3
San Luis Potosi, *Mexico*, 34 D3
San Marino, *Europe, country*, 90 E3
San Matias, Gulf of, *Argentina*, 45 F8
San Miguel de Tucuman, *Argentina*, 44 E5
San Nicolas de los Arroyos, *Argentina*, 44 F6
San Pedro, *Ivory Coast*, 101 D8
San Pedro de Atacama, *Chile*, 44 E4
San Rafael, *Argentina*, 44 E6
San Remo, *Italy*, 90 C3
San Salvador, *Ecuador*, 42 N10
San Salvador, *El Salvador, national capital*, 34 G5

ACKNOWLEDGEMENTS

Every effort has been made to trace the copyright holders of the material in this book. If any rights have been omitted, the publishers offer to rectify this in any subsequent edition, following notification. The publishers are grateful to the following organizations and individuals for their contributions and permission to reproduce material (t=top, m=middle, b=bottom, l=left, r=right):

Cover © Jacques Descloitres, MODIS Land Science Team; (globe) © Digital Vision; **Endpapers** © Ric Ergenbright/CORBIS; **p1** © Jim Zuckerman/CORBIS; **p2–3** © Art Wolfe/Science Photo Library; **p4–5** Stephen Moncrieff, Digital Vision; **p4** (tr) © Geospace/Science Photo Library; **p6** (bl) © CNES, 1988 Distribution SPOT Image/Science Photo Library; (mr) Stephen Moncrieff; **p7** (tm & tr) European Map Graphics Ltd; (b) © Paul A. Souders/CORBIS; **p8–9** (background) © Digital Vision; **p8** (mr) PHOTO ESA; **p9** (tl) © NERC Satellite Station, University of Dundee www.sat.dundee.ac.html; (br) Science Photo Library/European Space Agency; **p10** (b) Stephen Moncrieff; (tr) © Dan Guravich/CORBIS; **p11** (bl) European Map Graphics Ltd; (tr) © W. Perry Conway/CORBIS; **p12** (b) © Christopher Cormack/CORBIS; **p13** Stephen Moncrieff, Craig Asquith; **p14** (tr) © Bill Ross/CORBIS; (b) Craig Asquith; **p15** Craig Asquith; **p16–17** European Map Graphics Ltd; **p22–23** © Richard Cummins/CORBIS; **p23** (br) © W. Perry Conway/CORBIS; **p24** (tr) © Worldsat International/Science Photo Library; (m) © NASA/JSC; (b) © Raymond Gehman/CORBIS; **p25** © NASA/CORBIS; **p26–27** (b) © Richard Cummins/CORBIS; **p26** (t) © Dave G. Houser/CORBIS; **p27** (tr) © Joe McDonald/CORBIS; **p28** (l) © Angelo Hornak/CORBIS; (tr) © Carl & Ann Purcell/CORBIS; **p29** (tl) © Schafer & Hill/GettyImages; (br) © Michael & Patricia Fogden/CORBIS; **p36–37** © Galen Rowell/CORBIS; **p37** (tr) © Eye Ubiquitous/CORBIS; **p38** (m) © Julian Baum & David Angus/Science Photo Library; (bl) © Yann Arthus-Bertrand/CORBIS; (mr) © NASA/JSC; **p39** (r) © CNES, 1986 Distribution SPOT Image/Science Photo Library; (bl) © CNES, Distribution SPOT Image/Science Photo Library; **p40–41** (b) © Robert Frerck/GettyImages; **p40** (tr) Claus Meyer/GettyImages; **p41** (tl) Walter Bibikow/GettyImages; (tr) Peter Oxford/BBC Wild; **p46–47** © Still Pictures/Pascal Kobeh; **p47** (br) © Bates Littlehales/CORBIS; **p48–49** (b) © Amos Nachoum/CORBIS; **p48** (ml) © 1995, Worldsat International and J. Knighton/Science Photo Library; (tr) © NASA/JSC; **p49** (tr) © CNES, Distribution SPOT Image/Science Photo Library; (ml) © CORBIS; **p50** © Yoshio Tomii/Bruce Coleman; **p51** (tr) © Klein/Hubert/Still Pictures; (bl) © Zefa visual media; **p56–57** © Michael S. Yamashita/CORBIS; **p57** (br) © Keren Su/CORBIS; **p58** (tr) © Worldsat International/Science Photo Library; (m) © CNES, 1986 Distribution SPOT Image/Science Photo Library; (b) © Liu Liqun/CORBIS; **p59** (t) © NASA JPL; (br) © CNES, 1987 Distribution SPOT Image/Science Photo Library; **p60** (l) © Keren Su/CORBIS; (tr) © Keren Su/China Span/Alamy; **p61** (tl) © www.pictor.com; (b) © Papilio/CORBIS; **p62** (tr) © Richard T. Nowitz/CORBIS; (b) © Archivo Iconografico, S.A./CORBIS; **p63** (ml) © www.pictor.com; (tr) © Wolfgang Kaehler/CORBIS; (b) © Brian & Cherry Alexander Photography; **p76–77** © Digital Vision; **p77** (br) Agripicture/© Peter Dean; **p78–79** (b) © Peter Adams/GettyImages; **p78** (tr) NASA/GSFC/MITI/ERSDAC/JAROS, & U.S./Japan ASTER Science Team; (ml) © NASA GSFC Scientific Visualization Studio; **p79** (tr) © CNES, 1994 Distribution SPOT Image/Science Photo Library; (m) © German Remote Sensing Data Center; **p80** (tr) © The Art Archive/Historiska Muséet Stockholm/Dagli Orti; (bl) © Enzo & Paolo Ragazzini/CORBIS; **p81** (t) © Zefa visual media; (br) © Frans Lanting/Minden Pictures; **p82** © Paul Hardy/corbisstockmarket.com; **p83** (t) © Bob Krist/CORBIS; (b) © Araldo de Luca/CORBIS; **p92–93** © Tom Brakefield/CORBIS; **p93** (br) © Gallo Images/CORBIS; **p94** (tr) © Worldsat International/Science Photo Library; (bl) © Yann Arthus-Bertrand/CORBIS; (br) © NASA JPL; **p95** (r) © Jacques Descloitres, MODIS Land Science Team; (bl) © NASA/JSC; **p96** © Roger Wood/CORBIS; **p97** (ml) © Charles O'Rear/CORBIS; (tr) © Wolfgang Kaehler/CORBIS; (b) © Karl Ammann/CORBIS; **p106** (tr) © Worldsat International/Science Photo Library; (m) © Jan Jordan; **p107** (t) © NRSC Ltd/Science Photo Library; (b) © Digital Vision; **p110–111** (b) © Paul A. Souders/CORBIS; **p110** (tl) © Peter M. Wilson/CORBIS; (tm) © Joe McDonald/CORBIS; (ml) © Charles O'Rear/CORBIS; (mr) © Vanni Archive/CORBIS; **p111** (br) Galen Rowell/CORBIS; **p112–125** (background) © Digital Vision; (Afghanistan, Bahrain, Comoros, Rwanda, Turkmenistan and East Timor flags) © Shipmate Flags, Vlaardingen, The Netherlands; (all other flags) © Flag Enterprises Ltd; **p125** (b) AFP Photos/Henry Ray Abrams; **p126** (b) Craig Asquith.

Managing editor: Gillian Doherty
Managing designer: Mary Cartwright
Cover design by Zöe Wray
With thanks to Ruth King

Usborne Publishing is not responsible and does not accept liability for the availability or content of any Web site other than its own, or for any exposure to harmful, offensive, or inaccurate material which may appear on the Web. Usborne Publishing will have no liability for any damage or loss caused by viruses that may be downloaded as a result of browsing the sites it recommends.

First published in 2002 by Usborne Publishing Ltd, 83–85 Saffron Hill, London EC1N 8RT, England. www.usborne.com
Copyright © 2002, 2001 Usborne Publishing Ltd. The name Usborne and the devices 💡 🐝 are Trade Marks of Usborne Publishing Ltd. All rights reserved. No part of this publication may be reproduced, stored in a retrieval system, or transmitted in any form or by any means, electronic, mechanical, photocopying, recording or otherwise, without the prior permission of the publisher. UE. First published in America in 2003. Printed in Spain.